Studies in Emotion and Social Interaction

Paul Ekman
University of California, San Francisco

Klaus R. Scherer
Université de Genève

General Editors

Affect and Social Behavior

Studies in Emotion and Social Interaction

This series is jointly published by the Cambridge University Press and the Editions de la Maison des Sciences de l'Homme, as part of the joint publishing agreement established in 1977 between the Fondation de la Maison des Sciences de l'Homme and the Syndics of the Cambridge University Press.

Cette collection est publiée co-édition par Cambridge University Press et les Editions de la Maison des Sciences de l'Homme. Elle s'intègre dans le programme de co-édition établi en 1977 par la Fondation de la Maison des Sciences de l'Homme et les Syndics de Cambridge University Press.

Affect and social behavior

Edited by
Bert S. Moore and Alice M. Isen

School of　　　　*Graduate School of Management*
Human Development　*Cornell University*
University of
Texas at Dallas

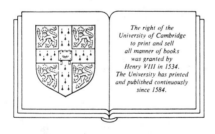

The right of the
University of Cambridge
to print and sell
all manner of books
was granted by
Henry VIII in 1534.
The University has printed
and published continuously
since 1584.

Cambridge University Press

Cambridge
New York　*Port Chester*
Melbourne　*Sydney*

Editions de la Maison des Sciences de l'Homme
Paris

Published by the Press Syndicate of the University of Cambridge
The Pitt Building, Trumpington Street, Cambridge CB2 1RP
40 West 20th Street, New York, NY 10011, USA
10 Stamford Road, Oakleigh, Melbourne 3166, Australia
and
Editions de la Maison des Sciences de l'Homme
54 Boulevard Raspail, 75270 Paris, Cedex 06

First published 1990

Printed in the United States of America

Library of Congress Cataloging-in-Publication Data

Affect and social behavior / edited by Bert S. Moore and Alice M.
　Isen.
　　p.　cm. – (Studies in emotion and social interaction)
　　1. Affect (Psychology)　2. Interpersonal relations.　I. Moore,
Bert S.　II. Isen, Alice M.　III. Series.
BF531.A57　1989
152.4–dc20　　　　　　　　　　　　　　　　　　　　　89-9789
ISBN 0-521-32768-7　　　　　　　　　　　　　　　　　　　CIP

British Library Cataloguing-in-Publication Data

Affect and social behavior. – (Studies in emotion and
　social interaction)
　1. Man. Social interactions. Role of emotion
　I. Moore, Bert S.　II. Isen, Alice M.　III. Series
302

　ISBN 2-7351-0311-0 France only
　ISBN 2-521-32768-7 hard covers

Contents

Contributors

Robert A. Baron
Department of Psychology
Rensselaer Polytechnic Institute

C. Daniel Batson
Department of Psychology
University of Kansas

Paul A. Bell
Department of Psychology
Colorado State University

Ellen Berscheid
Department of Psychology
University of Minnesota

Nancy Cantor
Department of Psychology
University of Michigan

Joel Cohen
Marketing Department
University of Florida

Elaine Hatfield
Department of Psychology
University of Hawaii

Alice M. Isen
Department of Psychology
Graduate School of Management
Cornell University

John C. Masters
Psychology Department
Vanderbilt University

Charles L. McCoy
Department of Psychiatry
Duke University

Bert S. Moore
School of Human Development
University of Texas at Dallas

Julie K. Norem
Department of Psychology
Northeastern University

Richard L. Rapson
Department of Psychology
University of Hawaii

Gifford Weary
Department of Psychology
Ohio State University

Preface

The study of emotional processes has had a long and checkered history in psychology. Scientists have studied emotion partly because of its pervasiveness and inherent interest, and partly because emotions are seen as organizers and regulators of a variety of behaviors. The centrality of affective processes in human behavior has an axiomatic quality: most theoretical positions address in some fashion questions centered on how affect influences behavior. However, for all of the consensus regarding the important regulating role of affect in behavior, the empirical investigation of that role has often been stymied by the difficult issues of definition and operation. So little agreement exists among investigators regarding the phenomena to be investigated that the development of any sort of coherent view of affective processes has been difficult to achieve. Investigative tactics have often been so heterogeneous as to render agreement that they were investigations of the same phenomena difficult.

The last 20 years, however, have seen an important revolution in the investigation of affect's role as a moderator of social behavior. Laboratory and field investigations have begun to clarify the complex interplay among affect, cognition, and behavior. The literature that might support a coherent picture of the ways emotion influences behavior has been scattered. Relevant elements exist in such work as the effects of success and failure on behavior; clinical literature on emotion; laboratory investigations of happiness, sadness, anxiety, and anger; and correlation work that relates mood to a variety of personality measures and day-to-day behavior. What has begun to emerge from these diverse domains is a picture that emphasizes that affect is an important moderator of social behavior and that the relationships are often subtle ones.

The present volume brings together some of the foremost contributors to this "affective revolution" and reviews work in a number of important social domains. It is in the area of social behavior that we might expect affective processes to have the most important role and, indeed, much of the empirical work of recent years has been in relation to social responses. However, that research has advanced piecemeal, and there have been few attempts to impose order on these diverse bodies of work. This volume grew out of our perception of the need for one resource that brings together work from different areas and tries to establish common principles, as well as acknowledging domain-specific phenomena. The authors of these chapters have addressed important questions of how affect influences such important behaviors as aggression, prosocial behavior, and consumer behavior, and what the mechanisms of those influences are. In addition, the authors have provided a number of important distinctions that are likely to influence research in these areas in the future.

The lead chapter in this volume was prepared by the editors and attempts to provide an integrative overview of affect's role in regulating social behavior. In Chapter 2, Ellen Berscheid addresses the fundamental question of the definition of emotional terms and explores the issue of how we speak about emotional processes and how our choice of terminology influences our understanding of the relation between affect and social behavior. In Chapter 3, Julie Norem and Nancy Cantor provide an overview of affective and cognitive processes and outline the ways in which the interplay of these processes act to influence social behavior. In their chapter they examine traditional distinctions between "affect" and "cognition" and provide an integrative reformulation to serve as a guide for thinking about our traditional tripartite division of affect, cognition, and behavior.

The chapter by Paul Bell and Robert Baron examines the mediating role of affect in aggressive behavior. Bell and Baron pose the question of why affect has been so little examined in the aggression literature, in distinction to such explanatory mechanisms as frustration and social context. By examining older literature in a new way and relating it to investigations in other domains, Bell and Baron provide a provocative model for examining aggression. Counterposed to Bell and Baron's discussion of aggression is Batson's examination of the other side of human social action: altruism. Altruism is a domain where a great deal of empirical work has been conducted regarding the mediating role of affect, and also where there have been a number of conceptual debates. Dan Batson provides an illuminating review of the existing research and points the direction to new understanding of affect's role in understanding altruism.

Elaine Hatfield and Richard Rapson address the challenging topic of romantic love in their chapter. In their extensive review of the growing literature in this domain, Hatfield and Rapson relate traditional literatures in attraction to try to understand the emotional underpinnings of passionate love.

From romantic love, we turn to the Joel Cohen's chapter on "Attitude, affect, and consumer behavior," where he brings together, in a new fashion, the affective underpinnings of attitude formation and activation and examines how they influence consumer behavior. This extension of the affect literature into consumer behavior affords Cohen the opportunity to provide a integrative examination of attitude and decision-making and the subtle and not-so-subtle ways that affect influences them.

In Gifford Weary's chapter entitled "Depression and sensitivity to social information," she examines the ways in which affect acts to bias our processing of social information with a focus on depression. Dr. Weary provides some recent findings that provide a new focus on the selective function that affect serves as we respond to social stimuli.

In the final chapter, Charles McCoy and John Masters present a comprehensive review from a developmental perspective of how children acquire the capacity for regulating emotional expression, as well as the emotions of others. Their examination of these issues leads them to pose general questions regarding processes of self-regulation and how children learn to respond to and moderate social exchange.

This book is the first comprehensive attempt to bring together experts from different domains of social research to address the various roles that affect plays in mediating social exchange. In addition, the authors have provided blueprints for future directions in research that utilizes a more comprehensive approach to understanding the affect-cognition-behavior nexus.

Alice M. Isen
Bert S. Moore

1. Affect and social behavior

BERT S. MOORE AND ALICE M. ISEN

The last 20 years has seen a resurgence of interest in the role of affect as a mediator of a variety of kinds of behavior. Although, there has long been an acknowledgment within the field of psychology of the central role played by affect as a governor of behavior, until recently empirical investigation of those relations had not had a great impact because of the thorny methodological and conceptual issues involved in the investigation of affect. In the early 1970s there began a period of intense interest in the mediating role affect plays in behavior. It might be fair to say that if the 1960s marked the advent of a "cognitive revolution" in psychology, the 1970s and 1980s have seen an analogous turning to the critical role of affect in both social behavior and cognition.

That our behavior, our reactions to our world, are colored by our affect requires only a moment's introspection. We can point to numerous ways that our responses to ourselves and others depend on our feelings. This intuition regarding the role that affect plays in moderating our social reactions and self-reactions has been extensively investigated during the past 20 years, and these investigations have provided a much clearer picture of how affect influences such important social behaviors as altruism, aggression, interpersonal attraction, consumer behavior, and decision making. In addition, during the past 10 years cognitive and social psychologists have turned their attention to how affect influences such phenomena as selective attention, schematic organization, state-dependent memory, and selective retrieval. These parallel movements, an examination of the influence of affect on social behavior and the explication of affect–cognition relations, have enabled increasingly comprehensive statements to be formulated about the interactive role played among affect, cognition, and social behavior. However, while there have been several volumes published on affect and cognition, there has not been a comprehensive work focusing on the area in which the

1

preponderance of the affect research has been conducted – social behavior. In this volume we bring together some of the most distinguished contributions in the domain, to provide the reader with an illustration of the richness and variety of the work and to clarify some of the contradictions that have appeared in the rather piecemeal evolution of research in this area.

While the intuitive plausibility of the relation between affect and social behavior may be a sufficient justification for the investigation of these effects, the accumulated research presented in this volume points out the increasing sophistication of our understanding of the processes underlying these relations. There have been several helpful distinctions drawn on the ways that affect may act to influence social behavior, but before we examine these inferred processes, we must clarify somewhat what is meant by "affect" in this volume. The literature in social psychology and personality contains many studies in which terms such as "emotions," "moods," and "affect" are used interchangeably. The relationship among these concepts is not well understood, but it may be possible to draw some distinctions among them.

Since at this stage in our knowledge such distinctions must be rather arbitrarily drawn, we would suggest that one important aspect of any definitional scheme selected should be its utility. In particular, it may be useful to focus on the dimensions of pervasiveness and specificity in considering the effects of feelings and emotions. Emotions may be seen as more "interrupting" types of experiences that are typically more focal in terms of both target and behavioral response than are feeling states. Feeling states may be pervasive but nonspecific affective events that are not directed toward any particular behaviors. Because of this pervasiveness and nonspecificity, feeling states may influence a variety of behaviors and judgments and may be able to redirect thinking and behavior. It appears that affect – which, as discussed here, primarily refers to feeling states – influences a wide variety of behaviors but that those influences are not the result of direct imperatives but rather are adventitious.

Feeling states have been found empirically to alter attention, memory, and behavior in a wide range of domains. The behavior affected by feeling states seems often to be determined by the chance encounters with behavioral alternatives offered by the environment after the induction of the feeling state. Thus, although a variety of social behaviors are influenced by affect, one would not expect all behavior to be equally affected. The pattern of influence is apt to be subtle, and the subtlety may be a partial explanation for the relative lack of attention that these relations have received until recently.

It is our contention that these relations are particularly important in understanding a variety of social behaviors because feeling states occur so frequently and may act to shade and shape people's reactions to themselves and others. We are all aware that our feelings can be potent determiners of how we respond to ourselves. We have all felt the flush of buoyancy and self-approbation that may accompany a "high"; we are also well acquainted with the self-criticism and self-doubt that may accompany our depressions. Of course, our affective states are subtle and multifaceted. Different shades of affect seem to be accompanied by specific forms of cognitive reactions to experience. Melancholy, guilt, nostalgia, exuberance, and joy all seem to produce specific reactions.

It is not critical for our purposes to go into the issues regarding the directionality of these associations – whether affect causes cognitive effects or cognitions cause affective reactions. Undoubtedly this relationship is bidirectional, with affective state engendering certain types of cognitive activity and cognitions leading to distinctive affective experiences. It is also the case, by and large, that these shades of affect, while pervasive and perhaps differing in important ways in their influences on behavior, have not received systematic investigation up to this point (for a comprehensive examination of these perspectives and data relative to them, see Mandler, 1984, and Isen, 1984). What is important for us is to see whether the relationships between cognition and affect suggest any comprehensive statement about how affect regulates behavior.

Later in the chapter we shall outline some of the presumed relations among affect, cognition, and social behavior, but first we shall discuss some of the ways that affective states have been discussed in terms of affective quality (positive, negative) and some of the methods that have been employed in the investigation of affect.

1.1. Affective quality

In a discussion of affect, the very use of the single word might imply a unidimensional phenomenon. There is, however, a continuing question as to the exact nature of the dimensionality of affect. Is it best thought of as a single, unitary dimension or as a series of perhaps interrelated dimensions? Do the common names for affective states (sadness, anger, happiness, fear, etc.) identify distinct affective dimensions? Are affective states unipolar (neutral–happy, neutral–sad, etc.) or are at least some of the bipolar (e.g., happy–sad)? These and similar questions are basic to our understanding of affect, and therefore to our choice of research strategies and questions.

It has often seemed that investigators think of affect in terms of a bipolar, unidimensional pleasant–unpleasant continuum. For example, a title such as "Affect and Altruism" (Moore, Underwood, & Rosenhan, 1973), attached to a report of a study of the effects of manipulations of happiness and sadness, may unfortunately imply that *all* affective states can be considered roughly equivalent to one examined in the study. Even more explicitly, a review of the literature on negative effect and altruism that lumps together studies of sadness, guilt, and sympathy without any real distinction among them (Cialdini & Kendrick, 1976) is also likely to promote a rather undifferentiated view of affect.

Similarly, it is sometimes suggested that a dimension of affect involves global "arousal." Yet the concept of "arousal" is itself a complex one (see Berlyne, 1971; Lacey, 1967; Lacey, Kagan, Lacey, & Moss, 1963; Martindale, 1981). Several authors have suggested that it may be misleading to think of arousal as global or unitary. Moreover, the relationship between arousal and affect is not simple: Some have proposed arousal to be orthogonal to valence as a component of affect; but the nonorthogonal relationship between valence and arousal has been noted for a century in psychology, dating back to the "Wundt Curve" (see Berlyne, 1971; Isen, 1984; Martindale, 1981, for discussion).

Whether we adopt such a view will have a definite impact on any review of the affect literature. Taking a unidimensional approach will increase the claimed generality for any mood effects noted in the literature, and will obviate the need for further studies with previously ignored affective states to complete the picture; a multidimensional approach will have opposite implications. Both to set the stage for the reviews that follow in this volume and to establish some sort of conceptual framework for affect, we shall address this issue in two ways: by brief reference to factor-analytic studies of affective self-reports and by examination of theoretically and conceptually based categorizations of affect.

Factor-analytic studies

Laboratory research on feelings over the past decade has produced a large number of affect self-report protocols. These have typically been adjective checklists based on Nowlis's Mood Adjective Checklist (MACL), but with additional descriptive adjectives included. Periodic factor analyses by one of the present authors have produced a strikingly similar pattern of (unpublished) results across the years: two large factors, one for positive affect and the other for negative affect, along with a few smaller factors that seem to us nonaffective in content (i.e., tired or concentrating; see also Watson, Clark, & Tellegen, 1988). In a similar vein, the conglomerate positive and negative mood scales used by Wispé, Kiecolt, and Long (1977) were chosen on the basis of the results of factor analyses (Wispé, personal communication). Such results would seem to support the notion of two large unipolar affect dimensions, one for "feeling good" and the other for "feeling bad." On the other hand, other investigators have provided numerous reports of factor analyses of mood scales resulting in a variety of specific mood factors, including Nowlis' (1965) report on the orignial MACL. Reviewing the results of 15 factor-analytic studies, Nowlis suggested "that twelve or more factors should be hypothesized and given futher study in mood research" (p. 361). In addition, contrary to his initial expectations, Nowlis found no evidence for bipolar mood dimensions. Similar results have been reported since (e.g., Izard, 1972), although it has been reported that bipolar mood dimensions may be obtained under certain circumstances (Russell, 1980). Although it is not clear why the results of factor analyses should be consistent with a relatively undifferentiated view of affect in some circumstances but reveal a much more differentiated pattern in others (see Watson & Tellegon, 1985 for more extensive discussion), the implications for our view of affect are quite clear. If there are *any* circumstances in which affect appears as a highly differentiated phenomenon, then it may be productive for it to be conceptualized as multidimensional (Shaver, Schwartz, Kirson, & O'Connor, 1987) even if there are some situations in which several of the dimensions cluster together to form a large superordinate dimension. The result of the factor analyses may vary depending both on how affect measures are elicited and the purposes for which they are to be used.

Conceptually based categorizations of affect

The diversity of affective dimensions is perhaps even more striking and ubiquitous within the realm of conceptually based categorizations of affect than it is in empirical studies relying on factor analyses. As an example, one of the reasons for rejection of the James–Lange theory of emotion was the fact that internal visceral reactions in emotional experience were not only too slow to explain the observed feeling states but also too uniform to hold any possibility of accounting for the wealth of distinct subjective experiences of affect. A later theory (Woodworth & Schlosberg, 1954) focused on facial expressions rather than visceral sensations as the key to affective distinctiveness and suggested an affect "wheel" on which individual states could be plotted to indicate their relatedness to one another.

This theoretical effort is of special interest in several ways. One point of interest is the early reliance on facial expressions, which have been the focus of continued theoretical interest over the past two decades. A second point of interest concerns the positing of distinct affects that nonetheless bear varying degrees of similarity to each other. This similarity might provide a basis for the occasional clustering of affect descriptions into large-scale superordinate dimensions in factor-analytic studies. A third interesting element of Woodworth and Schlosberg's (1954) approach is their attempt to explain the distinct-yet-related nature of affective states in terms of two primary dimensions: pleasantness–unpleasantness and acceptance–rejection. These hypothesized underlying dimensions might be another basis for the superordinate factor structure sometimes obtained. Indeed, in data from a number of studies over the past two decades the division into factors has seemed to be based on the pleasantness-unpleasantness distinction.

There have been many other theoretical approaches to affect, virtually all of which have hypothesized numerous distinctive affects. Another that might be mentioned is Plutchik's (1980a,b) both because of its currency and because of its similarity to the Woodworth and Schlosberg (1954) formulation. Although his approach is an explication of emotions rather than of the feeling states that are our central concern and is based upon conceptual rather than empirical grounds, it does raise some relevant issues. The similarity to Woodworth and Schlosberg is noticeable in the diversity of affects posited, in the use of a geometric figure to illustrate the relationships (a cone in the 1970 version, a circle in the 1980 formulation), and in the suggestion of underlying dimensions to explain relationships among affective states.

It is this attempt to reduce the diversity of affective states to a few explanatory dimensions (common to many theoretical approaches) that represents the only real tendency of conceptual treatments to place severe limits on the number of dimensions of affect. Of course, this sort of limitation is quite different from the suggestion that there are only a few basic affects, since it leaves open the question of when (and to what extent) different affects that happen to share a common position on some underlying dimension will have different effects. Indeed, some dimensions such as positive–negative may be much more central in their organizing influence on behavior than are other dimensions. In any event, most conceptual approaches to affect are very much in line with the results of most factor-analytic studies in suggesting a variety of distinct affective states. The results of several recent experiments (e.g., Barnett, King, & Howard, 1979; Thompson, Cowan, & Rosenhan, 1980) have even suggested that alterations in the focus of attention may change the quality of certain affective experiences, yielding still greater diversity of affect.

Implications of affective diversity

Because of important and complex differences in the relations between positive and negative affect (Isen, 1984) and behavior, which will be discussed later, the way in which feeling states are conceptualized has important implications for the conduct of research. One implication of the idea of affects as related but numerous and diverse states concerns the validation of experimental manipulations of affect.

1.2. Manipulations of affect

Much of the work in the area of affect over the past two decades has attempted to manipulate affect as an independent variable. Some of the chapters in the present volume describe research in this tradition, while others describe work that assesses but does not directly manipulate feeling states. A brief description of some of the methods employed to manipulate affect will provide a context for understanding some of the conceptual issues to follow.

Children learn very early what we mean when we use an emotional label (see McCoy and Masters in this volume). If you ask children of age 2 to make a happy face and a sad face, they can usually do so. Although the 2-year-olds are less adept at describing what makes them happy or sad, by age 3 children can readily come up with some examples for you. Undoubtedly, this early development of a shared meaning system regarding what is a subtle and complex private experience derives partially from the biological processes that are shared by all people and tied to emotional states. Also, as is discussed elsewhere in this volume, affective states undoubtedly have certain cultural specificities in their expression, and we surmise the experience, with certain emotions perhaps being differentially socialized across cultures and therefore having different behavioral concomitants. Therefore, part of children's developmental tasks is to learn the appropriate emotional repertoire suitable to their culture. Because of our different wirings and different experiences, however, we have idiosyncratic emotional experiences. While acknowledging the individual nature of affective experiences, investigators have increasingly tried to bring the study of affect into the laboratory. They have used a variety of methods for manipulating affect, and these will be briefly outlined here.

The design typically used in affect manipulation research is simple. One treatment group of subjects undergoes a short induction experience designed to elicit positive feelings. Another group experiences a negative mood induction, and a third group is given a suitable control experience. A behavioral or cognitive variable is assessed immediately following the induction phase, and analyses are computed to assess group differences on this response attributable to the induction variable.

The use of this design entails the assumption that affect levels can be readily manipulated within the person. Indeed, affect is conceived of as a within-person variable because an individual can be in a happier or sadder state, perhaps relative to a neutral affect balancing point, from moment to moment. Furthermore, it is assumed that shifts in affect level are predictable in relation to the nature of current experiences.

Experimental studies into affect manipulations have generally used one of four recognized procedures: the Velten technique (Velten, 1968), the success or failure experience (e.g., Isen, 1970), the reminiscence interview (Moore et al., 1973), and the serendipitous gift (e.g., Isen & Levin, 1972). Although different techniques are plainly better suited to different subject populations, the assumption is made that the different techniques achieve similar psychological consequences, that is, changes in a neutral to positive or a neutral to negative mood dimension.

The Velten technique involves assigning subjects to either elation, depression, or control treatments. Subjects are asked to read aloud 50 statements, each one having been typed onto a separate small card. The statements used in the elation treatment either connote physical energy or have positive self-referring connotations (e.g., "If my attitude is good then things go better and my attitude is good"). The depression treatment statements either connote tiredness, lethargy, ill health, or a negative self-view (e.g., "There are too many bad things in my life"). Control group statements are designed to have neutral connotations (e.g.,

"Peanuts are grown in Georgia"). Obviously, the Velten procedures are most suited for work with adults.

The success or failure experience involves subjects receiving information as to success, failure, or control experience applied to a task upon which they are unable to judge their own performance level or, alternatively, to a task upon which a predictable outcome is assured. For example, suitable tasks for young children could include matching-familiar-figure problems, the success-failure test, and the widely-used bowling game.

The reminiscence procedure consists of a short interview between a subject and an experimenter. The subject is asked to describe an experience that has happy or sad connotations, or that constitutes a neutral affect content. In a typical study, the experimenter will instruct the positive induction subjects, "I want you to tell me of something that really makes you happy, that makes you feel good." Negative induction subjects are asked to tell of something that makes them feel unhappy or sad. Control group subjects can be asked to verbalize innocuous content such as counting to 10 three times, to describe a scene in a picture, or to list the names of other children in their classroom. In the case of positive and negative induction treatment, the subjects are asked to dwell on the relevant experience for perhaps 20 or 30 seconds. A typical induction is likely to last about a minute.

A serendipitous gift is simply one that a subject receives unexpectedly. The gift need not be one of great value: Several studies have used free samples of items of merchandise or coupons valued at 50 cents or less.

Additionally, some investigators have used stories whose affective tone is varied, movies, audiotapes, music, humor, or even hypnotic inductions to create different feelings within their subjects. Although these manipulations rarely evoke profound emotional experiences, there is evidence that they can reliably alter affect.

It must be said, by the way of caveat, that it has become clear that experimenters are tapping complicated affective complexes when they call upon subjects to generate a specific affective state. It has been demonstrated recently by Polivy (1981) and Underwood, Froming, and Moore (1982) that laboratory inductions designed to influence a single affective state such as sadness, anger, or fear can actually cause significant alterations in all those states simultaneously as well as influencing still other affects, and therefore making difficult the conclusion which component(s) of the manipulation is (are) the critical one(s). All of this suggests that any procedure designed to validate an affect induction should attempt to measure multiple affective states so as to give a more complex and realistic picture of the effects of emotion. The typical validation has consisted of some form of subject self-report. Even these efforts, however, have often focused only on those affective dimensions presumed to have been influenced by the experimental manipulation.

In addition to the methodological implication of the multidimensionality of affect, there is also an interpretive implication. In any review of the literature, one must be careful to distinguish between the effects of different affective states, and if this has not been addressed directly by the researchers, one must remain aware that the empirical findings may be limited in generality or applicability by such factors.

In recent years, there has been a major effort to obtain behavioral validation of affect inductions. For example, Masters, Barden, and Ford (1979) collected independent ratings of children's facial expressions to validate their induction of mood. Bugental and Moore (1979) used a different approach to assess the validity of an affect manipulation: They recorded the voices of their elementary school subjects, and then subjected the recordings to a pass band filter that removes voice content while maintaining voice quality. Validation of the affect induction was obtained when raters listening to the filtered recording were able to distinguish between the affect and control conditions. A variety of more prosaic manipulation checks (adjective checklists, having children indicate the face most resembling their own feelings) have been used with child and adult subjects – generally finding differences among conditions. All of this is by way of saying that it does not appear that at least transient affective states can be successfully induced in both children and adults.

1.3. Overview of empirical relations

We have commented on the intuitive rationales for expecting there to be important relationships between affect and behaviors. There have also been numerous theoretical arguments advanced for such relationships (cf. Izard, 1977). However, most of the empirical work done in the past two decades has not grown out of any specific theoretical position. Indeed, most of the research has been rather piecemeal, with very few attempts to come up with an undergirding conceptual framework. Yet there is, of course, some sort of implicit framework that leads investigators to the topic in the first place.

The most general form of the framework (somehow the term "theory" seems too high-flown for the level of understanding in the area) is that affective states have their behavioral concomitants. This does not mean that moods have necessary behavioral products, but rather that when individuals encounter certain types of situations, their feelings will affect how they respond to those situations. This does not seem like a terribly startling revelation, but what becomes interesting is what we can infer about the affect–cognition behavior links from the observed behavior patterns.

Psychodynamic theory sees behavior as "solutions" to emotional states. While we do not accept most of the trappings of the analytic position, perhaps this simple proposition, without the remainder of psychoanalytic theory, might be of value in interpreting much of the work on affect that has emerged. Affect is an important guide for behavior in that it influences the selection among the behavioral opportunities. That selection process is doubtlessly idiosyncratically organized, but to the extent that we can uncover affect–behavior links that have some generality, we can look at how these links may be socialized and how certain behaviors can act as solutions for different feelings. This is where we part company with the psychodynamic view, because it proposed on the basis of theory specific kinds of variables that were central and specific kinds of relationships that enabled various behaviors to be seen as solutions for various emotional states, in particular ways. In contrast, we encourage the empirical investigation of these kinds of relationships. A wider variety of affects, behaviors, and situations is considered than would be from a Freudian or neo-Freudian perspective. In fact, this might result in an interesting and useful way of categorizing feeling states and relating them to behavior.

Another interesting way to categorize some of the work that has been conducted on feeling is to examine separately how it influences reactions to self and reactions to others. Naturally some of the research on affect (e.g., state-dependent memory) does not lend itself to such categorization, but this dimension is relevant to the bulk of research related to social behavior.

Why should affect function as a setting condition for self- and other-oriented behavior? Negative affect by definition increases the psychological distance between self and other. Under negative affect, we suspect that natural tendencies arise to comfort self, by heightening self-reward, and, under some conditions, by withholding from others by decreasing their reward (but see work by Cialdini and his colleagues for examples of the complexity of this relationship). Positive affect in contrast, decreases psychological distance, making one feel good about the self and others. Especially with positive affect, one sees a high degree of generalization from the original source of the affect. Perhaps because the psychological distance between self and others is decreased, one feels about others as one does about oneself.

Recently, more sophisticated attempts to generate general theoretical arguments regarding the affect–social behavior link have begun to appear (Batson, Baron, & Berscheid, this volume; Isen, 1984, 1987). Some of the theoretical richness is the result of work in the domain of affect and cognition. As research has been conducted on the relation between affect and memory, perception, problem solving, and other indexes of cognitive performance, the findings have helped to illuminate general mechanisms underlying the relations between affect and social behavior. On the other hand, many of the affect and cognition links are complex and rely on particular setting conditions and should not be taken as rendering a full explanation in the domain of social behavior. That is, there is sometimes an implication that there is something "primary" about the affect–cognition relations that undergird the domains of social behavior. Whereas this is undoubtedly true at one level, we believe that there are aspects of the operations of feeling states that are particular to their influence in the social domain and are not apt to be manifested fully in purely cognitive measures. For instance, the relation between self-reward and being rewarding toward others doubtlessly has important cognitive underpinnings; however, the underpinnings may be difficult to observe except in social measures. It is not possible to explore here the extensive work that has been performed in the affect–cognition domain (see Isen, 1984, 1987; Blaney, 1986, for reviews), but we shall make some general brief comments on the emerging picture of processes relating affect and cognition and social behavior as an overview for the following chapters. Again, although most of the comments particularly apply to studies of induced affect, we feel that in general the principles also apply to discussions of nonmanipulated assessed affect.

The roles that feeling states play in influencing behavior occur at many levels and the general effects may be described in various ways, but at least three possible influences of affect have been suggested. Affect may serve both informational and directive functions (Wyer & Carlston, 1979). As an example of its informational function, people may use their momentary affective state as a basis for coming to various kinds of judgments, including assessments regarding their lives, abilities, and judgments of others, through processes like those involved in the attribution process. In the same context, feelings may serve a directive function in that they can direct one's attention to particular kinds of information in order to generate plausible causes for the feelings. Further, a substantial body of evidence suggests that affect may serve as a retrieval cue, influencing the material in memory that is most likely to be accessed. Mood may act to produce mood-congruent thought, or information. The impact of these general processes for social behavior are varied and depend on the type of behavior being assessed and the circumstances under which it is assessed. So, for example, sadness may produce either lower levels of altruism, or higher levels, depending on the conditions of assessment and the age of the subjects (e.g., Cialdini & Kendrick, 1976; Isen, Horn, & Rosenhan, 1973; Moore et al., 1973). Similarly, positive and negtive feeling states may produce similar levels of self-reward or opposite patterns, depending on how the behavioral measurement is constructed.

Additional complexity is added by the general finding that the effects of positive affective states are much more consistent than are those of negative feeling states, and the assumed symmetry between positive and negative feeling states may be an artifact of language rather than a reflection of the actual state of affairs. As was stated earlier, there is good evidence that affect influences retrieval of information from memory.

Affect alters attention and recall, and through them, cognitions about self and others. The power of feeling states in this regard is seen in a study by Mischel, Ebbeson, and Zeiss (1976), who induced success and failure to explore the relationship between affect and memory for personality information that purportedly was derived from previous personality testing. Subjects were subsequently tested for recall of the information. The subjects who experienced success were better able to recall personality strengths than liabilities. Those who experienced failure, however, did not differ from controls. Compatible findings were obtained by Isen (1970). Whereas these findings suggest that only positive affect has potent effects on recall of personality-relevant information, later studies indicate that negative emotion may have similar effects. Teasdale and Fogarty (1979) examined the personal memories that happy and sad moods evoke. On separate occasions, happy and sad moods were induced. On each occasion, subjects were presented with a series of words. For each word they were asked to recall a real-life experience, either pleasant or unpleasant, that they associated with the word. Using latency of retrieval for each experience, Teasdale and Fogarty found that happy subjects retrieved happy memories faster than they did sad ones, and that sad subjects retrieved sad memories faster than they did happy ones.

Affect determines both the tone and the availability of memories. For example, people who are happy give more favorable evaluations of the performance and service records of their cars than do those who are not. Moreover, happy people recall more positive (but no more neutral or negative) words than do control subjects (Isen, Shalker, Clark, & Karp, 1978; Nasby & Yando, 1982). Positive affect in particular may promote a "cognitive loop" that increases the salience and availability of positively toned memories.

Finally, another study has shown that the valence of an experienced emotion can determine the valence of personal memories that are re-called. In one study, subjects who had been maintaining daily diaries of emotional events were subsequently hypnotically induced to experience emotion. Those who were in a pleasant mood recalled more of their pleasant experiences than their unpleasant ones, while those who were in a negative mood recalled a higher proportion of their unpleasant memories (Bower, 1981). It should be noted that many of the studies showing such effects of negative affect did not contain control groups or did not compare the effect on negative vs. neutral material (but only compared retrievability of negative with that of positive material). Therefore, effects apparently showing facilitation of recall of negative material by negative feelings may actually reflect, instead, impairment of recall of positive material. In fact, one study designed specifically to look at that issue found that whereas positive affect facilitated recall of positive material, sadness did not facilitate the recall of negative material but did impair recall of positive material (Nasby & Yando, 1982). This suggests that studies investigating the influence of feelings on recall of material of different affective types should avoid the practice of just substracting the recall scores of the two types of material to come up with the "relative advantage" of the type targeted for interest.

Some of these findings have been corroborated in clinical populations. An investigation by Lloyd and Lishman (1975) used depressed patients and closely parallels the findings of Teasdale and Fogarty (1979). Sub-jects were instructed to recall a happy or sad personal incident in response to neutral words. The more severe their depression, the longer the subjects took to retrieve a pleasant as opposed to an unpleasant memory. Again, this could by the result of facilitated recall of the unpleasant or impaired access to the pleasant, under conditions of depression.

Proponents of cognitive models of affective disorders have marshalled an impressive number of studies that demonstrate differences between normals and both clinically and subclinically depressed subjects (see reviews by Miller, 1975; Coyne & Gottlieb, 1983). For example, depressed subjects evaluate themselves more negatively than do nondepressed subjects in the absence of differences in actual performance on ambiguous laboratory tasks (e.g., Lobitz & Post, 1979). Depressed subjects also recall receiving lower rates of rewards than they actually did receive on laboratory tasks (e.g., Nelson & Craighead, 1977). One interesting line of research has utilized an incidental learning paradigm in which subjects rate adjectives according to several variables, one being whether the particular adjective is self-referent or not. Davis and Unruh (1981) found depressed–nondepressed differences only for those adjectives rated as self-referent, with depressed subjects recalling fewer self-referent adjectives. Derry and Kuiper (1981) found that depressed subjects were superior to both normal controls and nondepressed psychiatric controls in their recall of self-referent depressive adjectives, with the opposite pattern occurring for recall of nondepressive self-referent adjectives.

However, it remains disputable whether these differences are the causal result of biased or distorted cognitive functioning. Some results may be a reflection of differences in self-presentational strategies. Both patient and nonpatient depressed samples are identified by self-report instruments as exhibiting self-blame, pessimism, and negative self-evaluation and are then compared on other measures of these specific tendencies. It is also unclear whether the results are due to specific mood-related disorders rather than level of psychopathology (Johnson & Magaro, 1987). The strong version of cognitive theories of depression requires proof of two premises. First, it needs to be demonstrated that cognitive factors rather than associated features were the cause of other symptoms such as depressed effect. Several studies (e.g., Manly, McMahon, Bradley, & Davidson, 1982) have been unable to predict subsequent depression from current cognitions. Second, it needs to be demonstrated that depression is associated with differences in cognitive processing rather than with similar cognitive processing of different materials. Laboratory tasks showing differences in attributions tend to be highly ambiguous, and differences in performance evaluation by depressed subjects may reflect differences in their prior experience. In this view, it is not that depressed subjects process information differently, but that they have different relevant background information or that information is organized differently as suggested by Isen (1985). These issues require greater knowledge of how normal subjects incorporate emotionally relevant events into their memories in order for adequate comparisons to be made with the processes used by depressed subjects. As Coyne and Gotlieb (1983) have pointed out, "In order to make unambiguous statements about the structure of cognitive processes, theorists may require data about the structure of subjects' extralab experiences" (p. 498).

Taken as a whole, results seem to indicate that people in positive affective states tend to have positive information more accessible in memory; tend to set higher estimations of performance and are more optimistic about future performance; make more favorable judgments; are more generous to themselves; and are more friendly, open, and giving to others. Negative affect often seems to produce conflicting tendencies. Sometimes negative material in memory may be more accessible and there may be greater pessimism. At other times, negative feeling states may act to produce behaviors designed to alter the negative state and those attempts may include behaviors that are affect incompatible – for example, focusing on more positive aspects of oneself or engaging in altruistic acts.

Isen (1984, 1987) has addressed both the problem of asymmetry in the results of positive and negative affect and some problems that current cognitive models have in accounting for the results of studies on affect. In the "contextualist view," the encoding and elaboration of stimuli are strongly influenced by the meaning of the context in which they are found. Isen believes that if affect is seen as functioning as both meaning and context cue in the associationist sense, many of the current ambiguities in affect-memory research can be explained. For example, the asymmetry in effects of positive and negative affect may result from the different cognitive contexts that they generate. Positive material is known to be diverse and extensive in mind (e.g., Cramer, 1968; Osgood, 1969), and thus anything that cues positive material also cues a complex cognitive context (Isen, Johnson, Mertz, & Robinson, 1985). The contextualist model also "implies a flexible, possibly multiple, and probably changing organization structure of memory" in which "affect may influence the way in which stimuli are grouped, organized, and related to one another" (Isen, 1984, p. 225). It may also be that negative material is less interconnected and elaborated in the memory system than is positive material.

It might also be of interest to think about the effects of feelings in the context of work on automaticity, which has been of interest recently (e.g., Udeman & Bargh, 1989). This work asks about the extent to which cognitive (and affective) processing may occur without attention, intention, or effort (e.g., Posner & Snyder, 1975; Shiffrin, 1988). The general findings in the area indicate that most processing is attentive rather than automatic, but that very familiar or frequently experienced material may come to be processed automatically. Thus, one suggestion that has been made (Isen & Diamond, 1989) is that positive affect may be more likely than other feeling states to be processed automatically or to have automatic influences on thought and behavior (because it tends to be the most frequently experienced affective state for most people). This is an area in which research is needed, however, to address some of these speculations.

We can draw several conclusions for this brief overview of the action of affect in relation to cognition and social behavior. In general, there seems to be evidence that positive affect is used as a way of organizing experience and storing material in memory, such that accessing one affective element activates other related elements. For a variety of reasons, these effects are more general and stronger for positive feeling states than for negative, at least in normal populations, although they may also be observed for some types of negatives feeling states, as well, under some circumstances. The evocation of congruent cognitive material may influence a variety of reactions to self and others for which judgments are required. However, other processes and motivations, such as motives to maintain or alter the particular feeling state may also be activated by feeling states and may influence behavior in complex ways. Since many of these processes and meanings are learned, we might expect to find some degree of developmental change in the ways in which affect influences behavior. But on the other hand, feeling states may be an area where individual stability of behavior is relatively high, in that different affect elicitors may activate learned associations. In addition, there may be some situations in which some affects operate relatively automatically. Research suggests that this can occur where material is very familiar and where the processing demands on the person are great and the situation is complex. It would seem that social situations might often present these very conditions. Thus, social behavior may be influenced by the joint action of automatic and attentive processes, and sometimes these processes will be producing similar effects and sometimes dissimilar effects. More research is needed into these processes, and the analysis of social behavior requires the careful delineation of the likely mode of action of such processes.

We are still a long way from describing precisely how affect influences reactions to self and others. That goal is remote for several reasons. In the first place, affect is not a unitary phenomenon: The different feeling states likely influence these reactions differently, and the full panorama of affect has not yet been explored. Second, the processes through which affects exert their influence are not yet fully understoood. Finally, perhaps as the result of these considerations, it is only recently that general theories or frameworks have begun to emerge to guide these explorations. The horizon is dotted with studies that separately are both interesting and challenging, but that together do not yet suggest the substantial fabric of theory.

Yet, for all these disclaimers, the literature on the relations between affect, self, and others is not without coherence. We begin with the assumption that the effects of feeling states on self are mediated through perception and memory. In general, the effects of feeling states on absolute memory performance levels are probably not large. Rather, we expect that the *accessibility* of memories, the readiness with which they come to mind, and the range of material cued will be differentially affected. Happy people retrieve pleasant information – whether that information consists of personality descriptions, memories, or pleasant words – more readily than they do unpleasant information and more readily than others. And that material is more diverse and extensive than other material.

Affect affects reactions to self and others (Moore, Underwood, & Rosenhan, 1984). Its power resides in part, in its pervasiveness: There is hardly an area of reaction to self or others that is not touched and altered by feeling states. Happiness affects attribution, perception of control, self-reward, task performance and evaluation, self-concept, and delay of gratification. Sadness can effect these aspects of self too, but complexly. The question of just how far the influence of affect on self-perception extends remains to be explored.

What holds for reactions to self seems also to hold regarding reactions to others. In the main, happiness promotes altruism, helpfulness, shar-ing, and sociability, while sadness retards them. These findings hold only when the effects are egocentric. When the effects are emphatic – that is, when one is happy or sad for others – the findings re-verse. Generally, as others have observed, the findings regarding positive affect are more consistent and stable than are those of negative states.

The chapters that follow offer a rich and comprehensive examination of the operation of affect on a variety of important social behaviors. This volume represents the first general examination of these diverse behaviors and provides a context for furthering understanding of these important relations.

References

Barnett, M. A., King, L. M., & Howard, J. A. (1979). Inducing affect about self or other: Effects on generosity in children. *Developmental Psychology, 15,* 164–167.

Berlyne, D. E. (1971). What next? In H. I. Day, D. E. Berlyne, & D. E. Hunt (Eds.), *Intrinsic motivation: A new direction in education.* Toronto: Holt, Rinehart, & Winston.

Blaney, P. H. (1986). Affect and memory: A review. *Psychological Bulletin, 99*(2), 229–246.

Boucher, J., & Osgood, C. E. (1969). The Pollyanna hypothesis. *Journal of Verbal Learning and Verbal Behavior, 8,* 1–8.

Bower, G. H. (1981). Mood and memory. *American Psychologist, 36,* 129–148.

Bugental, D. B., & Moore, B. S. (1979). Effects of induced moods on voice affect. *Developmental Psychology, 15*(6), 664–665.

Cialdini, R. B., & Kendrick, D. T. (1976). Altruism and hedonism: A social developmental perspective on the relation of mood states and helping. *Journal of Personality and Social Psychology, 34,* 907–914.

Clark, M. S., & Isen, A. M. (1982). The relationship between feeling states and social behavior. In A. H. Hastorf & A. M. Isen (Eds.), *Cognitive social psychology.* New York: Elsevier North-Holland.

Coyne, J. C., & Gotlieb, I. H. (1983). The role of cognition in depression: A critical appraisal. *Psychological Bulletin, 94,* 472–505.

Cramer, P. (1968). *Word Association.* New York: Academic Press.

Davis, H., & Unruh, W. R. (1981). The development of the self-schema in adult depression. *Journal of Abnormal Psychology, 90,* 125–133.

Derry, P., & Kuiper, N. (1981). Schematic processing and self-reference in clinical depression. *Journal of Abnormal Psychology, 90,* 286–297.

Isen, A. M. (1970). Success, failure, attention and reaction to others: The warm glow of success. *Journal of Personality and Social Psychology, 15,* 294–301.

Isen, A. M. (1984). Toward understanding the role of affect in cognition. In R. Wyer & T. Srull (Eds.), *Handbook of social cognition.* Hillsdale, NJ: Erlbaum.

Isen, A. M. (1987).Positive affect, cognitive processes, and social behavior. In L. Berkowitz (Ed.), *Advances in experimental social psychology* (Vol. 21). New York: Academic Press.

Isen, A. M., & Diamond, G. A. (1989). Affect and automaticity. In J. S. Uleman & J. A. Bargh (Eds.), *Unintended thought.* New York: Guilford Press.

Isen, A. M., Johnson, M. M. S., Mertz, E., Robinson, G. F. (1985). The influence of positive affect on the unusualness of word associations. *Journal of Personality and Social Psychology, 48,* 1413–1426.

Isen, A. M., Horn, N., & Rosenhan, D. L. (1973). Effects of success and failure on children's generosity. *Journal of Personality and Social Psychology, 27,* 239–247.

Isen, A. M., & Levin, P. F. (1972). The effects of feeling good on helping: Cookies and kindness. *Journal of Personality and Social Psychology, 21,* 384–388.

Isen, A. M., Shalker, T., Clark, M., & Karp, L. (1978). Affect, accessibility, of material in memory and behavior. *Journal of Personality and Social Psychology, 36,* 1–12.

Izard, C. E. (1972). *Patterns of emotions: A new analysis of anxiety and depression.* New York: Academic Press.

Izard, C. E. (1977). *Human emotions.* New York: Plenum.

Johnson, M. H., & Magaro, P. A. (1987). Effects of mood and severity on memory processes in depression and mania. *Psychological Bulletin, 101*(1), 28–40.

Lacey, J. I. (1967). Somatic response patterning and stress: Some revisions of activation theory. In M. H. Appley & R. Trumbul (Eds.), *Psychological stress: Issues in research.* New York: Appleton Century Crofts.

Lacey, J. I., Kagan, J., Lacey, B., & Moss, H. A. (1963). The visceral level: Situational determinants and behavioral correlates of autonomic response patterns. In P. H. Knapp (Ed.), *Expressions of the emotions in man.* New York: International Universities Press.

Lloyd, G. C., & Lishman, W. A. (1975). Effect of depression on the speed of recall of pleasant and unpleasant experiences. *Psychological Medicine, 5,* 173–180.

Lobitz, C. W., & Post, R. D. (1979). Parameters of self-reinforcement and depression. *Journal of Abnormal Psychology, 88*(1), 33–41.

Mandler, G. (1984). *Mind and emotion* (2nd ed.). New York: Wiley.

Manly, P. C., McMahon, R. J., Bradley, C. F., & Davidson, P. O. (1982). Depressive attributional style and depression following childbirth. *Journal of Abnormal Psychology, 91*(4), 245–254.

Martindale, C. (1981). *Cognition and consciousness.* Homewood, IL: Dorsey Press.

Masters, J. C., Barden, R. C., & Ford, M. E. (1979). Affective states, expressive behavior, and learning in children. *Journal of Personality and Social Psychology, 37,* 380–390.

Miller, W. R. (1975). Psychological deficit in depression. *Psychological Bulletin, 82*(2), 238–260.

Mischel, W., Ebbeson, E. B., & Zeiss, A. R. (1976). Determinants of selective memory about the self. *Journal of Consulting and Clinical Psychology, 44,* 92–103.

Moore, B. S., Underwood, B., & Rosenhan, D. (1984). Affect, self and other. In C. E. Izard, J. Kagan, & R. Zajonc (Eds.), *Emotion, cognition and behavior.* New York: Cambridge University Press.

Moore B. S., Underwood, W., & Rosenhan, D. L. (1973). Affect and altruism. *Developmental Psychology, 8,* 99–104.

Nasby, W., & Yando, R. (1982). Selective encoding and retrieval of affectively valent information: Two cognitive consequences of children's mood states. *Journal of Personality and Social Psychology, 43,* 1244–1253.

Nelson, R. E., & Craighead, W. E. (1977). Selective recall of positive and negative feedback, self-control behaviors, and depression. *Journal of Abnormal Psychology, 86,* 379–388.

Plutchik, R. (1980a). *Emotion: A psychoevolutionary synthesis.* New York: Harper & Row.

Plutchik, R. (1980b). A general psychoevolutionary theory of emotion. In R. Plutchik & H. Kellerman (Eds.), *Emotion: Theory, research and experience* (Vol. 1). New York: Academic Press.

Polivy, J. (1981). On the induction of emotion in the laboratory: Discrete moods or multiple affect states. *Journal of Personality and Social Psychology, 41,* 803–817.

Posner, M. I., & Snyder, C. R. R. (1975). Attention and cognitive control. In R. L. Solso (Ed.), *Information processing and cognition: The Loyola symposium.* Hillsdale, NJ: Erlbaum.

Russell, J. A. (1980). A circumplex model of affect. *Journal of Personality and Social Psychology, 39,* 1161–1178.

Shaver, P., Schwartz, J., Kirson, D., & O'Connor, C. (1987). Emotion knowledge: Further exploration of a prototype approach. *Journal of Personality and Social Psychology. 52*(6), 1061–1086.

Shiffrin, R. M. (1988). Attention. In R. C. Atkinston, R. J. Hernstein, G. Lindzey, & R. D. Luce (Eds.), *Steven's handbook of experimental psychology* (2nd Ed). New York: Wiley.

Teasdale, J. D., & Fogarty, S. J. (1979). Differential effects of induced mood on retrieval of pleasant and unpleasant events from episodic memory. *Journal of Abnormal Psychology, 88,* 248–257.

Thompson, W. C., Cowan, C. L., & Rosenhan, D. L. (1980). Focus of attention mediates the impact of negative affect on altruism. *Journal of Personality and Social Psychology, 2,* 291–300.

Uleman, J. S., & Bargh, J. A. (Eds.) (1989). *Unintended Thought.* New York: Guilford Press.

Underwood, B., Froming, W. J., & Moore, B. S. (1982). *Dimensions of affect.* Unpublished manuscript, University of Texas.

Velton, E. (1968). A laboratory task for the induction of mood. *Behaviour Research and Therapy, 6,* 473–482.

Watson, D., Clark, L. A., & Tellegen, A. (1988). Development and validation of brief measures of positive and negative affect: The PANAS scales. *Journal of Personality and Social Psychology, 54*(6), 1063–1070.

Watson, D., & Tellegen, A. (1985). Toward a consensual structure of mood. *Psychological Bulletin, 98,* 219–235.

Wispé, L., Kiecolt, J., Long, R. E. (1977). Demand characteristics, moods, and helping. *Social Behavior and Personality, 5,* 249–255.

Woodworth, R., & Schlosberg, H. (1954). *Experimental psychology.* New York: Holt.

Wyer, R. S., & Carlston, D. E. (1979). *Social cognition, inference and attribution.* Hillsdale, NJ: Erlbaum.

2. Contemporary vocabularies of emotion

ELLEN BERSCHEID

2.1. Psychology's new tower of Babel

My queries to others about the nature of the comments appropriate to a forum such as this yielded the opinion that it is a marvelous opportunity to speak ex cathedra about matters of deep concern to oneself, with the aim of instilling some degree of the same concern in one's brethren. For those who think of this platform as a pulpit of sorts, perhaps I should immediately say that the appropriate text for my sermon can be found in the eleventh chapter of Genesis, where what happened long ago in a city in the land of Shinar is recounted. As all graduates of Sunday school will recall, the citizens of that city embarked upon the most ambitious building project ever undertaken – the construction of a tower tall enough to reach heaven. But the workers' zeal and enthusiasm soon dissipated into confusion, disorder, and, ultimately, apathy, because they found that they could not communicate with one another. As a consequence, the raising of the great tower of Babel was abandoned.

The zeal with which psychologists of all stripes and persuasions are currently pursuing the venerable mysteries of emotion suggests that we, too, are ambitiously building our own kind of tower – one designed to reach, if not a piece of heaven, then certainly new heights in understanding human behavior, for it is not much of an exaggeration to say that we can truly appreciate very little about human behavior without understanding the emotional phenomena that pervade it.

For psychologists, then, the emotion "gold rush" is on. New books on the subject pour off the presses at a rate that overwhelms even the most devoted student of human emotion. In the last few years alone, we have

This chapter was first presented as the presidential address at the annual meeting of the American Psychological Association, Toronto, to the Society of Personality and Social Psychology (Division 8) in August 1984.

seen Mandler's revision of *Mind and Emotion* (1975; now called *Mind and Body*, 1984); Izard, Kagan, and Zajonc's edited book *Emotions, Cognition, and Behaviors* (1984); Malatesta and Izard's edited book *Emotion in Adult Development* (1984); de Rivera's edited issue of the *American Behavioral Scientist* addressed to "The Qualitative Analysis of Emotional Experience" (1984); Buck's book *The Communication of Emotion* (1984); and, finally, the volume of the *Review of Personality and Social Psychology* (1984) edited by Shaver and addressed to emotion, relationships, and health. In addition, the words "affect" and "emotion" appear with ever-increasing frequency in the titles of articles in virtually all journals, and the recent pages of the *American Psychologist* have carried at least one fevered debate.

It is not surprising that questions of human emotion are attracting so many laborers, for the potential harvest is plentiful. It is *so* plentiful, in fact, and so vital to our progress as a discipline, that I think it important that even more workers be enlisted and that those thinking about offering their service to the enterprise not be turned away in frustration and bewilderment. And – here comes the sermon – I think that is now becoming a very real danger. It is a danger because it is becoming increasingly difficult for a potential contributor or consumer to read intelligently in the area. It is difficult to read the emotion literature because there is not one vocabulary of emotion today but, as the title of my chapter suggests, there are many – almost as many as there are active theorists and investigators.

Thus, the budding student of human emotion who wishes to build upon a century of emotion theory and research must be multilingual. But unfortunately there is no easy way to learn the languages quickly. Indeed, there is little to warn the unsuspecting that all is not what it seems – that while the basic language of emotion is in English, there are so many dialects of meaning that what we have here is a city of Babel indeed. There is little or nothing to caution students that, despite the surface similarities in the languages used to talk about emotional phenomena, strong and conflicting undercurrents of meaning exist, and that the speaker's individual dialect may be shaped by his or her training, the kinds of research he or she was accustomed to doing before entering the field of emotion, the kinds of animals that were (or are) the subject of study, the methodology that the person knows well or favors, and the kinds of emotional phenomena he or she is focusing upon.

I should like, then, to illustrate briefly some of our vocabulary problems, to describe several of their consequences and to offer a modest proposal of my own.

My concern is not for the cognoscenti, whose sophistication is undoubtedly the result of knocking around the polyglot domain of emotion for a very long time. Rather it is for the student, or that person who seeks to become familiar with contemporary emotion theory and research, often not because he or she is interested in problems of emotion per se, but rather because these directly engage other problems of interest. That is, for many of us the only way to get from point A to Point C is to travel through point B, or the psychology of emotion. People such as we, for whom emotion is central but not identical to the phenomena of interest, cannot afford to spend years in the jungle of emotion, talking to the natives and learning their many dialects, if we are ever to get to where we were going in the first place.

2.2. Real vs. counterfeit emotions

The first problem for those who wish to partake of the fruits of psychological theory and research on emotion is that the natives do not agree on what an emotion is. They are in agreement on one thing, however, and that is that there are a lot of fakes floating around and masquerading as the real thing.

Thus, the emotion literature abounds with references to real emotion, pure emotion, true emotion, fundamental emotion, and so on, all of which, presumably, are to be contrasted with unreal, impure, superficial, and bogus emotion. Unfortunately, one person's idea of a true emotion is often someone else's counterfeit.

It was just this sort of thing that must have led Richard Lazarus to conclude in the pages of the *American Psychologist* recently that "the searching question [before us] is what an emotion is or is not" (1984, p. 122). I do not think that is the searching question facing us, but I do think the fact that it has been represented as such by so eminent an emotion theorist and researcher underscores the severity of our vocabulary problem. It is also, of course, symptomatic of the issues and controversies that thread throughout the psychology of emotion.

Perhaps I can quickly illustrate the current state of affairs by relating a recent brief encounter I had with a lawyer. Like many encounters between psychology and law, this one was definitely "of the third kind." It began with a telephone call just as I was leaving the office late one afternoon. The caller introduced himself as an assistant attorney in what I immediately recognized as one of the most celebrated criminal defense firms in the Midwest . . . celebrated, I might add, for winning hopeless cases. He said that he was calling from a phone booth, having just been sent out of the courtroom by the famous senior partner himself, who was at that very moment still in there battling for their client's life. He said it was urgent that he talk to me. Would I wait for him to come up to the university?

While I was waiting, I tried to remember the newspaper and television stories that had been flowing from that courtroom in the past weeks. The bare facts, as I recalled them, were that the man on trial had come home one afternoon and discovered that his wife had left him. He also found a note in which his wife explained, first, that she didn't love him anymore and planned to file for divorce and, second, that she did love her employer, an executive with the company for which she worked. The executive was also married and she apparently had been having an affair with him for some time. Later that afternoon, the husband went to the company headquarters, brushed aside his wife and others in the secretarial offices, and, gaining access to the executive's office, pumped the contents of a sawed-off shotgun into him at very close range.

When the assistant defense attorney arrived, he patiently explained to me that the question the judge and jury would be deliberating was not whether his firm's client had murdered the executive. He obviously had. The legal issue was, Murder in what degree? And, he said, the central question that had developed over the course of the trial and that now, at this eleventh hour, appeared to be critical, was whether or not their client was in an "emotional state" at the time he shot the executive. The prosecution was arguing that the man was not experiencing emotion at the time of the murder. The defense was arguing that their client *was* in an emotional state at the time the act was committed – that he was, in fact, a walking "emotional volcano" that had erupted.

I immediately responded, "You don't want me, a social psychologist; you need a forensic psychologist, one of my clinical colleagues upstairs, because surely you are pleading temporary insanity." "Oh, no," he replied, "we don't want our client locked up in Minnesota's institution for the criminally insane. No," he went on, "we want to argue, first, that our client was in an emotional state at the time of the murder and, second, that the provocation was such that any normal, average human being in this particular situation would have been in an intense emotional state and, just conceivably, could have taken the same action our client did." The light then dawned: They were endeavoring to show that their client's behavior was, in our terms, just part of the "psychopathology of everyday life" and so deserving of a lesser sentence, such as manslaughter, or even possibly acquittal.

Continuing on, the attorney said that he had just a couple of "simple" questions. The first one, he said, with his pencil poised over his legal pad, was: "How do you psychologists tell that someone is in an emotional state? Oh, and by the way," he added, "we'll also need the names of some experts we can call to testify in court about how you can tell that someone is experiencing an emotion."

It was my sad public duty to inform him that he had just asked the $64,000 question – or the "searching question," if you will. How an expert witness would answer that question in court would depend very much upon the expert witness he happened to ask. And, since there is no dearth of experts on emotion, for virtually every answer the defense could come up with the prosecution could find someone who would say something quite different, if not in direct contradiction.

The role of arousal

Because he looked bewildered at my response to what he had thought was a simple question, I outlined a scenario illustrating the kind of courtroom circus that could result from this line of pursuit. First, I said, you could call Mandler (1984) or Schachter (1964), or any of several others (e.g., Strongman, 1978) who would probably say that peripheral physiological arousal is a necessary, although not sufficient, condition for the experience of emotion. And then they might proceed to outline for the jury some of the usual visible symptoms of that arousal.

The prosecution, however, could easily counter you, I said, by calling a number of people to the stand who would say that arousal not only is not sufficient but is not necessary for emotional experience. Your adversary, for example, could call up Bernie Weiner, who might say: "There is, in fact, little evidence to support the position that arousal is necesssry for emotional experience, or that arousal is a needed concept in the field of emotion" (Valins, 1966; 1982, p. 204). As this suggests, I said, some experts would say that all we have to know to classify your client as having been in an emotional state is whether he had a negative cognitive appraisal of the executive – or, in other words, just did not *like* him very much. But, as Zajonc (1984) has observed, this probably isn't going to be very helpful to you or to anyone else because it suggests that virtually everyone is in some sort of an emotional state all of the time. You could also persist in your argument, I said, by calling James Averill to the stand, and he might testify: "It would be fatuous to argue that emotional reactions do not involve peripheral physiological change" (1974, p. 176). But even if you won that point, I explained, there would be complications. For example, Averill and others would go on to elaborate that not *all* emotions are characterized by marked physiological arousal and, further, that arousal is indicative of some nonemotional as well as emotional states. They will note, for example, that physical exercise also produces arousal symptoms. So, even if your client had been excited and agitated, flushed of face and tremulous of hand, some experts would want to know if he had been exercising or had run up a long flight of stairs before he committed the murder – or, in other words, if the peripheral arousal was extraneous to the events in question.

And it gets even more complicated than this, I warned. Someone like Dolf Zillmann (1978) or Peggy Clark (1982) would say that information about extraneous arousal is not entirely irrelevant because some of the arousal may have "transferred" to the marital situation and heightened the intensity of whatever emotional state your client may have been experiencing. In this regard, Clark and Isen (1982) also might be interested in the fact that there is evidence that your client had been in a bad mood for some time before the event, having lost two jobs in succession. But of course I had to point out to him that no one really knows how affective experience may cumulate and combine over time. The last research I heard of on that problem was being conducted by Richard Solomon (1979), and his subjects were chickens.

And then there is another complication, I continued. Even if you presented evidence that your client *was* experiencing arousal just before the murder, many experts would also have to know if he himself *perceived* the arousal. If he did not, they would say he probably was not experiencing an emotion.

This issue, too, I observed, is fraught with uncertainties. For example, someone like Mandler (1979) might testify that if he experienced it, he probably perceived it, for "the human organism is pre-programmed to represent certain events consciously" (1979, p. 82), and autonomic nervous system activity, he theorizes, is among these. Nevertheless, I had to point out that, as Blascovich and Katkin (1982) discuss, there clearly are wide individual differences in the perception of various autonomic or visceral responses; for example, many Vietnam War and other veterans of combat, it is said, eventually learned to "tune out" their arousal symptoms.

And then there is the further problem, I went on, that the event that precipitated the arousal also may have instantly triggered coping behaviors that so fully occupied consciousness that the person never was aware of the arousal. For example, the frail woman who manages to lift the two-ton car that is crushing her daughter after an automobile accident may be so focused on saving her child that she never perceives the adrenalin pumping in her veins. Later, when asked how she felt at the time, she responds that she did not really "feel" anything – she was concentrating on lifting the car. In any event, I said, some experts would conclude that people who *are* strongly aroused but who do not consciously perceive it are not in an emotional state. And there are still other problems with the arousal criterion, I started to explain, but the attorney held up his hand and cried: "That's enough! The role of arousal in emotional states sounds too complicated for us. Aren't there *other* kinds of evidence we could use?"

The role of facial musculature

Yes, I replied, you could call Carroll Izard to the stand and he might testify: "Sensory feedback from the face then generates the subjective experience of a particular fundamental emotion" (1980, p. 169). And thus, "for each subjective experience corresponding to a fundamental emotion there is a corresponding facial pattern or expression" (1972, p. 78). So, for evidence that your client was in an emotional state, someone like Izard, or others such as Paul Ekman (e.g., Ekman, Friesen, & Ellsworth, 1972) might like to know what his facial expression was. But I had to warn him that even if he could bring forth evidence on this dimension favorable to his client – for example, even if he could get the secretaries and the security guard to testify that his client *looked* angry – the prosecution could easily counter this evidence that his client was in an emotional state. They might simply cite, for example, a personal communication from Ekman to Mandler (cited on p. 170 of Mandler's 1984 book) in which Ekman states that "there is obviously emotion without facial expression and facial expression without emotion." Facial expressions of emotion, in other words, are regarded as neither necessary nor sufficient evidence of an emotional state even by some who regard them as a crucially important component of emotion.

The role of self-report

By this time the lawyer's pencil had drooped and his eyes had glazed, but he persisted. "Well, are there *other* kinds of evidence?" he asked.

"Yes", I replied, "there is verbal self-report." Many people, as I have implied, would require some evidence that your client was *consciously* experiencing an emotion before concluding that he was in an emotional state. Unfortunately, I told him, we have to rely heavily on what they tell us about their emotional experience. And what they tell us about it – their verbal expressions of emotion – is influenced by any number of things, as Ekman (1977) and others have detailed. Perhaps, I explained, your client is emotionally inarticulate; perhaps he was inadequately socialized in learning an emotional language and could not verbally express the feelings he was experiencing even if someone had thought to ask him at the time. And even if he had answered a question posed to him at the time by saying that he felt very "angry," what would this signify? Maybe nothing. Maybe he was lying. And maybe he is also a very good actor; actors can display rage and grief very well while experiencing nothing, while the person who truly is angry or grieving may look just like someone who is neither.

2.3. The attribution of emotion in others

By this time, the lawyer looked like *he* was in an emotional state. The partners' eleventh-hour brainstorm for a dazzling finale to their defense had fizzled. So I tried to console him by pointing out that the fact that different experts regard different behavioral events, or clusters of events, as critical in determining whether a person is experiencing an emotional state really should not concern him. That is, I told him that what the experts think an emotion is, or is not, was not going to make a big difference to his client. No amount of expert testimony was going to legislate that for the jury. The people on the jury, I explained, have their own vocabularies of emotion and what *they* believe constitutes evidence of an emotional state is what is going to make the difference here. "Well," he replied, "it's too late to tailor a defense to that. But just out of curiosity, what do they believe?" I replied that he could read Averill (1974), but that, really, investigators are just now trying to identify the situations conducive to the attribution of emotion; other investigators, such as Pennebaker (1983), are trying to identify the physiological symptoms people believe are associated with the different emotional states (whether they truly are or not); and still others are trying to identify the kinds of actions believed to be typical of people in emotional states of various kinds. He left shaking his head and sorry, no doubt, that he had ever asked the question.

2.4. Talking to each other about emotion

It is not just "heat of passion" defenses that founder on the shoals of myriad vocabularies of emotion and ideas of what an emotion is or is not. There are consequences for students of emotion, too. When it is painful and laborious for people to talk to one another, they usually stop trying. Perhaps this is one reason why people in different emotion camps often ignore each other and go about their separate businesses. And it may be why, when they do attempt to make contact, the result is frustrating, not only to them but also to those of us who witness the interaction.

As illustration, I need only point to the *American Psychologist* (1984) debate between Bob Zajonc and Richard Lazarus. Since each has contributed so much to our understanding of various kinds of emotional phenomena, many of us were eager to witness this confrontation, and those who did, know what happened. They never laid a glove on each other. They never made contact. Each theorist appeared to be talking about different behavioral events, or clusters of events, which may be regarded by some, and are of course by the authors respectively, as "emotional" events. Specifically, Lazarus referred, as do many others, to a cluster of physiological, cognitive, and molar behavioral events that occur either simultaneously or within a very limited time frame. Zajonc, on the other hand, seemed to be talking about a more limited array of events, if not a single event: a simple preference for one stimulus over another. And so, predictably, perhaps, Zajonc charges that Lazarus's arguments are "based entirely on an arbitrary definition of emotion" (1984, p. 117). Lazarus, in turn, questions whether "preferences should always be regarded as evidence of emotion" (1984, p. 125) and, having the last word, concludes, as I have noted, that the "searching question is what an emotion is or is not."

The problem of vocabulary not only foils those rare attempts by emotion theorists to talk to each other but, more seriously for the student of emotion (who in the above instances is at least warned that the discussion is controversial), it infects reviews of the literature and the conclusions drawn from them. Such reviews are more likely to be viewed as an impartial and objective weighing of the evidence. Therefore, the reader is not so likely to be alert to the role problems of vocabulary play, or to recognize that the author's notion of what an emotion is often lies unstated and hidden under the surface of the discussion.

An example is an otherwise excellent review of the evidence pertaining to Schachter's theory of emotion that appeared in the *Psychological Bulletin* (Reisenzein, 1983). While the review represents a masterful collection and organization of the work spawned by Schachter's theory in the past two decades, one is startled to read some of the author's conclusions, to wit: "It is concluded that there is no convincing evidence for Schachter's claim that arousal is a necessary condition for an emotional state, nor for the suggestion that emotional states may result from a labeling of unexplained arousal. It is suggested that the role of arousal in emotion has been over-stated" (p. 239). Now, whether or not you agree with that conclusion after surveying the evidence depends very much on what *you* personally want to call an emotional state and how well that corresponds to the author's notion of what an emotional state is.

The point I want to make here is not that the author's conclusion is right or wrong but rather that, first, its truth depends upon the definition of emotional state and that, second and more importantly, the author (while briefly discussing Schachter's conception of emotion) never tells us what his own notion of an emotional state is. From the context and the conclusions the author draws, however, one suspects that he believes evidence of an emotional state to be revealed by a strong positive or negative appraisal of anything – or what people such as Lazarus and others have called cold cognition, cold emotion, feelings, sentiments, or evaluations. Thus, translating this author's dialect from context, one presumes he is concluding that there is evidence that people sometimes express strong sentiments, or preferences, or evaluations, in the absence of arousal. (And no one, I might add, is going to argue with that – not even Stanley Schachter.)

There is yet another consequence of the present state of affairs. I said earlier that new, rather than old, students of emotion are really the major concern of my remarks, and I have observed that their reactions to the fact that there are many vocabularies of emotion in currency today take a variety of forms – none of them good. Some are simply "bewildered" by it all and conclude that the problems of emotion are much too difficult for them to grasp, let alone attack. Some quickly realize the impossibility of mastering myriad vocabularies and say "The heck with it all" and invent their own vocabulary – thus adding to the confusion but at least retaining interest in the problem. Perhaps worst of all, some simply take all that is said at face value, and inevitably come to recognize numerous apparent controversies and contradictions in the emotion literature. I say "apparent" because many of these are, in my opinion, pseudocontroversies that derive not necessarily from basic differences in viewing the behavioral events in question but, rather, from the use of the same word by different people to refer to different behavioral events – events that surely have different properties. As a result, much time seems to be spent pursuing these controversies to the neglect of more profitable questions about emotional phenomena.

I have characterized the current vocabulary situation as a problem, and have tried to illustrate just a few of its consequences, but I should also say that some people do not regard it as a problem. They have faith that from the ferment and confusion all will right itself in the end.

Needless to say, I do not share that faith. For one thing, it has been over 100 years now and the world is still waiting. For example, psychiatry and clinical and counseling psychology are booming businesses and scientific-quality knowledge of the dynamics of emotional phenomena ought to play a central role in them. It does not. As Unger pointed out in a lead article in the American Journal of Psychiatry: "Although Psychiatry has never entirely abandoned the principle that the understanding of mental illness and the analysis of the ordinary emotions . . . bear on each other . . . it has failed to develop a view of the passions that is anything other than the shadow of its particular conjectures about insanity, its therapeutic strategies, and its diagnostic vocabulary" (1982, p. 155). Within counseling and clinical psychology, too, practitioners have received little inspiration or aid from basic theory and research on emotion. Even the new cognitive therapies appear to have evolved largely out of the practitioners' richness of clinical insight and experience in actively dealing with emotional phenomena and owe rather little to a century of theory and research on emotion. Viewed historically, the emotion area has fallen into the doldrums after a period of feverish activity before.

Others share my pessimism and have offered possible solutions. Herb Simon, for example, observes: "Terminological problems are important, not because there are usually right and wrong answers to them, but because unless we settle them we will not understand each other" (1982, p. 333). He proposes that "if our science is to advance, we must identify the nuances [in our present vocabularies of emotion] and both construct and adhere to a vocabulary that makes the necessary distinctions in a consistent way" (1982, p. 334). He also details specific conventions to which we might adhere. For instance, he suggests that we use the word "valuation" (or evaluation), rather than "emotion", to refer to cognitive labels (so-called) that attribute positive or negative valence to objects or events.

2.5. A modest proposal

I personally despair that we shall uniformly adopt the convention he advocates. Therefore, my proposal is much more modest. First, because I think we can all agree that human behavior is virtually saturated with behavioral events that might reasonably be called emotional phenomena – that it is permeated with preferences, positive and negative appraisals of things and events, with approach and avoidance behaviors, with what we now variously call feelings, sentiments, and passions – I think we can also agree that the behavioral events that might legitimately be said to fall in the domain of emotion are very large in number and diverse in quality. This fact suggests that our vocabulary for describing the properties of these events, as well as their antecedents and consequences, also needs to be large, as well as consistently applied, as Simon and others have observed.

If we can agree to this, how do we explain our apparent reluctance to develop the extensive descriptive vocabulary we need? Why, for example, is the one word "emotion" so overworked that its behavioral referents are legion (not to mention frequently unspecified except by context)? Among the probable explanations is surely our implicit assumption, which Lazarus has nicely made explicit, that it is paramount that we find out "what an emotion is or is not" – in other words, that we identify "true" emotion and separate it from its many impostors. Given the assumption that this is the question, it follows that people will try to come up with answers even if there are no criteria for their validity. And given the status of the question as being the question in this field, it also follows that few working in the emotion domain can resist the temptation to justify their particular endeavors, or their focus on certain behavioral events to the exclusion of others, by claiming that these events are part or parcel of the real McCoy: "true" emotion.

My modest proposal, then, is that we exorcise a major source of our vocabulary problems, specifically our collective idea that the important question confronting us is "what an emotion is or is not." Actually, I suggest that we abandon this question for many reasons, not the least of which is that it is unanswerable. Apart from hearing a deep voice come rumbling down from the heavens saying "Yes, my child, *that's* what an emotion really is," it is not clear what the criteria for the correct answer would be.

If we abandon this quest to find true emotion, we shall have to base our individual claims of the importance of studying some behavioral events to the exclusion of others on something other than the assertion that those events in which we ourselves are interested constitute true emotion. And what our individual claims that certain behavioral events are more important and worthy of study than others has to be based on is the same criterion that scientists have always used to justify focusing on some events and relatively ignoring others, and that is on the basis of evidence that the consequences of those specific events ultimately (either directly or as part of a causal chain of events) make a significant difference to the person whose behavior we are observing or to the people who interact with him or her.

When that criterion is applied to most of the diverse events that workers in the emotion domain currently are addressing, it is clear that few of these cannot be demonstrated to make a significant difference. For example, who would like to argue that a person's gut-level, split-second preferences are not going to make a difference to him or her or to others? Whether preferences really quality for the honorific title of "true" emotion seems quite beside the point. Or, who would like to argue that ANS arousal is not an important event for the human organism, one that, for example, appears to affect the workings of the mind, as numerous investigations suggest (e.g., Harkness, DeBono, & Borgida, 1985; Clark, Milberg, & Ross, 1983), including recent studies of hormonal influences on memory storage (McGaugh, 1983). One consequence of ANS arousal sometimes seems to be the self-report of an emotional experience; but even apart from whatever consequences it has for the report of an emotional experience, such arousal clearly has been shown to have consequences for the person and for those with whom that person is interacting. Or, to take yet another example, who is going to argue that it is not of great importance that we understand the complex processes by which people arrive at positive or negative valuations of things or other people? The status of such appraisals as "real" emotions or not hardly changes their importance or interest value in the scheme of human affairs.

Finally, while I doubt that current investigations of the vocabularies of the man and woman on the street are going to tell us what an emotion really is – or what specific emotions such as anger, joy, or jealousy truly are – who would want to argue that people's perceptions of what an emotion is do not make an important difference, a difference not only to themselves but to those with whom they interact?

One person who is not going to argue that point is the abandoned husband I mentioned earlier. The jury in his case returned a verdict of murder in the first degree. And it is easy to see why his behavior probably did not fit popular ideas of a true emotional state. He did not read the note, pick up his shotgun, and rush to the executive's office. In fact, he did not own a shotgun and so he had to go to his local Sears store to buy one. Further, of course, Sears does not sell short shotguns, and so he had to take the gun home and saw it down before proceeding to the executive's office. Thus, given lay persons' perceptions of how people behave in emotional states, this man's behavior probably did not qualify as the "emotional volcanic eruption" the defense billed it as.

I am assuming that if we focus upon the specific behavioral events in which we are interested and lay claim to their importance by demonstrating their consequences, rather than by propounding their candidacy for the honorific title of "emotion," then when writing or speaking about emotion, we shall automatically be careful to describe the behavioral referents of the terms we are using and many of our present misunderstandings will disappear.

At least one set of editors of the books I mentioned previously recognized the problem and took the first step. Izard, Kagan, and Zajonc (1984), noting that "a serious problem exists in the definition of emotion terms" (p. 7), urged their contributors "to specify what they meant by emotion or the particular emotions they discuss" (p. 7). I confess I have not yet read the book and so do not know how successful their injunction was. They do provide a warning note in their introduction, however; specifically, they state that they "feel remiss in not requesting the authors to [also] specify what they mean by cognition" (1984, p. 7).

I should also like to mention that in the introduction to their edited book, Scherer & Ekman (1984) itemize many of the questions that thread through the field of emotion today and detail which authors and chapters treat which issues. They state that they "preserved the issues but removed, as best we could, terms specific to a particular theorist" (p. 1). Upon reading these questions, however (e.g., "What are the minimal cognitive prerequisites for the occurrence of emotion?" and "Must the organism be capable of being aware of the self, conscious of its behavior" for an emotion to occur?), one immediately realizes that the answer one will receive is going to depend very much upon what the author thinks an emotion is.

Finally, I must say that the vocabulary problem in the emotion area has a familiar ring to anyone who has worked in the interpersonal attraction area and who has had, therefore, even a passing interest in one of the most dramatic of the emotions, love. There, too, there was for years debate about what constitutes true love as opposed to its many so-called imposters. And there, also, numerous clusters of behavioral events were often offered, usually implicitly, as constituting true love.

Harold Kelley (1983) has discussed at some length the terminological problems in the love area, and what he says about them is as true for emotion in general as it is for love in particular. That is, any general theory of emotion, like any theory of love, has associated with it a cluster of ideas that includes one or more of the following components:

1. There are certain observable phenomena identified with it, particularly certain behavioral events that are believed to be the characteristic manifestations of emotion.
2. There are notions about the current causes believed to be responsible for the observed emotional phenomena.
3. There are ideas about the historical antecedents of the current causes and phenomena.
4. There are notions about the future course of the phenomenon.

As Kelley observes, various analyses presented by different scientists will differ in the particular part of the cluster used as a focal point, and it is in focusing on different components of the cluster that people use the concept with seeming inconsistency and divergency. What especially causes problems, however, is the tendency for us to argue that our starting point is the phenomenon of interest, because we then neglect the other necessary components of any comprehensive theory of emotion; these remain unspecified or ambiguous, as is the case with most theories of emotion today.

I cannot resist concluding with the observation that our situation in the emotion domain is not very different from that of scientists in Orwell's *1984* (1949). In that novel, scientists were allowed to have their own vocabulary in Newspeak, Vocabulary C, which contained separate lists of words for scientists working within a given specialty. "Any scientific worker or technician," Orwell tells us, "could find all the words he needed in the list devoted to his own specialty," but very few words were common to all lists and so no scientist had more than a smattering of words occurring in the lists of other scientists (1949,

p. 254). He does not tell us so, but knowing Big Brother well, I suspect the word "emotion," if it was allowed to appear in any list at all, was one of those all-purpose, over-worked words, and so Orwell's scientists could communicate with each other little better on this subject than we behavioral scientists in the real 1984 apparently can.

References

Averill, J. (1974). An analysis of psychophysiological symbolism and its influence on theories of emotion. *cf. Theory Soc. Behaviour, 4,* 147–190.

Blascovich, J. and Katkin, E. S. (1982). Arousal-based social behaviors: Do they reflect differences in visceral perception? In L. Wheeler (Ed.), *Review of personality and social psychology* (Vol. 3). Beverly Hills, CA: Sage.

Buck, R. (1984). *The communication of emotion.* Beverly Hills, CA: Sage.

Clark, M. S. (1982). A role for arousal in the link between feeling states, judgments, and behavior. In M. S. Clark & S. T. Fiske (Eds.), *Affect and cognition,* Hillsdale, NJ: Erlbaum.

Clark, M. S., & Isen, A. M. (1982) Toward understanding the relationship between feeling states and social behavior. In A. Hasdorf & A. M. Isen (Eds.), *Cognitive social psychology.* New York: Elservier/North Holland.

Clark, M. S., Milberg, S., & Ross, J. (1983). Arousal cues arousal-related material in memory: Implications for understanding effects of mood on memory. *Journal of Verbal Learning and Verbal Behavior, 22,* 633–649.

de Rivera, J. (Ed.). (1984). The analysis of emotional experience. *American Behavioral Scientists, 27,* 6.

Ekman, P. (1977). Biological and cultural contributions to body and facial movement. In J. Blacking (Ed.), A. S. A. Monograph 15, *The anthropology of the body.* London: Academic Press.

Ekman, P., Friesen, W. V., & Ellsworth, P. (1972). *Emotion in the human face.* Elmsford, NY: Pergamon.

Harkness, A. R., DeBono, K. G., & Borgida, E. (1985). Personal involvement and strategies for making contingency judgments: A stake in the dating game makes a difference. *Journal of Personality & Social Psychology, 49,* 22–32.

Izard, C. E. (1972). Anxiety: A variable combination of interacting fundamental emotions. In C. D. Spielberger (Ed.), *Anxiety: Current trends in theory and research* (Vol. 1). New York: Academic Press.

Izard, C. E., & Buechler, S. (1980). Aspects of consciousness and personality in terms of differential emotions theory. In R. Plutchik & H. Kellerman (Eds.), *Emotion: Theory, research, & experience* (Vol. 1). New York: Academic Press.

Izard, L. E., Kagan, J., & Zajonc, R. B. (Eds.) (1984). *Emotions, cognition, and behaviors.* New York: Cambridge University Press.

Kelley, H. H. (1983). Love and commitment. In H. H. Kelley, E. Berscheid, A. Christensen, J. H. Harvey, P. L. Huston, G. Levinger, E. McClintock, L. A. Peplau, & D. R. Peterson, *Close relationships.* New York: Freeman.

Lazarus, R. S. (1984). On the primacy of cognition. *American Psychologist, 39,* 124–129.

Malatesta, C. Z., & Izard, C. E. (Eds.) (1984). *Emotion in adult development.* Beverly Hills, CA: Sage.

Mandler, G. (1975). *Mind and emotion.* New York: Wiley.

Mandler, G. (1979). Thought processes, consciousness, and stress. In V. Hamilton & D. M. Warburton (Eds.), *Human stress and cognition: An information processing approach*. London: Wiley.

Mandler, G. (1984). *Mind and body*. NY: Norton.

McGaugh, J. L. (1983). Preserving the presence of the past: Hormonal influence on memory storage. *American Psychologist, 38*(2), 161–174.

Orwell, G. (1949). *1984*. Harcourt Brace Jovanovich.

Pennebaker, J. K. (1983). *The psychology of physical symptoms*. New York: Springer Verlag.

Reisenzein, R. (1983). The Schachter theory of emotion: Two decades later. *Psychological Bulletin, 94*(2), 239–264.

Schachter, S. (1964). The interaction of cognitive and physiological determinants of emotional state. In L. Berkowitz (Ed.), *Advances in experimental social psychology* (Vol. 1), New York: Academic Press.

Scherer, K. R., & Ekman, P. (Eds.). (1984). *Approaches to emotion*. Hillsdale, NJ: Erlbaum.

Shaver, P. (Ed.) (1984). Emotions, relationships, and health. *Review of personality and social psychology* (Vol. 5). Beverly Hills, CA: Sage.

Simon, B. A. (1982). Comments. In M. S. Clark & S. T. Fiske (Eds.), *Affect and cognition*. Hillsdale, NJ: Erlbaum.

Solomon, R. I. (1979). *Recent experiments testing an opponent-process theory of acquired motivation*. Unpublished paper available from author, University of Pennsylvania.

Strongman, K. T. (1978). *The psychology of emotion* (2nd ed.). New York: Wiley.

Unger, R. M. (1982). A program for late twentieth century psychiatry. *American Journal of Psychiatry, 139*, 155–164.

Weiner, B. (1982). The emotional consequences of causal attributions. In M. S. Clark & S. T. Fiske (Eds.), *Affect and cognition*, Hillsdale, NJ: Erlbaum.

Zajonc, R. (1984). On the primacy of affect. *American Psychologist, 29*, 117–123.

Zillmann, D. (1978). Attribution and misattribution of excitatory reactions. In J. H. Harvey, W. Ickes, & R. F. Kidd (Eds.), *New directions in attribution research* (Vol. 2). Hillsdale, NJ: Erlbaum.

3. Capturing the "flavor" of behavior: cognition, affect, and interpretation

JULIE K. NOREM AND NANCY CANTOR

It is our conviction that the understanding of complex social behavior requires greater understanding of the influence of affect than we currently have, and that inclusion of affect in our models of social behavior will also benefit our understanding of affect itself. Among social cognition researchers, an earlier emphasis on the "cold" (i.e., unemotional, nonmotivated) processes of perception and cognition, as studied by traditional cognitive psychologists, has given way to recognition that social phenomena require consideration of "hot" processes (i.e. processes that take into account affective and motivational variables believed to be a fundamental part of social behavior; Isen & Hastorf, 1982; Zajonc, 1984; Sorrentino & Higgins, 1986). Previous neglect of affective processes has given way to intensive interest in the extent to which cognition and affect interact in the determination of social behavior.

3.1. Interpretation and meaning

Consideration of the influence of affect on cognition, the influence of cognition on affect, and their mutual influence on social behavior presupposes the existence of the two constructs affect and cognition. Indeed, at first glance this hardly seems problematic. Casual introspection and perusal of our language categories reveal a gross division of human experience into affective and cognitive realms. Everyday conversation is filled with remarks such as "Don't sit there and stew about it, go with your feelings," "I know he's a jerk, but I love him anyway" and "Let's put feelings aside for a moment and discuss this objectively." Yet, as soon as one begins to look carefully at in vivo social behavior – real people in complex situations as they unfold over time – distinctions between affect and cognition become more difficult to maintain. Indeed, the statements above oppose "rational" or "objective" thought to

39

thought that reflects personal or self-centered considerations more than they do cognition per se to affect.

It is very clear that though what we believe to be rational or ideal thought is often not the thought in which people actually engage, the latter is much more central to our endeavors to understand complex social behavior. Consider a prototypical situation having to do with achievement: David has done well in his chemistry class all during the semester, has gotten good feedback from the professor, but goes out drinking the night before the final exam instead of studying. He thus takes the exam with a hangover, which one would suppose would impair his ability to perform well. Indeed, instead of receiving the A his professor predicted, David receives a B for the course. Surprisingly, however, David does not seem disappointed with his grade; instead, he feels relieved and vindicated that he was able to get a B even though he was hung over while taking the exam.

This example, of course, describes an individual using a self-handicapping strategy similar to those investigated extensively by Jones and Berglas (1978), Berglas (1985), and Smith, Snyder, and Handelsman (1982). What is potentially informative about this example, as well as other examples reviewed below of other strategies, is that a straightforward, consensually objective reading of the situation provides little help in understanding David's behavior. A student who has performed well in a circumscribed situation in the past, ought reasonably to expect to perform well in that situation in the near future (barring drastic changes in circumstances). Moreover, if performing well is at all important, that student ought not deliberately sabotage his or her performance by drinking the night before. Finally, if the professor and others truly believed that an A was well within the student's capacity, some disappointment when the lower grade was received would have been expected.

According to the theoretical formulation of self-handicapping, which has substantial empirical support, the key to understanding David's behavior in this situation is his interpretation of past success feedback (which is viewed as noncontingent, leaving an insecure sense of positive self-esteem); his interpretation of the achievement situation at hand, and his understanding of what an outcome will mean in the particular context of his behaviors. Specifically, given that he is not at all confident of his ability, he is loathe to put himself into a situation where there is the potential for unambiguous negative feedback about that ability, which would be the case if he were to study extensively before taking the test. Drinking serves as a self-handicap (or excuse, see Mehlman & Snyder, 1985) that makes performance feedback unclear in its implications for ability. This, in turn, effectively changes the meaning of receiving a B on the exam. It would have been a disappointing grade if received after furious and diligent study; however, a B achieved even though performance was impaired by external (non ability-related) factors turns into quite a successful accomplishment. After all, the reasoning goes, if one can get a B with a hangover, think what one could do if unimpaired! (A paradoxical implication of David's construction of the situation around the handicap is that it may end up taking enough pressure off to enable him to perform more effectively than he would have without a built-in excuse to alleviate his anxiety [see Berglas, 1985].)

Extensive consideration of David's behavior is meant to highlight three points. First of all, it is difficult, in this example, to isolate distinct affective and cognitive processes, but it seems clear that there are psychological processes involved that result in both affective and cognitive outcomes or products. Those processes involve the construction or interpretation of the situation by the individual involved. The process of interpretation, although cognitive in that it clearly involves reference to and processing of knowledge, is not unaffective, or cold; rather, it is saturated with hot consideration of the meaning or implication of the situation for activated parts of the self-concept, which in this case relate to ability. In this example a grade of B on a final exam has no inherent implications; its meaning derives from consideration of what the grade implies in reference to particular behaviors that resulted from a particular construal of the achievement situation as one that presents a potential threat to one's self-esteem or view of one's competence.

Second, even though it may be difficult to understand the episode above in terms of discreet cognitive and affective processes, and even though David's behavior does not seem to follow particularly well from a standard view of the contingencies involved, there is substantial internal coherence to his construction of the situation and the behavior that follows from that construction. Moreover, in the research cited above, it has not proved difficult to identify person and situation variables that effectively predict, and even modify, self-handicapping behavior. Thus, in this example, emphasis on the individual's interpretation of a situation provides a testable, cogent explanation of behavior that is grounded in underlying psychological processes.

Third, there is considerable research that points to the importance of interpretation of particular contexts – including internal states and external features – in the determination of performance, emotional reactions, selection of strategies, and expectations about future events. Examples include work on motivated strategies (Norem, 1989; Norem & Cantor, 1986 a & b; Showers & Cantor, 1985; Pyszczynski, 1982; Pyszczynski & Greenberg, 1983), self-fulfilling prophecies (Sherman et al. 1981), mood effects on memory and problem solving (Strack, Schwartz & Gschneidinger, 1985; Isen & Means, 1983; Isen, Means, Patrick & Nowicki, 1982; Snyder & White, 1982), and self-serving biases in attribution (Langer, 1975; Alloy & Abramson, 1979; Greenwald, 1980).

Interpretation is crucial even in laboratory situations designed to be relatively streamlined, or controlled, which present far less rich and potentially ambiguous environments for individual construal than those present in everyday interactions. If this is the case, then one might reasonably expect the importance of interpretative processes, and the fuzziness of any distinctions between affective and cognitive processes, to increase as the complexity of the behavior of interest increases.

Three considerations, then – that affective and cognitive processes are difficult to distinguish during the ongoing course of interpretation in a situation, that a focus on individuals' interpretations of situations can provide a powerful way of understanding the internal coherence of behavior, and that individual interpretations may have significant implications for behavior even in relatively clear-cut environments – form the core set of assumptions behind the research and arguments presented in this chapter. It is not our intention to present new definitions of affect and cognition, nor even to make proclamations concerning what we consider to be the "right" definitions among those offered by others. Instead, our premise is that social behavior is the result of an ongoing process of interpretation (Kelly, 1955; Bruner, 1957; Cantor & Kihlstrom, 1985). This process involves the determination of meaning, which depends on the assessed implications for the processing organism (Arnold, 1960; Leventhal, 1980; Lazarus & Averill, 1972; Mandler, 1982; Folkman, Lazarus, Dunkel-Schetter, DeLongis & Gruen, 1986).

3.2. Self-referent processing

Affect is encompassed within our emphasis on interpretation by our assumption that determining the implications of any set of stimuli involves a priori reference to some aspect of the self, because the self is a part of any context in which an organism is processing information.

Determining meaning with reference to the self is fundamentally a hot, or affective, process and our primary source of affective meaning (Freud, 1923; Kuhl, 1986).

This perspective does not necessitate particular assumptions about the structure of the self, or about its complexity; indeed, the basic assumptions apply to the processing of exceedingly simple organisms. For example, Plutchik (1977) argues that affect is (and has been) the primary adaptational system, in that organisms must process with reference to consequences for themselves if they are to survive. Cognition, he argues, has developed in the service of affect, as an adaptation that allows us to interpret our environment effectively according to the basic constructs of safety and danger – which are of course meaningful in reference to the self. Functioning in the service of self-preservation, cognitive processes must occur prior to, during, and as a result of any given affect. This interpretation of physiological and evolutionary evidence regarding affect and cognition views them as part of a single system involved in interpreting the environment in ways that are functional for the organism; it is quite congruent with the perspective taken here.

The research we discuss below involves sophisticated processing and very complex behaviors performed by human beings. Note however, that as formulated by Plutchik, our emphasis on interpretation applies to much more primitive processing. Research on the "mere exposure" effect supplies a useful example to illustrate this point (Zajonc, 1980), when considered in conjunction with evidence that some awareness of the significance of an object can be obtained before identification of an object is made (Marcel, 1980). Using safety–danger as a basic dimension of meaning, it may be that the structural relationship first encoded in a given situation (i.e., first appraised relative to one's expectations) is whether or not there is imminent danger. (One would not expect this appraisal necessarily to be conscious unless potential danger was discerned.)

This appraisal could be the very simple comparison of any feature(s) or stimulus configurations to prior knowledge (however primitive) about safety and danger: For example, the "meaning" of the looming light gradient for the safety of a rabbit (Zajonc, 1984) would be clear without the requirement that the rabbit recognize (categorize) a snake according to any particular set of stimulus features (Bandura, 1986). This process seems neither particularly affective nor particularly cognitive as those terms have been used in previous accounts. Clearly, however, it is an interpretative process. It may very well be the basic process from which more complex processes involving familiar affective and cognitive components arise.

Furthermore, this process could easily lead to the patterns of results that are found in the "mere exposure" studies. In a limited exposure situation, this rudimentary appraisal process may be all that is possible. If this is the case, and processing about specific feature characteristics does not occur, the only input available for storage about a particular stimulus would be the judgment that it did not have some implications for the well-being of the subject. In fact, even if longer stimulus exposure were allowed, it might be that "not dangerous" would be the only information coded about a given stimulus. Repeated brief exposures would not necessarily lead to elaboration of this initial schema in terms of the features necessary for recognition. Rather, repeated judgments of "not dangerous" might be expected to disinhibit a positive response (based on a "safety" judgment) or inhibit a negative response (based on a "not dangerous" judgment), and thereby lead to a preference judgment. The context or situation involved in the "mere exposure" studies is not particularly complex, nor is the behavior that results from the subjects' interpretation. Nevertheless, the subjects are interpreting that context. As a result of their interpretations, they develop subjective preferences that do not relate directly to specific features of the stimuli, but to their potential implications. Even in this quite simple situation, consideration of interpretative processes helps one realize that "mere" exposure may in part be quite *meaningful* exposure.

3.3. Of jelly beans and social behavior

We began this chapter by saying that understanding that affect and cognition are different is not difficult, but distinguishing precisely between them is more difficult. From our perspective, it appears that many of the distinctions that have formed the basis of previous work may have hidden the degree to which cognition is saturated with affect, and vice versa.

The implications and assumptions of this perspective may be best understood through use of analogy that considers affect as similar to flavor. If one has a lemon jelly bean and a cherry jelly bean it is possible to speak descriptively about the flavors of each. Because it is possible to abstract from the observed jelly beans a description of flavors, it is tempting to make the assumption that those flavors represent something that exists independently of the "essential" jelly bean. Indeed, one might make the further assumption that the essential jelly bean can be understood apart from its flavor. The problem then becomes how one is to go about understanding the phenomenon of the flavorless jelly bean. In fact, it may be that there is no such phenomenon in any meaningful sense. That is, though it may be possible to conceive of something like a flavorless jelly bean, it may be so far removed from the nature of real jelly beans that it offers very little help in understanding the original phenomenon of interest, jelly beans.

Our somewhat tongue-in-cheek contention, then, is that social behavior can be understood as analogous to jelly beans in that it seems pointless to try to distinguish between affect and cognition, from a process perspective, because it seems doubtful that there is much significant psychological activity (at least within the social realm) that is divorced from consideration of meaning. In other words, if interpretations of situations (contexts, cues, people, stimuli) are the fundamental psychological processes of interest, it is not clear that much is to be gained from trying to separate two processes – one affective, one cognitive – if both are almost always involved in the primary process of interpretation.

The central tenet of this argument, therefore, is that there is no such thing as affectless cognition just as there is no such thing as a flavorless jelly bean, and that failure to recognize the extent to which affect and cognition are intertwined in the context of social behavior will result in models that are unable to account for many phenomena of interest in a coherent manner, as well as in continual debates about a priori definitions. The central implication of this position is that a reorientation, away from models that at some level assume the possibility of "pure" cognition or "pure" affect, may provide for more comprehensive accounts of social behavior, while maintaining an emphasis on the process of interpretation.

Emphasizing interpretative processes allows one to capture the richness, flexibility, and internal coherence of social behavior as it unfolds. This advantage, however, brings with it potential difficulties (as is the case with any approach, of course). Specifically, the interpretative process may be so complex that nomothetic research attempts run the risk of becoming bogged down in idiographic description. The dimensions of meaning that people are able to use when making judgments and planning their behavior clearly extend far beyond a single dimension of safety and danger. Moreover, understanding how people construe situations is further complicated by the potential for relationships between dimensions that are idiosyncratic to individuals or changing across situations.

Nevertheless, one can find situations in which the probable interpretations are somewhat constrained. This is, of course, one of the primary objectives of controlled laboratory research. There also seem to be naturally occurring contexts in which normative demands provide some limit to the interpretation an individual is apt to construct, yet in which there is sufficient leeway to observe the effects of different constructs and rules being brought to bear according to individual objectives. One of these contexts is a major life transition (Cantor & Kihlstrom, 1987).

In the next section, we present examples of research that focuses on the interpretations individuals construct for the tasks they face as they make the transition from high school, home, and family, to college and living on their own. We believe this research nicely illustrates both the complex texture of the interpretative process and the potential of this approach for providing comprehensive accounts of social behavior.

The processes of interpretation on which we focus are not easy to categorize as either cognitive or affective, but they clearly generate both affective and cognitive products (feelings and thoughts) that are significantly related to important outcomes. Moreover, examination of the students' interpretative strategies reveals substantial internal coherence; these strategies tie together a variety of cognitive and affective products that include attributions, expectations, moods, feelings of stress and anxiety, behavior, and outcomes.

3.4. Interpretation and life tasks

Major life transitions offer a particularly appropriate staging for the study of individual interpretations because they generally encompass several situations for which the normative demands are consensually well defined. This, in turn, provides a background against which individual interpretations and their impact on behavior can be seen in vivid relief (Cantor & Kihlstrom, 1985; Cantor & Kihlstrom, 1987).

During the course of this study, we asked students entering the Honors College at the University of Michigan about their current life tasks (Cantor, Norem, Niedenthal, Langston, & Brower, 1987). Current life tasks are those problems, situations, issues, or concerns that individuals feel are central and important during a specific period (here, during the first year in college), and on which they expend considerable time, energy, and commitment. A life task provides a convenient unit of analysis for examining how individuals imbue normative tasks with personal meaning. Note, especially, that while the tasks themselves may be quite well defined (at least to the extent that they are consensual), the solutions for those tasks are often relatively ill defined. Thus there is ample room for unique construal and strategy selection by the individual. It is this construal and choice of strategies that are particularly well suited to illustrating the extent to which cognitive and affective variables are encompassed within interpretation. (Norem & Cantor, in press).

Life tasks and plans

During the middle of their first semester at college, students ($N = 147$) were asked to describe their experiences in terms of "the areas to which you have been and expect to be directing your energies; your thoughts about what will make this both a good and bad year for you; and the plans you have made for accomplishing some of your goals during your time here." These instructions were meant to orient the students toward the time-consuming and important activities in their ongoing school life that they construed as goal directed and personally demanding. Students, on average, listed eight or nine tasks on which they were currently working, and were themselves able to code more than seventy percent of these tasks into six normative task categories. These categories (generated through pretesting;) were making friends, being on their own, establishing an identity, getting good grades, establishing future goals, and managing time and getting organized.

Students rated each task according to 11 meaning dimensions developed by Little (1983). These dimensions were importance, difficulty, stress, initiation, enjoyment, progress, control, absorption, other's view, challenge, and time spent on the task. Within each task category, students generated plans for accomplishing their goals in particular situations. Following the format of the questionnaire, students constructed their plans in component parts of descriptions, actions, outcomes, and long-term consequences (Spivak, Platt, & Shure, 1976). Each plan was then coded for reflectivity or means–end thinking (Baron, 1981). Amount of reflectivity was computed by multiplying the number of alternatives within each component of the plan by the number of themes present in the plan as a whole.

Not surprisingly, students in general construed their academic tasks (getting good grades, establishing future goals, and managing time) as significantly more important, stressful, and difficult than the more interpersonal tasks of making friends, being on one's own, and establishing an identity. The latter tasks were also seen as more enjoyable, and students saw themselves as making more progress on interpersonal tasks than on academic ones (Cantor, et al., 1987).

During the second semester of their first year, students reported the grade point average (GPA) they had received the previous semester, and completed the 14-item Perceived Stress Scale (Cohen, Kamarick, & Mermelstein, 1984). Across the sample as a whole, being able to construe academic tasks as relatively enjoyable and not difficult, and being more reflective about those tasks, were related to higher GPAs and lower perceived stress scores.

These results indicate that students are clearly able to discriminate in their interpretations between different task domains (academic and social) and that the particular dimensions of their construals, as well as the amount of reflection that goes into those construals, significantly affect both GPA and level of perceived stress. The latter two outcome variables, one might argue, could be characterized as cognitive and affective products, respectively. However, the process of interpretation that determines the meaning of each task (and task domain) for the individual is harder to pigeonhole because it reflects the position and significance of each task relative to the individual, not in the abstract.

One could argue that reflectivity is primarily a cognitive, or cold, process. Further data, however, indicate that individual mood and subjective interpretation of these situations significantly alter the function of reflectivity such that it ends up looking like a very hot process indeed.

Although there is clearly a normative or consensual understanding of academic tasks, relative to interpersonal ones, along the dimensions of difficulty, stress, enjoyment, and so forth, some individuals fashion unique interpretations that exaggerate or even contrast with the normative relationship between appraisal and outcomes. They then select strategies corresponding to their individualized constructions, and those strategies guide their behavior as they work to achieve their goals. Of special interest here are the strategies of defensive pessimism and illusory glow optimism, which are particularly well suited to illustrating the internal coherence of individual interpretation.

Defensive pessimism and illusory glow optimism

Defensive pessimism is a strategy that individuals may use to protect their sense of self-esteem or self-efficacy, and to motivate themselves to work hard in situations where anxiety may be generated by the potential for failure (i.e., risky situations). The strategy involves emphasizing the possibility of failure or playing through a worst-case analysis – even though past performance in the same sort of situations has generally been good. Emphasizing potential bad outcomes and setting un-realistically low expectations seem to work to help the individual turn what could be debilitating anxiety into a motivating force. Having con-structed a given situation around low expectations at the outset, an individual using the strategy feels little need to go through protective ex post facto revision in the event of failure (Norem & Cantor, 1986 a & b).

Thus, unlike David, who got drunk the night before an exam in order to provide an excuse for potential failure, individuals using a defensive pessimist strategy are apt to go about bemoaning the inevitability of failure, and then rush home to work furiously all night before the exam – even though they have prepared conscientiously all semester and done very well on previous exams. In the unlikely event of a poor perform-ance, they are not apt to deny responsibility for a given outcome; there is no need to resort to self-protecting attributions because the initial strategic construction of the situation has prepared them for the possibil-ity of failure.

In contrast, individuals using an optimistic strategy enter perfor-mance situations with high expectations, which correspond to their generally positive past experience. They "psych up" for their perform-ance by thinking about the positive aspects of the situation (Showers, 1988). The illusory nature of the optimistic strategy stems from the self-serving biases used to restructure or revise interpretation of the situation after the fact – especially in the event of failure. Thus, people using this strategy are likely to take responsibility for successful out-comes, and deny having control when bad outcomes occur (Langer, 1975; Alloy & Abramson, 1979).

Laboratory research reveals that, among subjects prescreened several months earlier for self-reported used of these strategies, pessimists set significantly lower expectations than optimists for performance on stan-dard achievement paradigm tasks such as solving anagrams and com-pleting tracing puzzles. The differences in expectations remain highly significant even when past academic performance is held constant and when feedback about performance during the experiment is identical for both groups of subjects (Norem & Cantor, 1986a). There are no differences in actual performance between optimists and pessimists on these tasks (nor are there differences in GPA or general level of past success reported). However, when given failure feedback, optimist subjects deny having control over their performance more than do optimists receiving success feedback; optimists thus conform to a typical "attributional egotism" pattern (Snyder, Stephan, & Rosenfield, 1978). There is no difference in level of control between pessimistic subjects receiving failure feedback and those receiving success feedback. Within feedback conditions, pessimists and optimists are equally satisfied with their performances. Apparently the defensive pessimist strategy serves to cushion the blow of failure to the same extent as the post hoc self-serving biases of the optimists.

Other studies provide evidence that interpreting achievement situations using the defensive pessimist strategy may help subjects turn potentially debilitating anxiety into positive motivation (Norem & Cantor, study 1, 1986b). Subjects prescreened for use of defensive pessimism reported significantly more test anxiety than subjects prescreened for use of the optimist strategy. However, when subjects used their preferred strategies to interpret laboratory testing situations, there were no performance differences between groups – despite higher anxiety among the pessimists. For pessimists, there was a nonsignificant positive relationship between anxiety level and performance; for optimists, anxiety was strongly negatively correlated with actual performance.

Thus, a person using defensive pessimism is anxious about and aware of the potential for failure, but instead of withdrawing effort or sabotaging performance, like David the self-handicapper, he or she works very hard, as does the individual using an optimistic strategy. Defensive pessimism and optimism, as strategies, are thus less likely to interfere with good performance than is self-handicapping, yet they provide similar cushioning or protection for self-esteem.

Further research bolsters the argument that the defensive pessimist strategy works to "harness" potentially disruptive anxiety. Norem and Cantor (study 2, 1986b) found interesting effects on performance using a manipulation designed to alter subjects' initial structuring of an achievement task. There was a significant interaction between strategy use and this manipulation. That is, half of a group of prescreened defensive pessimists and optimists were told by the experimenter that their expectations seemed somewhat low given their previous academic performance, and that the experimenter thought it likely that they would do quite well on the task. The other half of each prescreened group received no encouragement before the task. Optimists responded to comments that their expectations were too low with higher performance, whereas pessimists' performance after those comments was impaired.

These data seem to indicate that the defensive pessimists' strategic interpretation of the situation was disrupted by the manipulation, and performance decrements resulted. Defensive pessimists whose strategy was not disrupted evidenced no impairment of performance. In contrast, the manipulation seemed to augment the strategic benefits of an optimistic interpretation of the situation. Pessimistic subjects whose strategy was disrupted showed protective post hoc attributional patterns similar to those of optimistic subjects who received failure feedback; whereas pessimistic subjects whose strategy was not interfered with showed no evidence of post hoc restructuring, even when they were not particularly satisfied with their performance.

Interpretive strategies and academic life tasks

The prescreening instrument used in the laboratory research discussed above was included among the questionnaires completed by students participating in the study of the transition to college. Of our sample of 147, 34 students reported using defensive pessimism in academic situations, and 43 students reported using optimism in those situations. Previous research has indicated a moderate correlation between use of these strategies in the academic domain and their use in interpersonal situations (see Norem, 1989; Norem & Cantor, 1986b), and roughly the same relationship was found in this sample ($r = .30$).

There is convergent evidence from this study that defensive pessimism and optimism can be strategic (motivating) ways of interpreting academic tasks (Norem & Cantor, 1986). Students using one of these two strategies had significantly higher GPAs at the end of their first semester than students who did not report using either strategy. Strategy use was not significantly correlated with past academic performance. (Norem, 1987)

A more direct measurement of students' actual behavior also supports the argument that these strategies are motivating. With a subsample of students ($N = 24$), a time-sampling study was conducted during which students responded to signals from electronic pagers at random intervals over approximately 10 days by filling out a report of their current activities, thoughts, and feelings. Approximately equal numbers of subjects in this subsample were classified as defensive pessimists, optimists, or neither. Corresponding to our previous motivational account of these strategies, planned comparisons showed that optimists and defensive pessimists spent significantly more time working on academic tasks (being in class, studying, etc.) than did students who were not using either strategy. (Norem, 1987)

A more detailed look at the meaning of academic life tasks to students using these strategies further clarifies their function, especially in relationship to reflectivity and the normative patterns described above. Defensive pessimists generally construe these tasks in harsher terms than optimists, finding them more difficult, less enjoyable, and so forth, which conforms quite nicely to the worst-case analysis pattern found in the laboratory. Moreover, the pessimists have significantly higher stress scores on the Perceived Stress Scales than the optimists. As in previous research, however, this stress and anxiety were *positively* related to performance (here, GPA) for pessimists, while stress scores and GPA were negatively related for optimists. (Cantor, et al., 1987)

There was also a significant interaction between reflectivity and strategy on GPA. When a median split on reflectivity scores for academic plans was used, high reflectivity pessimists and low reflectivity optimists had the highest GPAs (Norem & Cantor, 1986). It appears that pessimists who reflect a great deal on the negative dimensions of academic situations are able to motivate themselves effectively and achieve their academic task goals. Optimists, however, apparently experience difficulty in emphasizing the rosy side of academic tasks in a facilitative way during the course of their interpretations. They perform best on these tasks when they are relatively less reflective. An interaction trend on the Perceived Stress Scale scores supports this interpretation: Optimists with low reflectivity have lower stress scores than optimists with high reflectivity, while the opposite pattern holds for pessimists. Thus, optimists seem not to be able to emphasize the positive aspects of academic tasks past a certain point, and it appears that when they persist in reflecting on those tasks, more negative and stressful dimensions become salient. Higher negativity and stress among these students is then related to lower GPA. In contrast, pessimists are able to emphasize these negative dimensions strategically and perform well. They may pay a cost for their negative interpretations in higher stress scores, but that cost is not "deducted" from their GPAs. (Cantor & Norem, in press)

There are several points worth emphasizing from this research. First of all, there is a time gap of several months, in both the laboratory research and the life transition study, between the defensive pessimism and optimism prescreening and performance measures (scores on laboratory tasks and GPA at the end of the semester). Nevertheless, knowing how individuals typically construct academic task situations (i.e., what strategies they typically select from their repertoire) proves a powerful predictor of performance.

Moreover, considering students' interpretations of academic tasks reveals substantial coherence between their construction of situations, their behavior in those situations, their performance, and a variety of affective and cognitive products: thoughts about the task, feelings before and after the task, expectations, attributions, anxiety, and stress. That is, prescreening for strategy use allows us to predict the general dimensions along which students will construct academic situations (i.e., the meaning of those situations), from which we can also predict their expectations, the time spent preparing for their performance (relative to those not using the strategies), actual performance, attribution patterns, and feelings after performance.

In addition, it is important to note that the data from laboratory research converge with those from the field study – an indication that assessing the implications for the self in this task domain may be quite an automatic process, even in situations (such as a laboratory experiment) where the "real" significance of outcomes would seem to be negligible. In other words, what is often thought to be a relatively cold laboratory task seems to elicit the complex package of feelings, attributions, and so forth that we refer to as a strategy in much the same way that presumably important and involving real-life tasks do. It would seem, therefore, either that life tasks are considerably more boring to the individuals working on them than is generally assumed or that the affectless cognition presumed to prevail in laboratory contexts may be much more "contaminated" with self-relevant feelings and assessment than is often thought to be the case.

Our preference, of course, is for the latter conclusion, that cognition, even in simple or relatively controlled situations, is continuously saturated with affect. The research presented above, we believe, supports this contention inasmuch as students report that the academic life tasks they are currently working on are very important and involving.

Finally, our preference for regarding cognition as saturated with affect, as opposed to as affectless (both in the laboratory and in real-life contexts), is reinforced by the observation that our data are not easily or parsimoniously encompassed by explorations that rely on separate cognitive and affective systems. For example, anxiety (usually considered an affective product) does not predict particularly well to outcome in our research in the absence of more information about the dimensions of meaning individuals are using to construct situations. Those dimensions, in turn, are quite subjective, as are their motivational and performance consequences. Thus, the effects of seeing a situation as highly stressful and challenging are quite different for people using defensive pessimism and for those using illusory glow optimism. The ways in which anxiety is generated and the effects of anxiety on performance differ markedly for individuals using different strategies. These variables are clearly related to motivation and the individual's subjective or self-referent understanding of situations; it is much less clear how one would consider the variables discussed as generated by an independently operating cognitive system.

We find an emphasis on interpretive processes and strategies to be useful in providing convincing accounts of complex behavior. Work currently in process using this approach in both academic and interpersonal domains will provide further tests of our arguments (see Langston & Cantor, 1989; Norem, 1989; Zirkel & Cantor, in press). Nevertheless, there are some issues, typically discussed by those concerned with the relationship between affect and cognition, that we have yet to address directly. Thus, the final section of this chapter will give some consideration to these issues as they relate to our position.

3.5. Afterthoughts and conclusion

It might be argued that "solving" previous debates concerning the relationship between affect and cognition in the determination of social behavior by defining both constructs as functionally inseparable sidesteps a number of basic issues identified by other researchers. Accordingly, we will briefly review some of the distinctions that other authors have emphasized, and discuss the extent to which hypothesizing a primary interpretive process, is able to encompass or reconcile previous disputes.

Much of the previous work on affect and cognition can be distinguished according to the authors' emphasis on (1) emotion as a product of cognitive processes, (2) affective processes as distinct from or independent of cognitive processes, or (3) the influence of affective processes and products on otherwise cold cognition. There is little initial disagreement among theorists that affect and cognition are intrinsically different. Instead, discussion centers (especially among the first two groups above) on issues of hegemony: Which system or effect is more important? Which system is more independent? Is emotion "merely" a product of cognition, or are there significant emotional processes that must themselves be taken into account?

Researchers in the first group include those described as cognitive by Zajonc, Pietromonoco, & Bargh (1982): Schacter and Singer (1962), Mandler (1982), and Lazarus (1966), to which group Arnold (1960) might appropriately be added. These theorists all emphasize appraisal processes, considered fundamentally cognitive, that precede emotional experience and result in particular emotions depending on the implications of a given appraisal for the well-being of the individual. For the cognitive theorist, the particular "feel" of emotion (vs. cognition) is accounted for by the arousal level corresponding to the meaning or significance of an appraisal, that is, the phenomenology of emotion is a result of a cognitive interpretation of a bodily state.

In contrast, the second group of theorists, including those described as somatic by Zajonc et al. (1982), emphasize the phenomenological immediacy of emotional reactions, their motivational importance, or the apparent ontological primacy of emotions and the universality of emotional expressive patterns (Izard, 1977; Tompkins, 1982; Leventhal, 1980). All contend that the cognitive position does not adequately account for the psychological significance of emotions as primary processes, or for their potential impact on human behavior. All would probably maintain, as does Izard, that the mutual influence of cognitive and emotional processes is considerable, yet "it is practicable to delineate the affective and cognitive components of the response sequence at both theoretical and empirical levels" (Izard, 1977, p. 21). Understanding of mutual influence, from this perspective, must await a better understanding of "emotion qua emotion."

These two positions are perhaps most concisely contrasted in the published debates between Zajonc (1984) and Lazarus (1984). For those interested in understanding social behavior, however, it is difficult to know precisely what conclusions should be drawn concerning the role affect and cognition are to play in future research. Indeed, one is tempted to agree with Ellen Berscheid (this volume) that "they never laid a glove on one another." Armed with considerably different definitions of both emotion and cognition, each author seems to be discussing entirely different phenomena. Clearly, however, both authors recognize that the issues under discussion are far from "just" definitional, precisely because the definitions used in one framework make it all but impossible to consider phenomena presented in the other.

Thus, the somatic theorists end up focusing on different phenomena from the cognitive theorists, and each camp seems convinced that it is attacking the "real thing." Though this approach is not unproductive, the obvious drawback is the resultant difficulty of integrating work done in such different "languages" (Berscheid, this volume).

An alternative approach is to switch emphasis from the search for "true" emotion to attempts to explain specific phenomena that seem to be central to a particular domain of psychological inquiry (Berscheid, this volume; Isen, 1984; Lazarus, 1984). As a preliminary step in this direction, it is informative to examine somewhat more closely some of the central distinctions that have arisen, in terms of their significance in accounting for particular social behaviors.

For example, Zajonc seems to argue for the primacy of affect in two senses. The first is the potential for affect to occur prior to cognition in time – that is, before cognitive appraisal in a given individual, before the development of complex cognitive capabilities in children, and before evolution of advanced symbolic abilities within a species. Affect is potentially prior to, and thus has primacy over, cognition in each of these circumstances according to Zajonc. Moreover, he argues, if affect can be shown to develop prior to cognition, this provides de facto evidence of its potential independence from cognition. These arguments are based on evidence such as apparently innate patterns of emotional expression (Izard, 1977) and primitive brain structures (Izard, 1984). The evidence is similar to that used by Leventhal (1982) to support a realist position on the independence of affect, as opposed to a synthesist position such as that proposed here.

There are both specific and general problems, however, with the assumptions upon which arguments using these data are based. First, despite the appeal of physiological evidence, which may seem "harder" than psychological data, it is not valid to assume that structures identified as more primitive within an evolving system necessarily maintain their original function. In fact, it is likely to be the case that those functions have been to a large extent superseded or "taken over" with the evolution of more complex structures, such that their remaining functions are quite different from their original functions (Plutchik, 1977). Thus, an affect system developing prior to a cognitive system is not necessarily in any meaningful way independent of that system as it functions at a later point. Indeed, there is data to indicate that, in contrast to the hypothesis of independent structures, the tendency in brain development has been overwhelmingly in the direction of integration of function (Sperry, 1982).

Perhaps more importantly, at some point we should assess to what extent evidence concerning the physiological correlates of emotion will impact on a psychological account of the relationship between affect and cognition, and of their effects on social behavior. That is, none of the theorists cited above argue that some set of physiological events constitutes affect in the absence of "feeling" or psychological experience. If this experience, and its subsequent effects on cognition and social behavior, are in fact what is to be explained, it is not clear that our understanding of affective processes at a psychological level will be enhanced even if a complete account of corresponding physiological events is achieved. The latter explanation is at a different level of analysis; assuming it necessarily corresponds to or suffices for a psychological explanation is what Lazarus correctly identifies as a "reductionistic bias" (Lazarus, 1984; see also Simon, 1981).

Thus, while the available physiological evidence does not preclude the consideration of affect and cognition as independent systems, neither does it provide overwhelming support for the position that affect and cognition must be considered separate or independent systems. After this conclusion has been drawn, the second implication of the primacy of affect becomes important. Zajonc is explicitly trying to argue that affect is a crucial component of human psychology, and that it has not been properly taken into account in many "overly cognitive" psychological paradigms. In fact, as part of his advocacy of emotion, Zajonc admits that it is a matter of conceptual convenience to assert the independence of affect and cognition (Zajonc et al., 1982); but he maintains that it is important to begin with two systems, because one would be unable to move beyond the assumptions involved in starting with a single-system model. Throughout the debate above, the assumption has been made repeatedly that affect must be defined and explained as a concept distinct from cognition before its relationship to cognition can be well understood. Even Lazarus, who considers emotion to be dependent on cognitive processes, maintains that the concept of emotion must be clarified and distinguished from cognition, as he refers to the "searching question of what an emotion is and is not" (1984, p. 124).

The central questions being addressed are, What is emotion? and Can there be emotion without cognition? As Zajonc explains: "If we assume that there may be conditions of emotional arousal that do not require cognitive appraisal, we shall dedicate our research to the questions of what these conditions are" (1984, p. 122). This is undoubtedly the case, and it is precisely the problem this chapter is attempting to address. That is, while it is likely that the search for the conditions mentioned above may provide some interesting information, it also would seem to put off for some time advances in knowledge about the interrelationship among affect, cognition, and social behavior. Our interest, in contrast, is in formulating accounts of complex behavior that capture its richness and coherence. To do so would seem to require considering the relationship of affect and cognition, even if there are gaps in our understanding of specific affective or cognitive phenomena.

In a similar vein, the "cognitive revolution" of the past few years has come under fire for its neglect of affect. Indeed, following from the laboratory paradigms of cognitive and experimental psychology, much of this endeavor has focused on attempts to isolate pure cognitive processes in contexts designed to eliminate the contamination of affect, which seems to be regarded as distorting such basic processes as perception, encoding, retrieval, and categorization.

In attempts to expand the models thus developed in order to account for information processing in more complex situations (i.e., add heat to essentially cold processes), there has been considerable research in which affective components have been introduced into experimental situations in order to assess their impact on basic cognitive and perceptual processes (e.g., Bower, Gilligan, & Montiero, 1981; Isen, Shalker, Clark, & Karp, 1978; Fiske, 1982).

As evidence accumulates, however, existing cognitive models must be strained to account for the apparent extent of the mutual influence of affect and cognition (Isen, 1984; Niedenthal, in press; Johnson & Tversky, 1983). From this research, one is faced with reconciling data that indicate that affect may exert an organizational influence of cognitive processes, may influence particular categorization or retrieval processes, or may be viewed as a product of those processes. Though models exist to account convincingly for some of these effects, it seems doubtful that any of the traditional models of cognition is sufficiently flexible to encompass all the extant results.

It is precisely at this point that one sees the difficulty in applying models developed for the theoretical special case – affectless cognition in a highly constrained laboratory environment – to the more complex general case of information processing in a social context that is fundamentally saturated with affect. This concern is reflected in Kuhl's assertion that our designation of cognitive processes has become over-inclusive, while our use of information processing is underinclusive (Kuhl, 1986). Zukier offers a related argument that social cognition research often ignores the pervasive way that all our cognition is social in that it is purposive, context embedded, and action linked (Zukier, 1986).

In the absence of conclusive data necessitating the conceptual separation of affective and cognitive processes, and faced with mounting evidence of their continuous mutual influence, one again confronts the argument that the phenomena of interest be allowed to direct conceptualization of those processes. In the realm of complex social behavior, there is growing evidence that individuals' ongoing interpretations of situations may guide the strategies they select to address those situations and the behavior they exhibit.

In the study of the relationship between interpretations and social behavior, the interpretative cycle can be viewed as a continuous one in which both affective and cognitive products function as meaningful input into a process that is characteristically neither affective nor cognitive, but indistinguishably both. Thus, just as the flavor of a jelly bean is inseparable from the jelly bean itself, the flavor of social behavior is determined by an interpretative process within which affect and cognition are effectively inseparable. It is this flavorful process that reveals the coherence between an individual's construction of a situation and the behavior that follows from that construction.

References

Alloy, L. B., & Abramson, L. (1979). Judgment of contingency in depressed and nondepressed students: Sadder but wiser? *Journal of Experimental Psychology: General, 108*, 441–485.

Arnold, M. B. (1960). *Emotion and Personality.* New York: Columbia Press.

Bandura, A. (1986). *Social foundations of thought and action: A social cognitive theory.* Englewood Cliffs, NJ: Prentice Hall.

Baron, J. (1981). Reflective thinking as a goal of education. *Intelligence, 5,* 291–309.

Berglas, S. (1985). Self-handicapping and self-handicappers: A cognitive/attributional model of interpersonal self-protective behavior. In B. Maher (Ed.), *Perspectives in personality* Vol. 1. Greenwich, CT: JAI Press.

Bower, G. H., Gilligan, S. G., & Montiero, K. (1981). Selectivity of learning caused by affective states. *Journal of Experimental Psychology: General, 110,* 451–473.

Bruner, J. S. (1957). On perceptual readiness. *Psychological Review, 64,* 123–152.

Cantor, N., & Kihlstrom, J. F. (1987). *Personality and social intelligence.* New York: Prentice-Hall.

Cantor, N., & Norem, J. K. (in press). Defensive pessimism and stress and coping. *Social Cognition.*

Cantor, N., Norem, J. K., Niedenthal, P. M., Langston, C. A. & Brower, A. M. (1987). Life tasks, self-concept ideals and cognitive strategies in a life transition. *Journal of Personality and Social Psychology, 53,* 1178–1192.

Cantor, N., & Kihlstrom, J. F. (1985). Social intelligence: The cognitive basis of personality. *Review of Personality and Social Psychology, 6,* 15–33.

Cantor, N., Markus, H., Niedenthal, P., & Nurius, P. (1986). On motivation and the self-concept. In R. M. Sorrentino & E. T. Higgins (Eds.), *Motivation and cognition: Foundations of social behavior.* New York: Guilford Press.

Clark, M. S., & Isen, A. M. (1982). Toward understanding the relationship between feeling states and social behavior. In A. Hastorf & A. M. Isen (Eds.), *Cognitive social psychology.* New York: Elsevier.

Cohen, S., Kamarick, T., & Mermelstein, R. (1983). A global measure of perceived stress. *Journal of Health and Social Behavior, 24,* 385–396.

Fiske, S. T. (1982). Schema-triggered affect: Applications to social perception. In M. S. Clark & S. T. Fiske (Eds.), *Affect and cognition: The 17th Annual Carnegie Symposium.* Hillsdale, NJ: Erlbaum.

Freud, S. (1923). *The ego and the id.* New York: W. W. Norton & Co, 1960.

Folkman, S., Lazarus, R. S., Dunkel-Schetter, C., DeLongis, A., & Gruen, R. J. (1986). Dynamics of a stressful encounter: Cognitive appraisal, coping, and encounter outcomes. *Journal of Personality and Social Psychology, 50,* 992–1003.

Greenwald, A. G. (1980). The totalitarian ego: Fabrication and revision of personal history. *American Psychologist, 35,* 603–618.

Isen, A. M. (1984). Toward understanding the role of affect in cognition. In R. S. Wyer & T. K. Srull (Eds.), *Handbook of social cognition* (Vol. 3). Hillsdale, NJ: Erlbaum.

Isen, A. M., & Hastorf, A. H. (1982). Some perspectives on cognitive social psychology. In A. H. Hastorf & A. M. Isen (Eds.), *Cognitive social psychology.* New York: Elsevier.

Isen, A. M., & Means, B. (1983). Positive affect as a variable in decision making. *Social Cognition, 2,* 18–31.

Isen, A. M., Means, B., Patrick, R., & Nowicki, G. (1982). Some factors influencing decision-making strategy and risk-taking. In M. S. Clark & S. T. Fiske (Eds.), *Affect and cognition: 17th annual Carnegie Symposium on Cognition.* Hillsdale, NJ: Erlbaum.

Isen, A. M., Shalker, T. E., Clark, M., & Karp, L. (1978). Affect, accessibility of material in memory, and behavior: A cognitive loop? *Journal of Personality and Social Psychology, 36,* 1–12.

Izard, C. E. (1977). *Human emotions.* New York: Plenum.

Izard, C. E. (1984). Emotion-cognition relationships and human development. In C. E. Izard, J. Kagan, & R. B. Zajonc (Eds.), *Emotions, cognition and behavior.* New York: Cambridge University Press.

Johnson, E., & Tversky, A. (1983). Affect, generalization, and the perception of risk. *Journal of Personality and Social Psychology, 45,* 20–31.

Jones, E. E., & Berglas, S. (1978). Control of attribution about the self through self-handicapping strategies: The appeal of alcohol and the role of under-achievement. *Personality and Social Psychology Bulletin, 4,* 200–206.

Kelly, G. A. (1955). *The psychology of personal constructs.* New York: Norton.

Kuhl, J. (1986). Motivation and information processing: A new look at decision making, dynamic change and action control. In R. M. Sorrentino & E. T. Higgins (Eds.), *Motivation and cognition: Foundations of social behavior.* New York: Guilford Press.

Langer, E. J. (1975). The illusions of control. *Journal of Personality and Social Psychology, 32,* 311–328.

Langston, C. A., & Cantor, N. (1989). Social anxiety and social constraint: When making friends is hard. *Journal of Personality and Social Psychology, 56,* 649–661.

Lazarus, R. S. (1984). On the primacy of cognition. *American Psychologist, 39,* 124–129.

Lazarus, R. S. (1966). *Psychological stress and the coping process.* New York: McGraw Hill.

Lazarus, R. S., & Averill, J. R. (1972). Emotion and cognition. With special reference to anxiety. In C. D. Spielberger (Ed.), *Anxiety: Current trends in theory and research* (Vol. 2). New York: Academic Press.

Leventhal, H. A. (1980). Toward a comprehensive theory of emotions. In L. Berkowitz (Ed.), *Advances in experimental social psychology* (Vol. 13). New York: Academic Press.

Leventhal, H. A. (1982). The integration of emotion and cognition: A view from the perceptual-motor theory of emotion. In M. S. Clark & S. T. Fiske (Eds.), *Affect and cognition: 17th annual Carnegie Symposium on Cognition.* Hillsdale, NJ: Erlbaum.

Little, B. (1983). Personal projects – A rationale and methods for investigation. *Environmental Behavior, 48,* 575–584.

Mandler, G. (1982). The structure of value: Accounting for taste. In M. S. Clark & S. T. Fiske (Eds.), *Affect and cognition: The 17th annual Carnegie Symposium on Cognition.* Hillsdale, NJ: Erlbaum.

Marcel, T. (1980). Conscious and preconscious recognition of polysemous words: Locating the selective effects of prior verbal context. In R. S. Nickerson (Ed.), *Attention and performance VII.* Hillsdale, NJ: Erlbaum.

Mehlman, R. C., & Snyder, C. R. (1985). Excuse theory: A test of the self-protective role of attributions. *Journal of Personality and Social Psychology, 49,* 994–1001.

Niedenthal, P., Cantor, N., & Kihlstrom, J. F. (1985). Prototype-matching: A strategy for social decision-making. *Journal of Personality and Social Psychology, 48,* 575–584.

Neidenthal, P. M. (in press). Implicit perception of affective information. *Journal of Experimental and Social Psychology.*

Norem, J. K. (1989). Cognitive strategies as personality: Effectiveness, specificity, flexibility, and change. In D. M. Buss & N. Cantor (Eds.), *Personality psychology: Recent trends and emerging directions.* New York: Springer-Verlag Publishers.

Norem, J. K. (1987). Strategic realities: Optimism and defensive pessimism. Unpublished doctoral dissertation, University of Michigan, Ann Arbor, MI.

Norem, J. K., & Cantor, N. (1986). Development of appraisal and planning among college "novices." Paper presented at the annual meeting of the Midwestern Psychological Association, Chicago.

Norem, J. K., & Cantor, N. (1986a). Anticipatory and post-hoc cushioning strategies: Optimism and defensive pessimism in "risky" situations. *Cognitive Therapy and Research*, *10*(3), 347–356.

Norem, J. K., & Cantor, N. (1986b). Defensive pessimism: "Harnessing" anxiety as motivation. *Journal of Personality and Social Psychology*, *51*, 1208–1217.

Norem, J. K., & Cantor, N. (in press). Cognitive strategies, coping and perceptions of competence. In R. J. Sternberg & J. Kolligian, Jr. (Eds.), *Perceptions of competence and incompetence across the lifespan*. New Haven, CT: Yale University Press.

Plutchik, R. (1977). Cognitions in the service of emotions: An evolutionary perspective. In D. K. Candland, J. P. Fell, E. Keen, A. I. Leshner, R. Plutchik, & R. M. Tarpy, *Emotions*. Monterey, CA: Brooks/Cole.

Pyszczynski, T. (1982). Cognitive strategies for coping with uncertain outcomes. *Journal of Research in Personality*, *16*, 386–399.

Schacter, S., & Singer, J. E. (1962). Cognitive social and physiological determinants of emotional state. *Psychological Review*, *69*, 377–399.

Sherman, S. T., Skov, R. B., Hervitz, E. G., & Stock, C. B. (1981). The effects of explaining hypothetical future events: From possibility to probability to actuality and beyond. *Journal of Experimental Social Psychology*, *17*, 142–158.

Showers, C. (1988). The effects of how and why thinking on the perception of future negative events. *Cognitive Therapy and Research*, *12*, 225–240.

Showers, C., & Cantor, N. (1985). Social cognition: A look at motivated strategies. *Annual Review of Psychology*, *36*, 275–305.

Simon, H. A. (1981). *The sciences of the artificial* (2nd ed.). Cambridge, MA: MIT Press.

Smith, T. W., Snyder, C. R., & Handelsman, M. M. (1982). On the self serving function of an academic wooden leg: Test anxiety as a self-handicapping strategy. *Journal of Personality and Social Psychology*, *42*, 314–321.

Snyder, M. L., Stephan, W. G., & Rosenfield, D. (1978). Attributional egotism. In J. Harvey, W. Ickes, & D. Kidd (Eds.), *New directions in attribution research* (Vol. 2). Hillsdale, NJ: Erlbaum.

Snyder, M., & White, P. (1982). Moods and memories: Elation, depression and remembering the events of one's life. *Journal of Personality*, *50*, 149–167.

Sorrentino, R. M., & Higgins, E. T. (1986). *Motivation and cognition: Foundations of social behavior*. New York: Guilford Press.

Sperry, R. (1982). Some effects of disconnecting the cerebral hemispheres. *Science*, *217*, 407–467.

Spivak, G., Platt, J. J., & Shure, M. B. (1976). *The problem solving approach to adjustment*. San Francisco: Jossey-Bass.

Strack, F., Schwartz, N. & Gshneidinger, E. (1985). Happiness and reminiscing: The role of time perspective, affect and mode of thinking. *Journal of Personality and Social Psychology*, *49*, 1460–1469.

Teasdale, J. D., & Fogarty, S. J. (1979). Differential effects of induced mood on retrieval of pleasant and unpleasant events from episodic memory. *Journal of Abnormal Psychology*, *88*, 248–257.

Tompkins, S. S. (1982). Affect theory. In P. Ekman (Ed.), *Emotion in the human face* (2nd ed.). Cambridge, England: Cambridge University Press.

Wyer, R. S., & Srull, T. K. (1981). Category accessibility: Some theoretical and empirical issues concerning the processing of social stimulus information. In E. T. Higgins, C. P. Herman, & M. P. Zanna (Eds.), *Social cognition: The Ontario Symposium* (Vol. 1). Hillsdale, NJ: Erlbaum.

Zajonc, R. B. (1979). Cognition and social cognition: A historical perspective. In L. Festinger (Ed.), *Four decades of social psychology.* New York: Oxford University Press.

Zajonc, R. B. (1984). On the primacy of affect. *American Psychologist, 39,* 117–123.

Zajonc, R. B., Pietromonoco, P., & Bargh, J. (1982). Independence and interaction of affect and cognition. In M. S. Clark & S. T. Fiske (Eds.), *Affect and cognition: The 17th annual Carnegie Symposium on Cognition.* Hillsdale, NJ: Erlbaum.

Zajonc, R. B. (1980). Feeling and thinking: Preferences need no inferences. *American Psychologist, 35,* 151–175.

Zirkel, S., & Cantor, N. (in press). Personal construal of life tasks: Those who struggle for independence. *Journal of Personality and Social Psychology.*

Zukier, H. (1986). The paradigmatic and narrative modes in goal-guided inference. In R. M. Sorrentino & E. T. Higgins (Eds.), *Motivation and cognition: Foundations of social behavior.* New York: Guilford Press.

4. Affect and aggression

PAUL A. BELL AND ROBERT A. BARON

Over the years many possible mediators have been proposed by social psychologists to explain the relationship between aggression and a variety of independent variables. Frustration (Dollard et al. 1939), arousal (Berkowitz, 1978; Zillmann, 1979), and social learning (Bandura, 1973) are some of the most notable mediators that have been widely followed in the literature. These mediators are by no means mutually exclusive, and each may have its own best predictive domain (Baron, 1977). It is certainly possible to build models that incorporate several mediators, and indeed it is helpful to have a complex model if one is to venture across the predictive domains of individual mediators. Yet the parsimony afforded by a simple model with one mediator is appealing in its own right, even though others may well explain various components of the simpler model. Such is the case with affect as a mediator of aggression. Where it has been employed in this context in the aggression literature, it has led to at least one appealingly simple model that has shown generalizability to several related antecedent conditions as well as to multiple measures of aggression. Interestingly, however, it is rare to see affect mentioned in the aggression literature as a potential mediator of anything, perhaps because researchers assume that one type of affect, anger, is extremely basic in aggression and thus research focuses on circumstances provoking anger and subsequent determinants of its expression or lack of expression. Even a cursory glance at research on other behaviors studied in social psychology, though, reveals that affect is employed extensively to explain a wide variety of social phenomena, including attitude formation and change, attraction, and helping behavior, to name a few (e.g., Baron & Byrne, 1987). As a careful examination of the research literature will show, affect is probably just as important in aggression as in these other behaviors.

In the present chapter we will explore the literature on affect as a mediator of aggression. In the process we will see that its potential is greater than is generally assumed in the aggression literature as a whole. First, we will review some relevant physiological and animal research and associated theoretical interpretations. Then we will see how, following from other social psychological and physiological models employing affect, the relationship between environmental stress and aggression is especially amenable to interpretation through an affective mediator. We will next consider how an extension of a basic affect–aggression relationship can be incorporated into a strategy for reducing and controlling aggression. Finally, we will turn from individual aggression to see how affect might be used to predict and assess organizational conflict.

4.1. Physiological aspects of aggression

Research over the last 50 years has shown convincingly that there are distinct connections between neural organization and aggressive behavior, especially in lower animals. Reviews of this line of research can be found in Johnson (1972) and Moyer (1976). Essentially, the evidence shows that several areas of the brain, most notably the limbic system, contain nuclei that facilitate or inhibit aggression (e.g., Flynn et al., 1970; Kluver & Bucy, 1937; MacDonnell & Flynn, 1966). Electrically or chemically stimulating certain areas of the hypothalamus, amygdala, or hippocampus will elicit attack in the rat or cat, and stimulating other nearby areas will inhibit attack. Alternatively, surgical or electrical lesions of these areas generally have the opposite effects of stimulation. The specific areas responsible for facilitation or inhibition of attack vary somewhat from species to species, and can involve areas outside the limbic system, such as the frontal and temporal lobes. Innervation of some centers seems to be specific to individual neurotransmitters. Moreover, some centers seem to be specific to predatory aggression, others to fear-related defensive attack, and others to sexually related dominance fighting. It should be emphasized that most of this neural research has been conducted on subhuman species, primarily rats and cats. The higher we move up the phylogenetic scale, the greater the role of higher cortical areas in influencing the primitive limbic system, so we should be very cautious in generalizing to humans the substantial findings from animal research on physiological mechanisms of aggression.

We do know, however, that at least some instances of bizarre expression of human violence can be attributed in part to tumors or other lesions in the limbic system, temporal lobes, or other areas (see Moyer, 1976, for numerous examples). Especially pertinent to the present discussion of affect and aggression are two other mechanisms controlled by the limbic system. First, the limbic system plays a key role, and quite likely the primary role, in the experience of affect, including pleasure, anger, and fear. Second, the hypothalamus plays a primary role in the thermal regulation of the body, a fact that will become important in our discussion of temperature and aggression.

To summarize, animal research demonstrates a strong connection between neural substrates and the expression of both aggression and affect. Such connections are also present in humans, although the influence of higher cortical functions is very strong in moderating the behaviors controlled by these more primitive neural centers.

4.2. An animal model

Blanchard and Blanchard (1984) have proposed an "emotional calculus" interpretation of the relationship between affect and aggression. Largely on the basis of research with rats, with corroborative evidence from other species, including humans, they propose that a cost–benefit analysis underlies the expression of offensive or defensive aggression. Offensive attack, typically elicited through territorial invasion by a conspecific, is proposed to be preceded by the emotion of anger (or in the case of lower animals, something akin to anger). Defensive attack, typically elicited through attack by another, appears to be accompanied by the emotion of fear. Although anger and fear appear to be emotional opposites, Blanchard and Blanchard suggest that they can occur at the same time. The experience of anger and fear is to some extent prewired in the brain in response to certain situations, and has survival value for the organism (e.g., fear in the face of threat probably helps keep the animal from getting deeper into an already bad situation). Both emotions can also be conditioned through experience, so that their expression will vary from individual to individual. A given situation, then, elicits a particular level of fear and anger. If fear predominates and escape is possible, flight results. If flight is not possible, defensive attack occurs. If anger predominates and the probability of success (i.e., benefit) seems relatively high, offensive attack will result. If the probability of success seems low, offensive attack is less likely. If attack does occur, and the battle gets costly, fear may become more dominant than anger and flight will then result. In lower animals, the emotional calculus may be quite rapid, since few higher cortical processes are involved. In higher animals, however, considerable time may be spent evaluating, monitoring, and reevaluating the situation.

In humans (and in other organisms), it is conceivable that a very intense level of attack-provoking anger may override higher cortical information that some other strategy (e.g., negotiation, retreat, stalling) would be more beneficial and less costly. Thus, anger may be so intense that attack occurs even when a more objective analysis would suggest that not attacking would be a better alternative. Social learning would certainly play a major role in determining an individual's tendencies to respond in a situation with anger or fear, and in determining whether aggression or some other behavior would be chosen in the expression of that affect. Certainly both the limbic system and higher cortical processes would be involved. Whether this animal model holds as well for humans as for other species remains to be seen. We will return to the question of its relevance to human affect and aggression after reviewing some basic findings in human research.

4.3. The experimental study of human aggression

Scientific study of human aggression is much more complicated than that of animal aggression for two reasons. First, although it is influenced by limbic and other primitive brain structures, human aggression is much more complex than animal aggression because of the vast influence of cognitive factors (e.g., Zillmann, 1979, 1988). Second, clean manipulation of independent variables is much more difficult with humans because of ethical considerations, especially in the study of aggressive behavior. Nevertheless, some standard laboratory procedures have been developed that allow manipulation of several types of affect as well as other variables, and that have at least some degree of external validity (see Baron, 1977, for a review). The most common procedure involves the use of a Buss "aggression machine" (Buss, 1961), which is a metal box about the size of a breadbox. The front of the device contains a series of buttons or switches (usually about 10 of them) or even a dial with several settings that can be used to deliver electric shocks of varying intensity. An accomplice and a subject are introduced to the apparatus, and the accomplice is selected to be the "victim." Ostensibly, the experiment concerns the effects of painful stimulation on learning or some other task, and the subject is assigned the role of administering electric shocks to the accomplice, either as punishment for errors on a learning task (teacher–learner paradigm) or to examine the physiological reactions of the victim to pain (physiological paradigm). The accomplice enters another room where he or she is allegedly attached to the machine through shock electrodes. The accomplice never actually receives the shocks, but a record is made of the intensity and duration of shocks chosen by the subject.

The experimenter manipulates independent variables in several ways. Anger can be examined by having the accomplice provoke the subject to varying degrees, either through verbal insult ("I don't want to work with this jerk"), through negative written evaluation of the subject (e.g., unwarranted criticism of an essay written by the subject for another part of the experiment), or by giving the accomplice a chance to shock the subject first (in which case the shock is real). Humor, sexual arousal, or other affective reactions can be elicited by asking the subject to review and evaluate a set of pictures or other stimuli (ostensibly to help standardize the materials for a future study) while the experimenter takes time to adjust the apparatus or give further instructions to the victim. High or low ambient temperatures, noise, odors, and other irritating factors can be introduced into the laboratory, allegedly to see what effects they might have on the pain reactions of the victim.

Although widely used, these procedures are not without drawbacks. There is some evidence of external validity (e.g., Shemberg, Leventhal, Allman, 1968; Wolfe & Baron, 1971), though in the teacher–learner paradigm the subject's selection of shocks is influenced both by motivation to hurt the victim and by motivation to help the victim learn the task (Baron & Eggleston, 1972). The physiological paradigm removes this helping motivation, but tends to greatly increase error variance in the dependent measures. Moreover, the aggressor does not appear to face any retaliation from the victim, and the means of expressing intent to harm are highly restricted to intensity and duration of ostensible shock. This whole external/internal validity issue has been addressed by Berkowitz and Donnerstein (1982), who argue in part that as long as subjects believe they can hurt the victim, some degree of external validity is assured. Most important of all, this standard laboratory procedure provides considerable experimental control over the situation, and postexperimental questionnaires do indeed indicate that the various manipulations of affect are effective in inducing the intended feeling states.

4.4. Using heat to manipulate affect

During and following the urban and campus riots of the 1960s and 1970s, there was considerable speculation that heat wave conditions in some way created a "long, hot summer effect" such that high temperatures, high tempers, and violence were interrelated. Indeed, the presidential commission appointed to examine the circumstances surrounding the collective violence noted the tendency for temperatures in the 80s (°F) and above to occur just prior to the outbreak of massive violence (U.S. Riot Commission, 1968). Anecdotes abounded about tempers flaring in excessive heat and minor incidents or altercations erupting into uncontrollable riots. Very little if any scientific evidence existed about temperature–aggression relationships, so researchers took the issue into the lab. It was known that the hypothalamus, a key component of the limbic system, was responsible for thermoregulation of the body as well as for some aspects of fight/flight responses in lower animals.

Animal experiments had also shown that high temperatures were associated with both increased and decreased aggressive activity. Ginsberg and Allee (1942), for example, studied several strains of mice in temperatures ranging from 64°F to 82°F and noted sluggishness and generally lowered levels of aggression at higher temperatures. Supporting this finding, Scott and Frederickson (1951) found reduced fighting in mice above temperatures of 78°F. On the other side of the coin, two animal studies found that elevated temperatures increased aggression. Wallis (1962) noted that ants were more aggressive at 68°–72°F than at 63°–66°F, and Berry and Jack (1971) reported that male Wistar rats were more aggressive at 100°F than at 39°F or 70°F, but only in response to electric shock. The absence of electric shock resulted in no effects of temperature on aggression. Thus, animal research showed both increases and decreases in aggression associated with rising ambient temperatures.

Such research, along with knowledge that the hypothalamus controls thermoregulation and some components of antagonistic behavior, and along with anecdotal evidence about riots in heat wave conditions, led researchers to question whether laboratory studies would show that human aggression would increase in a hot environment. Human research on attraction (Griffitt, 1970; Griffitt & Veitch, 1971) had demonstrated that temperatures in the neighborhood of 95°F could make people feel uncomfortable, irritable, and more prone to dislike strangers.

Moreover, high temperatures were known to increase some measures of arousal and decrease others, while either facilitating or impairing task performance (e.g., Poulton, 1970; Provins, 1966). Since heightened arousal was known to increase aggression under at least some circumstances (e.g., Berkowitz, 1969), it was reasonable to expect that high-temperature laboratory conditions would increase aggression. Indeed, Rohles (1976) observed juveniles in a heated laboratory room and noted heightened agitation, needling, provocation, and an attempted knifing, although a group of presumably more mature graduate students displayed no such heightened aggressiveness.

A more experimental approach to the issue occurred when Baron (1972) used the teacher–learner paradigm described above with subjects participating in a room kept at either 73°F or roughly 94°F. Half the subjects were angered by the accomplice's negatively evaluating an essay written by the subject (through both written criticism and delivery of electric shocks to signify poor performance), and the other half were treated in a more favorable manner by the accomplice's making a positive evaluation of the essay (and not delivering shock). As expected, the provocation led to considerably heightened levels of ostensible shock delivered to the victim. However, high temperatures actually reduced the level of attack, in both the angered and nonangered conditions. Although consistent with some of the animal research cited above, these results were unexpected, since it had been anticipated that at least under the hot, angry condition, the temperature would increase the intensity of hostile feelings, and the resulting heightened anger would be reflected in enhanced attack behavior.

Perhaps high temperatures could increase the likelihood and intensity of collective violence, but the necessary conditions were not present in the first Baron laboratory experiment. For example, only one attacker was present, hardly the type of situation that occurs in collective violence. Since social learning is known to play a major role in establishing the circumstances under which individuals will express irritation in the form of aggression, Baron and Lawton (1972) suggested that the presence of a model would make a major difference in the influence of heat on laboratory aggression. Following the procedures of Baron (1972) above, all the subjects were provoked through the negative evaluation technique. With the lab at either 73°F or 96°F, half the subjects administered shocks to the victim under the usual teacher–learner circumstances. Before the other half delivered their shocks, however, they first observed a second accomplice administering exceptional shock levels to the victim. That is, an aggressive model was present for this half of the subjects. Results indicated that the greatest aggression occurred under the hot, model condition. Presumably, the anger-enhancing effects of the heat, when combined with the aggression-disinhibiting effects of the model, produced the anticipated heightened aggression under at least some elevated temperature conditions. The Baron (1972) study, however, and some animal research, suggested that under other circumstances heat could actually decrease aggression.

Were these disparate findings perhaps methodological artifacts or were they systematically robust and explainable with more thorough experimentation? To start answering this question Baron and Bell (1975) had the accomplice either provoke or compliment the subject through a written evaluation of the subject's personality. The experiment took place in either a comfortably cool (73°F) or an uncomfortably hot (94°F) room, and an aggressive model either shocked the victim before the subject had a chance to, as above, or did not attack the victim before the subject did. This study was conducted in the winter in Indiana, whereas the Baron (1972) and Baron and Lawton (1972) studies were conducted in South Carolina in the summer. In the summer studies the subjects may have been acclimatized to a very hot and humid environment, whereas in the winter study the subjects were not accustomed to the hot conditions. Results indicated that the model increased aggression under all circumstances. Surprisingly, nonprovoked subjects were more aggressive in the hot than cool condition, but provoked subjects were less aggressive in the hot than cool condition (see Figure 4.1). In essence, some of the findings of the previous two laboratory experiments were replicated under different procedural circumstances and under apparently different degrees of acclimatization. Contrary to expectations, however, the hot, angry condition resulted in somewhat reduced aggression, rather than the anticipated heightened aggression thought to occur through heat enhancing the aggression-eliciting effects of anger. This unusual pattern of results was replicated by Baron and Bell (1976) using three levels of temperature (73°F, 82°F, 94°F). In this latter study both male and female subjects participated, whereas in earlier studies only male subjects were employed. Both the 82°F and 94°F conditions revealed the same pattern: Elevated temperatures increased aggression for nonprovoked subjects, but decreased it for provoked subjects. Although unexpected, the pattern was becoming more and more robust with respect to minor methodological variations. How could these puzzling results be explained? One possible answer rested

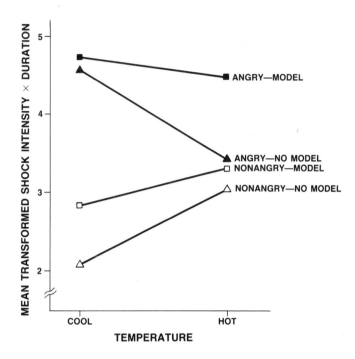

Figure 4.1. Mean level of aggression (shock) as a function of temperature, provocation, and presence of an aggressive model. Aggression and heat: mediating effects of prior provocation and exposure to an aggressive model. (Reprinted from Baron and Bell, 1975, by permission of the American Psychological Association.)

in an interpretation of the influence of affect as a moderator in the heat–aggression relationship. Before being explicit about this relationship, we need to examine the theoretical underpinnings of a closely related model of attraction that relies heavily on affect and that helps subsume the complex effects of the independent variables of the above aggression experiments under the simpler mediating effects of affect.

4.5. An affective model of attraction

As indicated previously, affect has been employed as a mediator with respect to a very wide range of social behaviors. One affective model of attraction particularly relevant to our present discussion is the reinforcement–affect model proposed by Clore and Byrne (1974) and completely reviewed by Byrne (1972). This model defines affect as lying on a pleasant–unpleasant continuum. Any stimulus with reinforcing properties appears to generate positive or negative affect: Rewarding stimuli produce positive affect and punishing stimuli generate negative affect, much as would occur in a classical conditioning paradigm. That is, the affect is an unconditioned response to unconditioned pleasurable or unpleasurable stimuli. Such stimuli might include attitude statements that agree or disagree with the subject's own beliefs, compliments or insults, prize winnings or painful punishments, and a host of other positive and negative events. Any previously neutral stimulus that is associated with such events serves as a conditioned stimulus, such that it becomes capable of eliciting positive or negative affect as well. The person delivering a compliment or insult, for example, becomes associated with the positive or negative affect generated by the unconditioned stimulus. That person then elicits a similar amount of affect in the subject the next time the subject encounters him or her. Since there are probably many different associations with a given conditioned stimulus, the affect elicited by that conditioned stimulus in the end is a weighted average of the affect produced by all the associated circumstances. Attraction toward the conditioned stimulus is a linear function of the associated affect. Thus, a target person delivering three agreeing attitudes and two insults to a subject will be somewhat disliked, since empirical evidence suggests that the affect generated by one insult is equivalent to the affect generated by three such attitudes. On average, then, three agreeing attitudes and two insults generate more negative than positive affect. Interestingly, an individual's affective state can be raised or lowered by factors independent of a target person, such as from watching a humorous or sad movie or from experiencing success or failure on a task. This additional fluctuation in affect must also be factored into the weighted average of affective associations when one is predicting attraction toward a target person. Thus, a subject receiving three agreeing attitudes and two insults will dislike the target less if the subject has just seen a humorous movie, and will dislike the target more if the subject has just experienced a failure.

The reason this model is relevant to our discussion of affect and aggression is that the independent variables used to study aggression are often the same independent variables used to study the reinforcement–affect model of attraction. If these variables generate affect in attraction research, they certainly generate similar affect in aggression research. For example, the anger or provocation manipulations in aggression research are essentially the same as insult or compliment manipulations in attraction research. In addition to generating anger, the insult also makes the subject's affective state more negative. Further-more, heat is known to lead to an unpleasant affective state, and also to reduce attraction, at least under some circumstances (Griffitt, 1970; Griffitt & Veitch, 1971). Thus, the simultaneous manipulation of anger (insult) and temperature is also manipulating affect in positive and negative directions. For the most part, these manipulations are simply adding different magnitudes of negative affect to the situation. That is, insult with heat should generate more negative affect than no insult with heat, and a cool room with no provocation or with a compliment should produce little if any negative affect. Could these seemingly simple affective relationships be used to explain the apparently complex results of the temperature–aggression studies described thus far? We turn now to a series of studies purporting to do just that.

4.6. Negative affect and aggression: a curvilinear relationship

Baron (1972) upon finding that high temperatures decreased aggression, first suggested that the discomfort of the hot laboratory produced so much misery that subjects would rather escape the situation than attack the accomplice. That is, under extreme discomfort, flight responses predominated over dispositions to fight. Indeed, Palamarek and Rule (1979) demonstrated that if given a choice, subjects experiencing con-siderable misery in a hot laboratory would prefer to escape the situation rather than attack a potential victim. Incorporating this notion, and the knowledge that provocation and heat were at least in part adding de-grees of discomfort to the experience of subjects, Baron and Bell (1976) proposed an inverted U curvilinear relationship between negative affect and aggression (see Figure 4.2). That is, moderate degrees of negative affect increase aggression, but more extreme levels of discomfort actual-ly reduce aggression since flight begins to predominate over fight tendencies. Thus, provocation in the absence of heat, or heat without provocation, was hypothesized to produce moderate levels of dis-comfort and consequently to produce heightened aggression. More ex-treme levels of discomfort, in the form of heat and provocation com-bined, reduce aggression since flight tendencies predominate at these high levels of negative affect. Such an interpretation would be consistent with all previous laboratory results, provided the degree of negative affect for the circumstances with the highest levels of aggression was in between the degree of negative affect for those conditions with less aggression.

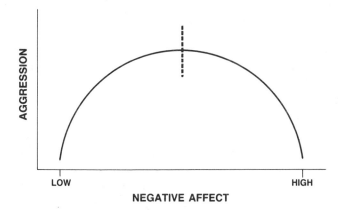

Figure 4.2. Theoretical relationship between negative affect and aggression. Aggression and heat: the influence of ambient temperature, negative affect, and a cooling drink on physical aggression. (Reprinted from Baron and Bell, 1976, by permission of the American Psychological Association.)

In support of this interpretation, Baron and Bell (1976) reported one more experiment with the same procedures as indicated above. That is, male subjects were either provoked or not provoked by an accomplice in a room that was either 72°F or 94°F. Prior to delivering the ostensible shocks to the victim, half the subjects were given a cooling glass of lemonade, and the other half were not. The hypothesis was that if the negative affect–aggression curve were to hold true, the lemonade would reduce the impact of heat and make the otherwise most uncomfortable subjects (hot, angry condition) less uncomfortable, and thus actually increase their level of aggression relative to the hot, angry group not receiving lemonade. That is, these subjects are on the extreme right side of the inverted U curve, with high negative affect and reduced aggression. Somewhat alleviating their negative affect with the lemonade would move them back toward the left side of the curve, but would increase their level of aggression if they followed the curve. In contrast, the relatively high aggressive, hot, nonprovoked subjects should be somewhere near the middle of the curve. Reducing their negative affect with lemonade should also move them toward the left side of the curve, but, following the curve, they should show reduced aggression relative to hot, nonprovoked subjects not receiving lemonade. For subjects in the cool room, lemonade should not particularly influence their negative affect (indeed, a methodological problem was getting these subjects to drink the lemonade), and thus should not influence their level of aggression. Results generally supported these hypotheses.

Still, even with the apparent support from several studies for the inverted U interpretation, there had been no direct efforts to scale the affective feelings of subjects prior to giving them an opportunity to aggress, so that a mathematical relationship between negative affect and aggression could be described. That is, there was no direct evidence that the conditions with the highest aggression were intermediate in negative affect. Bell and Baron (1976) reported an experiment that did indeed allow assessment of affect. Recall that Byrne (1972) reviewed numerous studies assessing the level of positive or negative affect generated by variables that influence attraction. Among the most studied variables have been attitude statements that are similar or dissimilar to the subject's own, and personal compliments and insults. The affect associated with heat has also been measured (e.g., Griffitt, 1970). Thus, Bell and Baron (1976) exposed male subjects to an accomplice who was made to appear attitudinally similar or dissimilar to the subject. The accomplice also delivered a personal compliment or insult to the subject. These procedures were carried out in a lab maintained at either 72°F or 94°F, and resulted in eight different combinations of attitude similarity, personal evaluation, and temperature. These eight conditions were scaled for their level of affect with subjects' responses to a semantic differential instrument. Subjects then aggressed against the accomplice using ostensible electric shock. As expected, conditions leading to moderate negative affect increased aggression the most, and conditions leading to the most extreme levels of negative affect resulted in less aggression than did the moderate negative affect conditions. Thus, a curvilinear trend between negative affect and aggression had been demonstrated.

4.7. Further studies of the negative affect – aggression relationship

We have presented much laboratory evidence that the relationship between high ambient temperatures and aggression can be conveniently described by an inverted U relationship between negative affect and aggression. As we will note below, alternative explanations are possible, and further support for the curvilinear hypothesis needs to be obtained. Two lines of work move in this direction. First, the curvilinear function should appear in research that studies the relationship between aggression and other determinants of negative affect. Second, this function should be found when other measures of aggression are employed outside the laboratory. We now turn to a review of both of these lines of research.

It is known that cold temperatures affect the body differently from hot temperatures, yet the affective experience of unpleasantness is similar whether the environment is excessively hot or excessively cold (e.g., Bell & Greene, 1982). It stands to reason, then, that the negative affect–aggression relationship should hold whether the negative affect is generated by heat or by cold. Bell and Baron (1977) tested this idea in the laboratory by placing subjects in an uncomfortably cool, comfortably cool, moderately hot, or very hot laboratory while they were either provoked or not provoked by an accomplice and then given the opportunity to deliver the customary ostensible electric shocks to this victim. Results supported the curvilinear interpretation: Moderate discomfort, whether associated with cold or hot temperatures, increased aggression, and more extreme discomfort reduced aggression.

Another environmental stressor with affective consequences is air pollution. Rotton et al. (1979) examined the curvilinear relationship between negative affect and aggression by employing foul odors to manipulate affect. Prior to administering the traditional electric shocks to an accomplice, subjects were exposed to either no foul odor, a moderately foul odor (ethyl mercaptan), or an extremely foul odor (ammonium sulfide). In consistency with the curvilinear hypothesis, the moderately foul odor increased aggression, and although it was not statistically significant, the extremely foul odor tended to reduce aggression.

Still another environmental stressor with affective consequences is noise. Loud, unpredictable, uncontrollable noise is especially known to produce irritation and discomfort (e.g., Glass & Singer, 1972). Noise has also been shown to produce heightened aggression, at least under some circumstances (Donnerstein & Wilson, 1976; Geen & O'Neal, 1969) when aggression is measured in the lab with the usual shock procedures. Whether extreme levels of noise will actually reduce aggression has not been demonstrated. In an effort to study this possibility, Bell (1980) combined noise and heat to produce an extreme level of discomfort. Male subjects were exposed to either 55 dB or 95 dB of white noise and to either 72°F or 94°F temperature. Half the subjects were verbally attacked by an assistant for allegedly not cooperating with the experimental procedures and the other half were not so abused. The measure of retaliation, rather than the usual shock procedure, was a written evaluation of the assistant by the subject that ostensibly could be used to influence the assistant's chances of employment. Unexpectedly, noise did not influence the evaluation, and heat influenced it only in the hot, angry condition, with subjects in this condition being particularly negative in their appraisal of the victim. Although seemingly inconsistent with the negative affect–aggression curve, these results should be considered tentative without further study of differences in measures of aggression. Verbal attack may be influenced differently from physical attack at different levels of negative affect. For example, whereas extremely negative levels of affect may decrease physical attack, even more unpleasant conditions may be required before verbal attack is displaced by flight tendencies.

A number of studies have sought to examine the generalizability of the curvilinear negative affect–aggression relationship to archival data on temperature and violence. Consistent with this relationship, Schwartz (1968) reported that coups, assassinations, revolts, and other forms of violence around the world are more likely to occur in the two temperate quarters of the year than in the hottest or coldest quarter for a given region. Baron and Ransberger (1978) examined urban riots of 1967 through 1971 and found that their frequency peaked at temperatures in the mid-80s to upper 80s, and declined thereafter. Carlsmith and Anderson (1979), however, noted that if one controls for frequency of temperatures across the year (temperatures are more likely to be in the 80s than in the 90s regardless of whether or not violence occurs on those days), the relationship between temperature and riots appears to be linear rather than curvilinear. Other researchers, examining the relationship between temperature and the incidence of various types of crime, also report linear rather than curvilinear relationships (Anderson & Anderson, 1984; Cotton, 1986; DeFronzo, 1984; Harries & Stadler, 1983; Rotton & Frey, 1985). Some of these findings may be due to the absence of enough extremely high-temperature days to test the curvilinear hypothesis (e.g., Cotton, 1986); that is, if only moderately high temperatures are studied, one should not expect to find a decrease in aggression since the decrease should occur only at extremely high discomfort. Similarly, residents of normally high-temperature areas might well acclimatize somewhat to otherwise uncomfortably hot conditions, so that the inflection point of the curvilinear function might be shifted toward very high temperatures. Some studies (e.g., Harris & Stadler, 1983), however, did observe very high temperature days and still found a linear rather than curvilinear relationship. Interestingly, DeFronzo (1984) found that the influence of temperature on violence was trivial when compared to the influence of socioeconomic and other factors.

Quite possibly, temperature influences some types of violence differently than others. For example, domestic violence may increase in hot
temperatures if the family cannot escape from circumstances that produce friction among individuals in the same house. Aggravated assault
against strangers may decrease with rising temperatures, but riots and
other forms of collective violence may increase. Definitive studies
addressing such speculation have not been reported. Moreover, the
type of aggression studied in the lab might respond differently to heat
than would some types of violence recorded in police reports. Com-
plicating factors such as increased consumption of alcohol and availability of deadly weapons have not been studied in lab research on heat and
aggression, yet such factors are almost inevitably involved in real-world
violence (Anderson, 1989).

Bell and Fusco (1986) offered another possibility for resolving the
differences between lab and field results. They reanalyzed Cotton's
(1986) data on police reports and noted that the variability in violence
increased with the temperature. Moreover, such an increase in variability seems to appear in other data sets as temperature increases. What
Bell and Fusco (1986) suggested was that both linear and curvilinear
trends are in the data. As temperatures, and discomfort, increase, violence is more likely. However, at higher levels of discomfort, there are
numerous instances of decreases in violence, consistent with the laboratory data, suggesting that lethargy or flight tendencies begin to suppress
overt expression of violence. At the same time, other factors increase
aggressive tendencies with increases in temperature, with the net result,
averaged across all the data, being a linear trend of increasing violence
but also increasing variance, with increasing temperatures reflecting
forces that tend to suppress aggression. The joint presence of
aggression-facilitating and aggression-inhibiting factors with increasingly negative affect would certainly be consistent with the Blanchard and Blanchard (1984) hypothesis of an anger-based and fear-based
emotional calculus determining the expression of fight or flight tendencies. Other interpretations are possible, of course, and we turn now to
some of these alternatives.

4.8. Alternative interpretations

We have noted that many, if not all, of the independent variables that
influence aggression also seem to influence affect. Accordingly, it
certainly seems legitimate to suggest affect as a mediator in aggres-

sion relationships. Manipulations of anger, heat, noise, and other aggression-related factors also produce internal changes beyond affect, however, and it is just as legitimate to examine these other factors as potential mediators of aggression.

One interesting interpretation of temperature–aggression relationships, which might be termed a "thermoregulatory interpretation," has been proposed by Boyanowsky et al. (1982–82). Recall that the hypothalamus controls thermoregulation of the body, as well as some components of the fight/flight response. The body's physiological reaction to excessive heat is fairly complex (Bell, 1981). Essentially, the body tries to maintain a constant core temperature through a homeostatic process. When overheated, the body makes efforts to lose excess heat. Heat loss procedures include peripheral vasodilation, or dilation of blood vessels in the extremities, in order to get more heat to the skin surface where it is lost primarily by convection and evaporation of sweat, and reduction of metabolism and physical activity in order not to produce so much internal heat in the first place. In the process, at least some measures of autonomic nervous system activity appear to show a reduction of autonomic arousal. For example, blood pressure will drop with peripheral vasodilation, as essentially the same amount of blood fills a larger space. The hypothalamus is heavily involved in these changes. However, in the face of anger-provoking situations, the hypothalamus works through the autonomic nervous system to prepare the organism for attack or flight: Heart rate, blood pressure, and other autonomic processes become elevated in order to maximize the intensity of fight or flight and thus maximize the chances for survival, whichever alternative is ultimately chosen. At least some of the autonomic processes for heat response run counter to the responses for fight/flight preparation. The resulting conflict in signals, according to Boyanowsky et al., increase irritation and physiological distress and also increases aggression. Were there an explanation present for the mixed signals, however, the irritation might not be so great and the aggression consequently reduced. In consistency with this expectation, Boyanowsky et al. reported that the presence of a thermometer within visual range of the subject reduces the level of aggression, apparently because it provides an explanation of the discomfort that is independent of the autonomic response to provocation. Should this process occur at low to intermediate levels of negative affect, it would certainly be compatible with the curvilinear negative affect interpretation.

As indicated above, the adaptive response to heat is complex and at some point may suggest a decrease in arousal. At other points, the response may suggest very high levels of arousal (Bell, 1981). Generally, provocation leads to an increase in arousal. Quite possibly, then, various combinations of arousal-reducing and arousal-enhancing forces could explain much of the relationship between heat, noise, anger, and other determinants of aggression (e.g., Geen & O'Neal, 1976). As indicated above, the arousal response to heat is complex and it is difficult to specify what is meant by "arousal." Blood pressure, for example, will initially rise on exposure to heat (as in a startle response), but will fall as peripheral vasodilation occurs, and may rise again as the heart pumps harder. Still later it will fall as coma and death approach in severe heat stress. Heart rate, galvanic skin response, and reticular activity increase more or less linearly with length of heat exposure (Bell, 1981). Because of this complexity and the difficulty of specifying just what is meant by arousal, our own preference is to stick with affect rather than arousal as the mediator in the heat–aggression relationship.

More cognitive interpretations of some of the above relationships are also possible, and certainly in humans cognitive processes are important in aggression. The Boyanowsky et al. finding mentioned above that viewing a thermometer leads to a reinterpretation of one's discomfort obviously relies in part on cognitive processes. Zillmann (1988, 1983) notes that arousal enhances aggression only if one interprets the arousal as relevant to the aggression-provoking situation. Attributing arousal to other factors (e.g., exercise) prevents that arousal from being interpreted as due to anger and reduces the impact of that arousal on subsequent aggression. It is certainly possible that extremely high levels of negative affect lead to decreased aggression in part because individuals attribute the discomfort to factors unrelated to aggression (e.g., angry individuals attribute their discomfort to heat rather than to anger). Berkowitz (1984) has noted that cognitions consistent with aggression can prime subsequent aggressive behavior. Discomfort of any form (pain, heat) could certainly lead to such cognitive priming, and extreme discomfort could even prime flight behavior.

All of these interpretations are obviously compatible with each other, and components of each interpretation may be necessary to explain the totality of determinants of aggression. These interpretations also rely to some extent on a trade-off of two or more factors, much as the Blanchard and Blanchard emotional calculus relies on a cost–benefit analysis of the particular circumstances.

4.9. Reducing aggression through incompatible affective responses

We noted in the Blanchard and Blanchard emotional calculus discussion that fear and anger seem to some extent to be emotional opposites, even though they can occur together. Moreover, the tendency to aggress when provoked can be overridden by an excess of fear. Is it possible that other emotions might also be able to counteract the influence of anger, and in effect reduce aggression by producing responses incompatible with attack? Baron (1977) has elaborated upon a number of such possibilities, including empathy, mild sexual arousal, and nonhostile humor.

Laboratory studies using the standard shock procedures have shown that anger will elicit strong attack against the victim. Several studies, however, have demonstrated that some events occurring between the provocation and the opportunity to aggress substantially decrease the level of attack. For example, the presence of a "pain meter" that ostensibly reflects the level of suffering of the victim will, when indicating substantial pain on the part of the victim, reduce aggression in the attacker (e.g., Baron, 1971a,b), although under extreme anger conditions pain may actually enhance aggression (Baron, 1974a). Similarly, asking angry subjects to evaluate a set of mildly erotic stimuli before they administer shocks to the accomplice seems to reduce their level of aggression (e.g., Baron, 1974b; Baron & Bell, 1977). Intriguingly, Donnerstein, Donnerstein, and Evans (1975) note that presenting the erotic stimuli before the provocation seems to enhance subsequent aggression. They suggest that when presented after provocation, mildly erotic stimuli distract attention from the provocation. When the erotica are presented before provocation, however, Donnerstein et al. propose that the distraction component is ineffective in reducing aggression and the arousal from the anger and the arousal from the sexual stimulation combine to intensify the level of attack. It is also intriguing to note that the hypothalamus controls not only fight/flight and temperature regulation but sexual behavior as well. A third affective factor, nonhostile humor, also reduces aggression by angry subjects (e.g., Baron & Ball, 1974). Fittingly, pleasure, including the pleasure of laughter, is in part a function of activity of the septal region of the limbic system.

A particularly interesting experiment has examined all three of these aggression-reducing factors in conjunction with heat. Baron (1976) measured the amount of horn honking drivers employed when stuck behind a car that did not move (because an assistant of the experimenter's was driving the 'stalled" car) when a traffic signal changed from red to green. Prior to the changing light, another (female) assistant passed the subject's car either walking normally (control), wearing a clown mask (humor), using crutches (empathy), or wearing a highly revealing outfit (mild sexual arousal). The experimenter also monitored temperature. The results indicated that honking was more likely at moderately warm temperatures (if drivers were in unair-conditioned cars), and that humor, empathy, and mild sexual arousal all decreased hostility as measured by horn honking.

Apparently, then, some types of affect (e.g., anger, fear) may well facilitate aggression under the right circumstances, but other affective reactions (e.g., humor, empathy, mild sexual arousal, fear) may well be incompatible with aggression under given conditions. To some extent these affective states are controlled by mechanisms within the primitive limbic system, although cognitive factors (e.g., interpretation of an event as humorous) must also be involved. As Moore and Isen discuss elsewhere in this volume, affect and cognition are closely intertwined, and affect influences numerous processes in social cognition, including the organization of cognitive structures and associations across categories of memory. (See also Isen, 1984; Isen et al., 1985). It is quite likely, then, that incompatibility of affective reactions is cognitively influenced and has cognitive consequences.

4.10. Some affective factors in organizational conflict

Conflict within an organization can have disastrous consequences (e.g., Robbins, 1974), so there is growing interest in finding ways to reduce its costly impact. Baron (1984) has noted that the emotions, motives, and overt behavior of aggression are often the same as those involved in organizational conflict. If so, could it be that the effective relationships described above for aggression also apply to organizational conflict? To study this possibility, Baron had a subject and accomplice role-play executives in an organization. The confederate was instructed to disagree with the subject as much as possible on the course of action for the organization. In some cases the disagreement was made in a condescending and arrogant manner, and in other cases it was expressed in a calm and rational manner. During a pause in the experiment, either nothing happened (control), the accomplice offered the subject some candy (gratitude), the accomplice attributed his or her own attitude to a busy schedule with many tests that week (sympathy), or the accomplice asked the subject to help evaluate some cartoons for another project (humor). As expected, disagreement expressed arrogantly produced more negative responses overall than did disagreement expressed calmly. More importantly, relative to the control condition, the gratitude, sympathy, and humor conditions enhanced subjects' moods, improved their impressions of the accomplice, and led to greater preferences for constructive (e.g., collaboration) as opposed to destructive (e.g., avoidance) means of handling future conflict, following the framework described by Thomas (1976). Thus, emotions found to be incompatible with aggression also proved to be incompatible with exacerbating components of conflict. In a second study, Baron (1985) found that the most positive reactions to a conflict-inducing accomplice occurred when the accomplice's behavior appeared, to derive from sincere beliefs about his or her stand. Thus, some degree of cognitive processing of conflict-related information, and attributions about apparent motives for conflict-related behavior appear to influence the manner in which we respond to conflict. Although affect is important, cognitive factors moderate their impact.

Summary and conclusions

We have seen that the physiological organization of the brain places the regulation of both aggression and affect in the primitive limbic system. Certainly with higher organisms, more cortical areas of the brain play a role as well. Other factors known to influence mood, such as sexual arousal, humor, anger, fear, and high ambient temperatures, are also closely tied into the limbic system. Moreover, empirical evidence does indeed indicate that all of these factors can increase or decrease aggression. According to the Blanchard and Blanchard emotional calculus approach, a cost–benefit analysis occurs between the odds of success and the odds of failure in a given situation, with anger and fear weighing heavily in the analysis. Attack or flight results, depending on the outcome of the analysis.

In humans, environmental stressors appear particularly amenable to an affective interpretation of their effects on aggression, with considerable evidence present for an inverted U relationship between negative affect and aggression. Laboratory evidence for heat, cold, and foul odors seems to support such a relationship, although many archival data suggest a more linear trend. Whatever the case, at extremely high levels of negative affect, escape or flight responses seem to occur as much as or more than attack tendencies. Perhaps other mediators, such as arousal, mixed hypothalamic signals, or cognitive assessments, account for some apparent discrepancies in the data.

Some affective responses, such as nonhostile humor, empathy, or mild sexual arousal, appear to be incompatible with aggression. At least under some circumstances, these emotions reduce both physical attack and factors that enhance organizational conflict.

References

Anderson, C. A. (1989). Temperature and aggression: Ubiquitous effects of heat on occurrence of human violence. *Psychological Bulletin, 106,* 74–96.

Anderson, C. A., & Anderson, D. C. (1984). Ambient temperature and violent crime: Tests of the linear and curvilinear hypotheses. *Journal of Personality and Social Psychology, 46,* 91–97.

Bandura, A. (1973). *Aggression: A social learning analysis.* Englewood Cliffs, NJ: Prentice-Hall.

Baron, R. A. (1971a). Magnitude of victim's pain cues and level of prior anger arousal as determinants of adult aggressive behavior. *Journal of Personality and Social Psychology, 17,* 236–243.

Baron, R. A. (1971b). Aggression as a function of magnitude of victim's pain cues, level of prior anger arousal, and aggressor victim similarity. *Journal of Personality and Social Psychology, 18,* 48–54.

Baron, R. A. (1972). Aggression as a function of ambient temperature and prior anger arousal. *Journal of Personality and Social Psychology, 21,* 183–189.

Baron, R. A. (1974a). Aggression as a function of victim's pain cues, level of prior anger arousal, and exposure to an aggressive model. *Journal of Personality and Social Psychology, 29,* 117–124.

Baron, R. A. (1974b). The aggression-inhibiting influence of heightened sexual arousal. *Journal of Personality and Social Psychology, 30,* 318–322.

Baron, R. A. (1976). The reduction of human aggression: A field study of the influence of incompatible reactions. *Journal of Applied Social Psychology, 6,* 260–274.

Baron, R. A. (1977). *Human aggression.* New York: Plenum.

Baron, R. A. (1984). Reducing organizational conflict: An incompatible response approach. *Journal of Applied Psychology, 69,* 272–279.

Baron, R. A. (1985). Reducing organizational conflict: The role of attribution. *Journal of Applied Psychology, 70,* 434–441.

Baron, R. A., & Ball, R. L. (1974). The aggression-inhibiting influence of nonhostile humor. *Journal of Experimental Social Psychology, 10,* 23–33.

Baron, R. A., & Bell, P. A. (1975). Aggression and heat: Mediating effects of prior provocation and exposure to an aggressive model. *Journal of Personality and Social Psychology, 31,* 825–832.

Baron, R. A., & Bell, P. A. (1976). Aggression and heat: The influence of ambient temperature, negative affect, and a cooling drink on physical aggression. *Journal of Personality and Social Psychology, 33,* 245–255.

Baron, R. A., & Bell, P. A. (1977). Sexual arousal by males: Effects of type of erotic stimuli and prior provocation. *Journal of Personality and Social Psychology, 35,* 79–87.

Baron, R. A., & Byrne, D. (1987). *Social psychology: Understanding human interaction* (5th ed.). Boston: Allyn & Bacon.

Baron, R. A., & Eggleston, R. J. (1972). Performance on the "aggression machine": Motivation to help or harm? *Psychonomic Science, 26,* 321–322.

Baron, R. A., & Lawton, S. F. (1972). Environmental influences on aggression: The facilitation of modeling effects by high ambient temperatures. *Psychonomic Science, 26,* 80–83.

Baron, R. A., & Ransberger, V. M. (1978). Ambient temperature and the occurrence of collective violence: The "long hot summer" revisited. *Journal of Personality and Social Psychology, 36,* 351–360.

Bell, P. A. (1980). Effects of heat, noise, and provocation on retaliatory evaluative behavior. *Journal of Social Psychology, 40,* 97–100.

Bell, P. A. (1981). Physiological, comfort, performance, and social effects of heat stress. *Journal of Social Issues, 37,* 71–94.

Bell, P. A., & Baron, R. A. (1976). Aggression and heat: The mediating role of negative affect. *Journal of Applied Social Psychology, 6,* 18–30.

Bell, P. A., & Baron, R. A. (1977). Aggression and ambient temperature: The facilitating and inhibiting effects of hot and cold environments. *Bulletin of the Psychonomic Society, 9,* 443–445.

Bell, P. A., & Fusco, M. E. (1986). Linear and curvilinear relationships between temperature, affect, and violence: Reply to Cotton. *Journal of Applied Social Psychology, 16,* 802–807.

Bell, P. A., & Greene, T. C. (1982). Thermal stress: Physiological, comfort, performance, and social effects of hot and cold environments. In G. W. Evans (Ed.), *Environmental stress.* London: Cambridge University Press.

Berkowitz, L. (1969). The frustration-aggression hypothesis revisited. In L. Berkowitz (Ed.), *Roots of aggression.* New York: Atherton Press.

Berkowitz, L. (1978). Whatever happened to the frustration-aggression hypothesis? *American Behavioral Scientist, 21,* 691–708.

Berkowitz, L. (1984). Some effects of thoughts on anti- and pro-social influences of media events: A cognitive neo-association analysis. *Psychological Bulletin, 95,* 410–427.

Berkowitz, L., & Donnerstein, E. (1982). External validity is more than skin deep. *American Psychologist, 37,* 245–257.

Berry, R. M., & Jack, E. C. (1971). The effect of temperature upon shock-elicited aggression in rats. *Psychonomic Science, 23,* 341–343.

Blanchard, D. C., & Blanchard, R. J. (1984). Affect and aggression: An animal model applied to human behavior. In R. J. Blanchard & D. C. Blanchard (Eds.), *Advances in the study of aggression* (Vol. I). New York: Academic Press.

Boyanowsky, E. O., Calvert, J., Young, J., & Brideau, L. (1981–82). *Journal of Environmental Systems, 11,* 81–87.

Buss, A. H. (1961). *The psychology of aggression.* New York: Wiley.

Byrne, D. (1971). *The attraction paradigm.* New York: Academic Press.

Carlsmith, J. M., & Anderson, C. A. (1979). Ambient temperature and the occurrence of collective violence: A new analysis. *Journal of Personality and Social Psychology, 37,* 337–344.

Clore, G. L., & Byrne, D. (1974). A reinforcement-affect model of attraction. In T. L. Huston (Ed.), *Foundations of interpersonal attraction.* New York: Academic Press.

Cotton, J. L. (1986). Ambient temperature and violent crime. *Journal of Applied Social Psychology, 16,* 786–801.

DeFronzo, J. (1984). Climate and crime: Tests of an FBI assumption. *Environment and Behavior, 16,* 185–210.

Dollard, J., Doob, L., Miller, N., Mowrer, O. H., & Sears, R. R. (1939). *Frustration and aggression.* New Haven, CT: Yale University Press.

Donnerstein, E., Donnerstein, M., & Evans, R. (1975). Erotic stimuli and aggression: Facilitation or inhibition. *Journal of Personality and Social Psychology, 32,* 237–244.

Donnerstein, E., & Wilson, D. W. (1976). Effects of noise and perceived control on ongoing and subsequent aggressive behavior. *Journal of Personality and Social Psychology, 34,* 774–781.

Flynn, J. P., Vanegas, H., Foote, W., & Edwards, S. (1970). Neural mechanisms involved in a cat's attack on a rat. In R. E. Whalen, R. F. Thompson, M. Verzeano, & N. M. Weinberger (Eds.), *The neural control of behavior.* New York: Academic Press.

Geen, R. G., & O'Neal, E. C. (1969). Activation of cue-elicited aggression by general arousal. *Journal of Personality and Social Psychology, 11,* 289–292.

Geen, R. G., & O'Neal, E. C. (1976). *Perspectives on aggression.* New York: Academic Press.

Ginsberg, B., & Allee, W. C. (1942). Some effects of conditioning on social dominance and subordination in inbred strains of mice. *Physiological Zoology, 15,* 485–506.

Glass, D. C., & Singer, J. E. (1972). *Urban stress.* New York: Academic Press.

Griffitt, W. (1970). Environmental effects on interpersonal affective behavior: Ambient effective temperature and attraction. *Journal of Personality and Social Psychology, 15,* 240–244.

Griffitt, W., & Veitch, R. (1971). Hot and crowded: Influence of population density and temperature on interpersonal affective behavior. *Journal of Personality and Social Psychology, 17,* 92–98.

Harries, K. D., & Stadler, S. J. (1983). Determinism revisited: Assault and heat stress in Dallas, 1980. *Environment and Behavior, 15,* 235–256.

Isen, A. M. (1984). Toward understanding the role of affect in cognition. In R. Wyer & T. Srull (Eds.), *Handbook of social cognition.* Hillsdale, NJ: Erlbaum.

Isen, A. M., Johnson, M. M. S., Mertz, E., & Robinson, G. (1985). The influence of positive affect on the unusualness of word associations. *Journal of Personality and Social Psychology, 48,* 413–426.

Johnson, R. N. (1972). *Aggression in man and animals.* Philadelphia: Saunders.

Kluver, H., & Bucy, P. C. (1937). Psychic blindness and other symptoms following bilateral temporal lobectomy in Rhesus monkeys. *American Journal of Physiology, 119,* 352–353.

MacDonnell, M. F., & Flynn, J. P. (1966). Sensory control of hypothalamic attack. *Animal Behavior, 14,* 399–405.

Moyer, K. B. (1976). *The psychobiology of aggression.* New York: Harper & Row.

Palamarek, D. L., & Rule, B. G. (1979). The effects of ambient temperature and insult on the motivation to retaliate or escape. *Motivation and Emotion, 3,* 83–92.

Poulton, E. C. (1970). *The environment and human efficiency.* Springfield, IL: Charles C. Thomas.

Provins, K. A. (1966). Environmental heat, body temperature, and behavior: An hypothesis. *Australian Journal of Psychology, 18,* 118–129.

Robbins, S. P. (1974). *Managing organizational conflict.* Englewood Cliffs, NJ: Prentice-Hall.

Rohles, F. H. (1976). Environmental psychology: A bucket of worms. *Psychology Today, 1*, 54–63.

Rotton, J., & Frey, J. (1985). Air pollution, weather, and violent crimes: Concomitant time-series analysis of archival data. *Journal of Personality and Social Psychology, 49*, 1207–1220.

Rotton, J., Frey, J., Barry, T., Milligan, M., & Fitzpatrick, M. (1979). The air pollution experience and interpersonal aggression. *Journal of Applied Social Psychology, 9*, 397–412.

Schwartz, D. C. (1968). On the ecology of political violence: The "long hot summer" as a hypothesis. *American Behavioral Scientist*, July–August, pp. 24–28.

Scott, J. P., & Frederickson, E. (1951). The causes of fighting in mice and rats. *Physiological Zoology, 24*, 273–309.

Shemberg, K. M., Leventhal, D. B., & Allman, L. (1968). Aggression machine performance and rated aggression. *Journal of Experimental Research in Personality, 3*, 117–119.

Thomas, K. W. (1976). Conflict and conflict management. In M. Dunnette (Ed.), *Handbook of industrial and organizational psychology*. Chicago: Rand McNally.

United States Riot Commission (1968). *Report of the National Advisory Commission on Civil Disorders*. New York: Bantam Books.

Wallis, D. I. (1962). Aggressive behavior in the ant *(Formica fusca)*. *Animal Behavior, 10*, 267–274.

Wolfe, B. M., & Baron, R. A. (1971). Laboratory aggression related to aggression in naturalistic social situations: Effects of an aggressive model on behavior of college student and prisoner observers. *Psychonomic Science, 24*, 193–194.

Zillmann, D. (1979). *Hostility and aggression*. Hillsdale, NJ: Erlbaum.

Zillmann, D. (1983). Transfer of excitation in emotional behavior. In J. T. Cacioppo & R. E. Petty (Eds.), *Social psychophysiology*. New York: Guilford Press.

Zillman, D. (1988). Cognition excitation interdependencies in aggressive behavior. *Aggressive Behavior, 14*, 51–64.

5. Affect and altruism

C. DANIEL BATSON

Consider the following eight statements:

1. "Please don't bother me, I'm feeling rotten today."
2. "I got the job – I feel great!"
3. "I'm so happy for you."
4. "I felt so sorry when I heard what happened to you."
5. "It's awful seeing her suffer like that."
6. "I'm so relieved to know you're feeling better."
7. "I would have felt really bad if I hadn't done something."
8. "When you see something like that, it's hard not to feel lucky yourself."

Each of these statements alludes to affect. But in no two is the affect quite the same.

The first two statements refer to moods, negative and positive; one is of unspecified but possibly health-related in origin; the other, the result of a specific event. The next four statements all refer to emotional reactions to the perceived welfare of someone else; in statements 3 and 4 the speaker seems to be resonating with the other person's condition (as the speaker perceives it), whereas in statements 5 and 6 the speaker reacts to the other's condition as a stimulus for the speaker's own emotional response. The emotions described in statements 5 and 6 are not unlike emotions the speaker might feel on encountering any of a variety of pleasant or unpleasant experiences; the experience need not concern another person. Statements 7 and 8 involve emotional reactions to situations viewed from a more abstract perspective. In these statements, the speaker seems to pull back to look at the situation from the outside. Roles for self and other are defined, principles of duty and justice are applied, and the emotional response occurs as a product of these evaluations.

Preparation of this paper was supported in part by NSF grants BNS-8507110 and BNS-8906723, C. Daniel Batson, principal investigator.

There is empirical evidence that each of these different types of affective response is related to helping behavior. This fact may seem to
suggest that we can ignore the different nuances in these affective states
and speak of a general relationship between affect and helping. My
main thesis in this chapter is that such a suggestion is misguided. I wish
to argue that we cannot ignore subtle shades of difference in affective
responses if we hope to progress beyond a superficial mapping of
co-occurrences of affect and helping, which we need to do. We need to
progress beyond this superficial level to develop an understanding of
the more fundamental psychological processes that underlie these surface relationships. As Lewin (1951) pointed out in discussing his
"method of construction," such progress is essential if our effort is to
merit the label "science" in the Galilean sense.

When we begin to consider the ways different affective reactions
influence the desire to benefit someone else, we find that several distinct
motivational processes seem to be involved. Exactly how many is as yet
unclear. Naturally, for the sake of simplicity and parsimony we are well
advised to keep the number of different processes proposed as small as
possible. Yet, if we are to consider the subtle shades of difference in
affective responses, we must run the risk of erring in the direction of
complexity and lack of parsimony. It is my present belief – based on
some by no means incontrovertible empirical evidence – that the conceptual distintions I shall make (or some very similar ones) are necessary, and that the number of processes I shall invoke is not excessive.
But this belief may be quite wrong.

To set the stage for my attempt to make sense of the relationship
between affect and altruism by identifying underlying constructs, let me
briefly list some major empirical findings in the area and some important
attempts to understand the psychologial processes underlying the
empirical relationships.

5.1. Some major empirical findings concerning the relationships between affect and altruism

In the last few years the research on affect and altruism has been nicely
reviewed by Dovidio (1984), Krebs and Miller (1985), and Rosenhan et
al. (1981b). Reviews of research on affect and altruism are also standard fare
in most introductory texts in social psychology. There is no need for me to
provide another review; I shall simply list what we think we know.

First of all, we know that positive moods increase helping. Experiences such as succeeding at a task (Berkowitz & Connor, 1966; Isen, 1970), receiving an unexpected cookie, finding a coin in the return slot of a phone booth (Isen & Levin, 1972; Levin & Isen, 1975), being given free stationery (Isen, Clark, & Schwartz, 1976), or enjoying a sunny day (Cunningham, 1979) all increase the likelihood of adults helping persons who were not the source of the mood-enhancing experience. Similar effects have also been found with children. Increased sharing and charity among children occur following success (Isen, Horn, & Rosenhan, 1973; Rushton & Littlefield, 1979) and thinking about happy memories (Moore, Underwood, & Rosenhan, 1973; Rosenhan, Underwood, & Moore, 1974). The one case in which elevated mood does not increase helping seems to be when the helping involves subjecting someone else (Isen & Levin, 1972) or oneself (Isen & Simonds, 1978) to an unpleasant experience.

Second, we know that negative moods sometimes increase and sometimes decrease helping. The negative affective state associated with harming someone or with seeing someone harmed has been found to lead to increased helping of a third party by adults (Carlsmith & Gross, 1969; Cialdini, Darby, & Vincent, 1973; Cunningham, Steinberg, & Grev, 1980; Freedman, Wallington, & Bless, 1967; Konecni, 1972; Rawlings, 1968; Regan, 1971; Wallington, 1973), as has remembering sad experiences (Manucia, Baumann, & Cialdini, 1984). But this relationship between negative mood and increased helping does not exist for young children; if anything, the relationship for them is the opposite. After recalling sad memories, children up to about 12 years are no more charitable than before, and they are sometimes less charitable (Cialdini & Kenrick, 1976; Isen et al., 1973; Moore, Underwood, & Rosenhan, 1973; Rosenhan, Underwood, & Moore, 1974).

Even among adults, there is evidence that after their reading a series of depressing statements (Aderman, 1972), receiving failure feedback (Berkowitz & Connor, 1966; Berkowitz, 1972; Isen, 1970), or imagining the personal pain and sorrow caused by the death of a friend (Thompson, Cowan, & Rosenhan, 1980), the likelihood of helping is either reduced or not changed relative to controls. On the other hand, Weyant (1978) found that failure feedback increased helping, but only when the reward value of helping was high (i.e., when the cause being helped was especially worthy and the cost of helping was low).

Third, we know that seeing someone suffer can lead to aversive arousal, and the arousal can lead to increased helping. Berger (1962) found more physiological arousal among research participants who thought that the person they were watching receive electric shocks found the shocks painful than he found among participants who thought that the person either was not receiving shocks or did not find the shocks painful. Increased physiological arousal to witnessing another person suffer has also been reported by Craig and Lowery (1969), Craig and Wood (1969), Gaertner and Dovidio (1977), Hygge (1976), Krebs (1975), Lazarus, Opton, Nomikos, and Rankin (1965), and Vaughn and Lanzetta (1980). This physiological arousal is associated with self-reports of unpleasantness, tension, nervousness (Stotland, 1969), and feeling bad (Krebs, 1975). Moreover, this unpleasant affective arousal is associated with higher rates of helping and more rapid helping of the person whose suffering caused the arousal (Clark & Word, 1974; Gaertner & Dovidio, 1977; Piliavin, Dovidio, Gaertner, & Clark, 1981).

Fourth, we know that feelings of personal distress caused by witnessing another's suffering are associated with more helping of that person only when it is difficult to escape exposure to the other's suffering without helping; feelings of empathy caused by witnessing another's suffering are associated with increased helping even when it is easy to escape exposure to the other's suffering without helping. Harris and Huang (1973), Krebs (1975), and Coke, Batson, and McDavis (1978) all provided evidence that increased emotional arousal attributed to witnessing another person suffer leads to increased helping of that person. Each of these researchers interpreted the emotional arousal of participants in their research to be empathic. Batson, Duncan, Ackerman, Buckley, and Birch (1981), Batson, O'Quin, Fultz, Vanderplas, and Isen (1983), and Toi and Batson (1972) reported evidence that the emotional reactions of personal distress (i.e., feeling alarmed, upset, troubled, and the like) and empathy (i.e., feeling sympathetic, compassionate, softhearted, tender, and the like) are experienced as qualitatively distinct. Moreover, these researchers provided evidence that when it is relatively easy to escape from exposure to another person's suffering without helping, there is reduced helping of that person by individuals feeling a predominance of personal distress as a result of seeing the person suffer, but not by individuals feeling a predominace of empathy.

Fifth, we know that persons attending to the suffering of another person will, at least under certain circumstances, help a third party more than persons attending to their own suffering caused by the other person's suffering; persons attending to another person's joy will, under certain circumstances, help a third party less than persons attending to their own joy. Thompson et al. (1980) found that research participants who focused on the worry, anxiety, and pain of a friend dying of cancer subsequently spent more time trying to answer difficult multiple-choice questions for an unknown graduate student in education than did either participants in a control condition or participants who focused on their own pain and sorrow caused by the friend's death. Rosenhan, Salovey, and Hargis (1981) found that participants who attended to their own joy at being given a trip to Hawaii subsequently spent more time answering the multiple-choice questions than did participants in a control condition, who in turn spent more time than subjects who attended to a close friend's joy at being given a trip to Hawaii.

5.2. Some attempts to understand the processes underlying the empirical evidence

As with the research itself, extensive discussion of the explanations proposed to make sense of part or all of what we know about the relationship between affect and altruism is not necessary. Different explanations have been discussed in detail, by Batson (1987), Dovidio (1984), Krebs and Miller (1985), Piliavin et al. (1981), and Rosenhan, Salovey, Karylowski, and Hargis (1981b). I shall simply allude to seven major explanations.

Positive mood maintenance

One of the first explanations of the positive relationship between good mood and helping was that a person in a good mood seeks to maintain this mood (Isen & Levin, 1972; Levin & Isen, 1975). To maintain the positive mood, the person must eliminate from his or her environment unpleasant and discomforting events, including the suffering of others. The person must also avoid the depressing effect of guilt. Pursuing either or both of these strategies for maintaining positive mood could lead to increased helping. (Alternatively, the person might maintain a positive mood simply by becoming callous to the suffering of others.)

The research cited above about positive moods increasing helping is entirely consistent with a positive mood maintenance explanation of the positive mood–helping relationship. But some recent empirical evidence suggests that a mood maintenance explanation may not alone account for this relationship. Manucia, Baumann, and Cialdini (1984) found that undergraduates whose mood was enhanced by having reminisced about a happy experience were as likely to acquiesce to a request for help when they thought their mood had been fixed by a drug (and so helping or lack of helping could not change their good mood) as when they thought their mood was labile. If these undergraduates were simply concerned to maintain their good mood, helping should have been unnecessary for them. Interpretation of the Manucia et al. (1984) positive mood results is, however, considerably clouded by the lack of evidence for a significant increase in helping relative to controls for enhanced-mood subjects in either the fixed or labile mood conditions (both $ts < 1.0$). Still, Isen (1987) argues that mood maintenance is not the only reason positive mood leads to increased helping.

Positive mood makes cognitions about the positive aspects of helping more accessible

Isen, Shalker, Clark, and Karp (1978) have suggested that being in a good mood may bias our memories about the positive and negative aspects of various activities, including helping. They suggest that when we are in a good mood we are more likely to recall and atttend to positive rather than negative aspects of our experience, and to have a more positive outlook on life (Isen, Clark, & Schwartz, 1976; Isen et al., 1978).

Applied to helping, this logic suggests that being in a good mood makes us more likely to remember and attend to the positive, rewarding features of helping, and less likely to attend to the negative features, such as the costs involved. Consistent with this explanation of the positive mood–helping relationship, Clark and Isen (1981) found that when people are in a good mood, they are more likely to recall the positive aspects of their past experiences involving helping, as well as to be more optimistic about their ability to help.

Hornstein (1982) has used a similar logic to predict that hearing good news will make more accessible positive cognitions about various activities, including helping, and therefore will lead to increased helping. Conversely, Hornstein suggests that hearing bad news will make more accessible negative cognitions and therefore lead to reduced helping. Hornstein and his colleagues (Hornstein, LaKind, Frankel, & Manne, 1976) have provided some evidence consistent with these predictions.

As noted earlier, however, bad mood is not always associated with reduced helping. Sometimes it leads to precisely the opposite – an increase in helping. Clearly, a different explanation is needed to account for a positive relationship between bad mood and helping.

Guilt reduction or self-image repair

Early explanations of the positive relationship between negative affect and helping focused on situations in which the negative affect was induced by a failure or transgression on the part of the subsequent helper. The positive relationship in these situations was explained in terms of either guilt reduction or self-image repair. There is considerable empirical evidence consistent with such an explanation (e.g., Carlsmith & Gross, 1969; Freedman et al., 1967; Isen et al., 1973; Rawlings, 1968).

But Cialdini and his colleagues have pointed out that increased helping can result from observing another person harm someone (Cialdini, Darby, & Vincent, 1973; Regan, 1971) or from thinking about a sad experience (Manucia et al., 1984). In these cases it seems unlikely that guilt or self-esteem is at issue.

Negative state relief

Cialdini and his colleagues (Cialdini et al., 1973; Cialdini, Baumann, & Kenrick, 1981) have argued that a more adequate and parsimonious explanation of the negative affect–increased helping relationships is negative state relief: When we experience a negative mood – whether as a result of our own action or some external event – we want to feel better. Those of us who have internalized prosocial standards know that we can feel good about ourselves when we help someone in need. Therefore, when we are in a bad mood we are more likely to help, because helping will lead to self-rewards that will relieve our negative affective state.

Support for this view is to be found in experiments in which negative state subjects – subjects who observed one person harm another or were themselves the harm doer – subsequently help a third party more than do neutral mood controls, except when a positive experience (e.g., monetary reward, praise, or verbal reassurance) relieves the negative state prior to the opportunity to help (cf. Cialdini et al., 1973; Cunningham et al., 1980; Regan, 1971). In addition, support is found in the Manucia et al. (1984) observation that people who reminisce about experiences that made them feel sad help more than neutral mood controls, except when they perceive that their mood will not be changed by their actions.

These results clearly conform to negative state relief predictions. But Cialdini and his colleagues (1981) argue that there is support for their view even in the observed exceptions to the "feel bad–do good" principle: Children do not help more when in a bad mood because they have not yet internalized the prosocial standards necessary to make help rewarding (Cialdini & Kenrick, 1976). Adults experiencing extreme or chronic negative affect do not help more because they perceive that the rewards associated with helping will not be efficacious in relieving their negative state (Aderman, 1972; Manucia et al., 1984; Weyant, 1978). Adults in a sad mood who are self-focused and so less attentive to their environment help less than those in a neutral mood because they fail to recognize the opportunity for self-reward (McMillen, Sanders, & Solomon, 1977; Rogers et al., 1982). Cialdini et al. (1981) point out that this last effect reverses when the other's need and helping are made sufficiently salient.

Aversive arousal reduction

The negative state relief explanation of the negative affect–increased helping relationship is based on a reinforcement model of motivation. Negative mood increases the need for mood enhancement and, as a result, the likelihood of helping (or some other mood-enhancing response). Another explanation that predicts a positive relationship between negative affect and helping is the aversive arousal reduction explanation proposed by Piliavin and her colleagues (Piliavin & Piliavin, 1973; Piliavin et al., 1981). Although the arousal reduction explanation has some surface similarity to the negative state relief explanation, it is actually quite different. It is not based on a reinforcement model of motivation but on a tension reduction model.

Piliavin and her colleagues propose that witnessing another person suffer causes the observer to become emotionally aroused; this emotional arousal is aversive, and the observer wishes to reduce it. Helping the suffering individual is one way to reduce the aversive arousal because it eliminates the stimulus causing the observer's arousal. Note that in this analysis helping is necessarily directed toward the person whose suffering caused one's arousal, whereas in the negative state relief analysis helping a third person is also predicted (and observed). In the negative state relief analysis, it is assumed that some negative experience has created a need within the individual for the self-rewards associated with helping. The classic learning theory analogue is a food-deprived animal pressing a bar for any of a variety of types of food. In the aversive arousal reduction explanation, it is assumed that witnessing another's suffering is a noxious stimulus that the individual wishes to escape. The classic analogue is an animal on a shock grid doing whatever it can to get away from the shock.

As noted earier, there is considerable empirical evidence that seeing someone else suffer leads to negative affect – to feeling upset, anxious, disturbed, and distressed. There is also considerable evidence that individuals are motivated to escape this aversive affective arousal – either by helping the suffering individual or by escaping (see Batson, 1987; Dovidio, 1984; Piliavin et al., 1981, for extensive reviews).

Variations on the aversive arousal reduction theme have been proposed by a number of other researchers. For example, Hoffman (1981) proposed that "empathic distress, which is a parallel response – a more or less exact replication of the victim's actual feelings of distress . . . is unpleasant, and helping the victim is usually the best way to get rid of the source" (pp. 51–52). Hornstein (1978) proposed that a cognitive link to others as "we" rather than "they" leads "one person's plight to become a source of tension for his or her fellows," who, in turn, "reduce this tension by aiding" (p. 189). Reykowski (1982) proposed that perception of a discrepancy between the current and expected or ideal state of another's welfare arouses an aversive cognitive inconsistency and "intrinsic prosocial motivation" to reduce this inconsistency. Lerner (1970) proposed a similar but more specific view, arguing that much helping is motivated by a desire to maintain a belief in a just world. The aversive arousal reduction explanation in its various forms has probably been the most popular explanation of the negative affect–helping relationship.

Empathic emotion leads to altruistic motivation

Although popular, the aversive arousal reduction explanation has not gone unchallenged. Batson and his colleagues (Batson, 1987; Batson & Coke, 1981; Batson et al., 1981; Batson, Fultz, & Schoenrade, 1987) have proposed that a qualitative distinction must be made between two different vicarious emotions evoked by witnessing another person suffer: personal distress and empathy. The former involves feeling upset, anxious, troubled, disturbed, distressed, and the like; the latter involves feeling sympathetic, compassionate, warm, softhearted, and tender. Parallel distinctions have been proposed by Hoffman (1975), who distinguished "empathic distress" from "sympathetic distress," and much earlier by McDougall (1908), who distinguished "sympathetic pain" from "the tender emotion."

Batson and his colleagues claim that although feeling personal distress may lead to helping as a means of reducing one's own aversive emotional state, empathy does not. Instead, they claim that empathy leads to altruistic motivation – motivation directed toward the ultimate goal of reducing the distress of the suffering victim rather than the helper's own aversive emotional arousal. Batson and his colleagues have presented considerable evidence consistent with their view (see Batson, 1987; and Batson et al., 1987, for reviews).

Comparative efficacy

Rosenhan and his colleagues (Rosenhan, Salovey, & Hargis, 1981a; Rosenhan, Salovey, Karylowski, & Hargis, 1981b) and Thompson et al., (1980) have proposed an explanation of the affect–helping relationship based on "comparative efficacy." They suggest that when people have an opportunity to help another person, they compare their current state with the state of the person they could help, and if they perceive an imbalance between the two states, they act in a manner that minimizes this imbalance. More specifically, people compare their own emotional state with the emotional state of the person needing help. If that person is experiencing more sadness or less joy than the prospective helper, then he or she will help; if that person is experiencing less sadness or more joy, then the prospective helper will not help.

This explanation of the affect–helping relationship was derived post hoc from reflection on the results of two experiments. In one experiment (Thompson et al., 1980), subjects who focused on a friend's sadness were more likely than neutral mood control subjects to help a third person, although subjects who focused on their own sadness were not less likely than control subjects to help the third person. In the other experiment (Rosenhan et al., 1981), subjects who focused on a friend's joy were less likely than neutral mood control subjects to help a third person, and subjects who focused on their own joy were more likely than control subjects to help a third person.

The fact that the person helped by subjects in these experiments was an unknown third party complicates the comparative efficacy explanation of these results. Comparative efficacy might account for the effects when attention is focused on one's own sorrow or joy – except that focusing on one's own sorrow did not lead to reduced helping relative to a neutral mood control in the Thompson et al. study. It is far less clear how comparative efficacy could account for the results when attention is focused on the friend's sorrow or joy. Did the Stanford undergraduates who participated in these studies fail to differentiate between their friend's emotional state and the emotional state of the unknown graduate student in education whom they helped? That seems unlikely.

5.3. Yet another attempt

Each of these seven attempts to make sense of the relationship between affect and helping seems to fit some of the data. But none seems capable of explaining the data as a whole, and in several cases, different explanations seem to predict – and find – diametrically opposite effects. How can this be?

I think our failure to make clear conceptual distinctions has prevented us from recognizing that the different explanations are actually about different phenomena. As Leon Festinger (1984) observed about recent work on social comparison processes, for theory construction it is essential to know what goes together and what does not. Surface similarities can easily lead us to assume that two phenomena are the same when they are not. Unlike water and ice, water and gasoline are both liquids. But to treat these two liquids as the same when trying to quench a thirst or put out a fire would be disastrous. The relevant level of analysis in this case is not surface appearance but chemical composition. And at this level, it is water and ice that are the same. In an analogous way, I think we need to look beyond surface similarities in the phenomena we have labeled affect and altruism to try to identify more fundamental constructs (Lewin, 1951) that may allow us to put together those things that go together in structure and function and keep apart those things that – in spite of surface similarities – are different.

Some definitions and conceptual distinctions

It is probably impossible to convince other people of the rightness of one's definitions of the terms I wish to focus upon: altruism, egoism, affect, mood, and emotion. Appeals to common usage seem fruitless; discussions with colleagues and students have convinced me that there is remarkably little agreement about precise definitions of these terms. There is usually agreement about the general domain to which a term belongs – affect, cognition, motivation, or behavior. Interestingly, there is also fairly good agreement about major conceptual distinctions within a given domain. But there is very little agreement about the definitions of specific terms used to express these conceptual distinctions. In defining everyday psychological terms, our common usage is just not that common.

There is, perhaps, more value in an appeal to historical precedence – in arguing that one is using a term in the way it was used by its originator. Wispé (1986) recently took this tack to justify his definitions of empathy and sympathy, and I have resorted to this approach myself in an effort to define altruism (e.g., Batson & Coke, 1981). But I now see three problems with appeals to historical precedence. First, for many psychological terms we can point to no one originator; they go back as far as written records. To whose authority do we appeal? Second, even in those cases where we can identify an originator (e.g., Comte, 1851, as the originator of the term "altruism"), some version of the concept almost always predates the term, often by centuries. One can thus argue from historical precedence to take issue even with the definition proposed by the originator of the term. Third, language evolves. Even if one could pinpoint the original meaning of a term, it is not clear that that is the best meaning for current usage.

These difficulties lead me to shy away from any claim to provide right definitions and conceptual distinctions; my goal is more modest – to provide useful ones. If (1) I can be as clear as possible about what I mean by a term, (2) my definition does not do conspicuous violence to general usage, and (3) the conceptual distinctions outlined prove useful, then I shall rest content. Should other people prefer to define terms differently, or to employ different concepts and distinctions, that is certainly their prerogative. I can give no logically compelling justification for the ones I shall see. They seem important and useful to me, but another set may be at least as useful.

The altruism domain. The definitions and distinctions I shall propose lie in the two distinct domains suggested by the title of this chapter – altruism and affect. The most basic distinction in the broad domain of altruism or helping is between behavior and motivation. Help is behavior that benefits someone; it can be accidental or intentional. The intentional acts are of most interest to psychologists, because these acts introduce the issue of motivation. If I can split a hair between the noun and the gerund, "help" is the act that benefits, whereas "helping" is acting with an intent to benefit. Helping occurs within the context of the helper's perception of the situation and may or may not actually help.

If we are to gain psychological understanding of helping, then it is important to probe more deeply into the motivation for the act, asking why the person was helping: What was his or her goal? The terms egoism and altruism operate at this level. To the extent that the helper has an ultimate goal of some form of self-benefit (e.g., acquiring rewards, avoiding punishments, reducing his or her own distress), then the motivation is egoistic. In this case, helping – that is, the intent to benefit the other – is an instrumental goal, a means to reaching the ultimate goal of some form of self-benefit. On the other hand, to the extent that the helper has an ultimate goal of benefiting someone else, then the motivation is altruistic. Benefits to self may result from altruistically motivated helping, but they are no longer the ultimate goal; they are simply consequences.

It is possible to have more than one ultimate goal at a given time, and different goals may be complementary or in conflict. It is also possible to have motivation of some magnitude to pursue a goal without acting on this motivation. A person may be either egoistically or altruistically motivated, or both, without actually helping. Finally, if helping occurs, whether egoistically or altruistically motivated, or both, it still may not actually help the person in need.

Even these basic conceptual distinctions in the altruism domain highlight a problem in the affect–altruism literature. The term altruism is used to mean quite different things. Most often, it is used to mean acting with intent to benefit another; that is, as a synonym for helping. The selfless connotation of the term may be evoked, but it is given no denotative meaning. Research designs employed demonstrate helping; they do not address the question of underlying motivation. Less often in the literature, altruism is used in the more explicit motivational sense proposed here. But to use the term in this manner with legitimacy, it is necessary to employ more complex research designs – ones that permit inference about the nature of the underlying motivation (see Batson et al., 1981, for a discussion of how this might be done).

In line with the more common usage, the term altruism appears in the title and earlier sections of this chapter as a synonym for helping. But because this use obscures a crucial distinction between behavior and motivation, I think it is unwise. Throughout the remainder of the chapter I shall try to be more precise. The term altruism will be used to describe a specific motivation for helping, and not as a synonym for helping.

The affect domain. The most basic distinctions in the affect domain are among three concepts: affect, mood, and emotion. Typically in the affect–helping literature, these three terms are treated as synonyms. But I think it is important to distinguish among them.

Affect is the most general of the three. It is also phylogenetically and ontogenetically the most primitive, being present in the yelp of a dog, as well as the coo and cry of an infant. Affect has tone or valence (positive or negative) and intensity (weak to strong). Both the tone and intensity are expressed physiologically in some way closely related to the mid-brain (possibly the hypothalamus for tone; the reticular formation for intensity – Buck, 1985), but it is not yet clear how (see also Leventhal, 1980). For the present analysis, it is less important to be able to say precisely what affect is than to say how it functions. Affect seems to communicate preference (Zajonc, 1980); it tells the organism experiencing it which states of affairs it values more than others. The shift from a less valued to a more valued state is accompanied by positive affect; the shift from a more valued to a less valued state is accompanied by negative affect. Intensity of the affect reflects the magnitude of the value preference.

Whether value determines affect, affect determines value, or they are two sides of the same coin, is not clear (see Lazarus, 1982, 1984; Zajonc, 1980, 1984). But it does seem clear that without the preferences reflected by positive and negative affective responses, all of our experiences would be a neutral gray. We would care no more what happens to us or what we do with our time than does a computer. There is, it seems, a firm, invariant, inbred preference for positive affect over negative. This is not to say that our goal in acting is necessarily to gain pleasure (the strong version of the argument for psychological hedonism), only that a state associated with more positive affect is necessarily preferred (the weak version of psychological hedonism – see MacIntyre, 1967). Nor is it to say that we may not decide to forego an immediate pleasure to obtain more pleasure in the long run. But such delay of gratification (Mischel, 1973) takes us to a different level of analysis; it involves goal setting and goal-directed motivation. The most basic affective reactions seem to operate at the more primitive level of operant conditioning, where it might be said that affect is what makes possible the effect in Thorndike's Law of Effect: "Pleasure stamps in; pain stamps out."

Mood refers to an affective state involving tone and intensity, but moods are more complex than basic affective reactions. In addition to affect, moods involve a more or less well-formed set of beliefs about whether, in general, one is likely to experience pleasure or pain – positive or negative affect – in the future. The temporary change in expectation, conbined with the affective state this change evokes in the present, constitutes the mood. Moods deal only with that part of this set of beliefs that is subject to relatively temporary fluctuation, the fine-tuning of one's perception of the general affective tone of what lies ahead. Moods can last for days, sometimes even weeks. But a perennial optimist is not in a good mood; optimism is a dispositional quality.

A given mood may be instigated by a specific event or experience – for example, failure at a task or a pleasant surprise. Still, simply to experience displeasure or pleasure does not constitute a mood change. One can experience positive or negative affect, even intense affect, without experiencing a change of mood (as occurs for the newborn, who has not yet developed expectations about the affective tone of experiences). Only when an experience introduces some temporary change in the way the individual perceives the likelihood of receiving pleasant or unpleasant experiences in the future is there a change of mood. When, for example, failure leads one to expect an increased number of failures in the future, the result is a bad (gloomy, depressed) mood.

For adults, it is difficult to imagine the affective experience that does not have the potential to affect mood. Yet even for the adult, we can – and I think should – distinguish between the psychology of the affect itself ("I feel awful") and the associated mood ("I'm in a rotten mood"). The distinction is in structure and function, not circumstance for occurrence.

Emotion also refers to an affective state with tone and intensity that is more complex than basic affective reactions, but emotion differs from mood. Whereas mood is a function of a change in expectations for the general likelihood of positive or negative affect in the future, emotions are a function of a perceived change in one's relationship to a specific goal in the present. Linking emotions to goals embeds emotion in a motivational framework.

Goals reflect a person's values. As already noted, values may be defined most generally as relative preferences: A person values state A over state B if he or she would consistently choose state A over state B, other things being equal. Some values are very abstract and pervasive (e.g., a preference for personal freedom over oppression); others are very concrete and specific (e.g., a preference for chocolate ice cream over vanilla). Moreover, some values are genetically based and are determined by our structure as organisms (e.g., the preferences we have for certain environmental temperatures, for oxygen to breathe, etc.); other values are learned through classical or operant conditioning, through modeling (cf. Bandura, 1977), or as a result of the transformation of a means toward some valued end into an end in its own right (cf. Allport's concept of functional autonomy). What is preferred (valued) depends on our current situation: When one is starved, a steaming bowl of soup is likely to be highly valued; but after an elaborate Thanksgiving feast with all the trimmings, it is not.

Relatively complex cognitive processes are required to produce a goal from a value. One must be able to imagine alternative states to the one that currently exists, and be able to compare these states. If there is a perceived negative discrepancy between a current or anticipated state and a valued state, then obtaining or maintaining the valued state may become a goal (wish, desire). Moreover, if the person perceives there to be one or more viable behavioral routes to the goal and perceives that pursuit of these routes is not more costly (i.e., more negatively valued) than the goal is positively valued, then goal-directed activity will likely ensue.

Following the lead of those theorists pursuing the new functional approach to emotions (Abelson, 1983; Berscheid, 1983; Buck, 1985; Epstein, 1984; Mandler, 1975; Roseman, 1984; Scherer, 1984), I would suggest that many (if not all) emotions occur in the context of goal-directed action sequences. Emotions serve two functions in goal-directed action.

Two functions of emotions in goal-directed action

Providing information. One function of emotions is to provide information. As noted earlier in the discussion of affect, the shift from a less valued (less preferred) state to a more valued (more preferred) state will be accompanied by negative affect. Similarly, emotions associated with personal or situational changes that increase the probability of obtaining a goal will have a positive affective tone; those associated with changes that decrease the probability of obtaining a goal will have a negative affective tone. But emotions are further differentiated in a way that affect is not. There is a vast array of distinct emotions that communicate to the actor (and often to other people as well) information about the actor's relationship to the goal. To illustrate, when I perceive the possibility of reaching a goal but it is still far away, I may experience emotions of hope and yearning; if someone facilitates my approach to the goal, I may feel gratitude; at goal acquisition, I may experience joy and satisfaction – or if the goal state proves not to be clearly preferred over other states as had been anticipated (which is often the case), I may experience disappointment.

*Distinguishing three types of emotions.*Thinking of emotions as embedded within a goal-directed action sequence introduces the possibility of developing a taxonomy of emotions based on where one is in the sequence. We might, for example, differentiate among need state emotions, end-state (outcome) emotions, and means emotions: Need state emotions are provoked by the perception of a negative discrepancy between the preferred and current (or impending) state of affairs. These emotions may be located in a three-dimensional space of (1) valence of current or impending states (positivity/negativity), which serves to identify the specific goal as a goal, (2) intensity of preference, which serves to identify the power (or potential motivational force) of the goal, and (3) perceived probability of obtaining the preferred state, which serves to define the actual motivational force toward the goal (see Lewin's, 1951, distinction between power fields and force fields). If, for example, I expect to obtain a highly desired goal, then even before I make any progress toward that goal I may experience need state emotions of excitement, impatience, and anticipated joy. If I do not expect to obtain the goal, then I may instead experience yearning and oscillations of hope and sorrow.

End-state (outcome) emotions are provoked either by one's reaching the goal or by one's reaching a point from which goal attainment is perceived to be impossible. They may be located in the same three-dimensional space as need state emotions, but the perceived probability dimension is retrospective not anticipatory. If I expected to obtain the goal and I do, then I may experience the end-state emotion of satisfaction; if I did not expect to obtain the goal but do, then I may instead experience elation.

Means emotions are provoked by perceived personal or situational changes toward or away from a goal. They do not fit easily into a multidimensional analysis. Instead, they may be classified according to (1) valence, which is determined by direction of change (toward or away from the goal), (2) intensity of preference, and (3) agent of change (self, another person, impersonal events). If I facilitate my own progress toward a desired goal, then I may experience the means emotion of pride; if someone else facilitates my progress, then I may experience gratitude. If someone hinders my progress, I may experience anger; if some impersonal event hinders my progress, I may experience frustration.

Similar – but by no means identical – taxonomies that also attempt to locate different emotions at different points in the process of goal-directed action have been proposed by Abelson (1983), Roseman (1984), and Scherer (1984), among others. Taxonomies of this sort have received some empirical support from self-report descriptions of naturally occurring emotions (Epstein, 1984; Scherer, 1984) and reports of likely emotional reactions to systematically varied descriptions of hypothetical situations (Roseman, 1984).

To the extent that an emotional reaction or the experience that evoked it leads to a fluctuation in expectations of encountering positive or negative experiences in the future, there will also be a change in mood. But the emotion, which occurs as a result of a change in the relationship to a present goal, and the mood, which occurs as a result of a change in expectations about the future, are conceptually distinct. Once again, the distinction is in structure and function, not circumstance for occurrence.

Emotional response to the perceived welfare of another person. One class of goals that is of particular importance for the emotion-helping relationship includes goals concerning the welfare of one or more other persons. As a result of our special relationship to some other persons, we may come to value their welfare and happiness. If their welfare is then threatened, maintaining it may become a goal for us. This goal defines altruistic motivation, as discussed earlier, and events that promote or prevent the welfare of these other persons should evoke in us positive and negative emotions – feelings of sympathetic joy or sorrow, compassion, warmth, tenderness, and the like. But the welfare of others may be relevant to nonaltruistic goals as well. We may have learned to value a world in which people do not suffer or in which people are treated fairly (Lerner, 1970, 1980). If so, then the unjust suffering of others confronts us with a nonpreferred state, and as a result, with a goal. The existence of this goal may evoke a range of emotions – disgust, anger, moral outrage, and the like.

Note that the event instigating these very different emotions may be exactly the same – person A is suffering unjustly. The different emotional reactions are accounted for by the different goals. This relationship between emotion and goal suggests that we may be able to reverse the inference process. The qualitative shadings among emotions may tell us (and others as well) not only where we are in relation to our goals but also at least something about what our goals – and hence our values – are. The inference process proposed here is just the reverse of that proposed by Schachter (1964; see also Smith & Ellsworth, 1985). Rather than using the situational context to provide information about the nature of an emotional experience, I am proposing that different emotions are experienced as qualitatively distinct and can provide information about our goals and where we are in relation to these goals (see Batson, Fultz, & Schoenrade, 1987, and Buck 1985, for similar views).

We often deceive ourselves and others about our true values. We try to convince ourselves that we value what we think we should. This self-deception can lead us to pursue goals that bring disappointment. One way to look at the therapeutic process of "getting in touch with our feelings" is that, by attending more closely to our emotional reactions in different situations, we may be able to discover what our true values are. Attention to the precise nature of our emotional response to another's welfare may enable us to learn what we value – the other's welfare, some psychological state of our own, or some worldview.

The logic here may at first glance appear circular; we must at some level know what our goals are and where we are in relation to them in order to experience the emotions that are supposed to inform us about what our goals are and where we are in relation to them. But there is an important difference between the information necessary to experience an emotion and the information provided by the emotion. To experience an emotion, we must have some perception of the current state of affairs, of one or more possible or impending alternative states of affairs, and of the discrepancy between the current and possible states of affairs. This information is relatively "cold," answering questions like, What is happening? and Where am I? The information added by the emotion is "hot"; it concerns our evaluation of this perceived state of affairs, answering questions like, Do I care? and How much do I care?

Providing amplification. One function of emotion is, then, to provide information about what our goals (and hence our values) are, and where we are in relation to these goals. But this is not the only function. A second function of many emotions that has long been recognized by those who have focused upon the motivational consequences of emotion (e.g., Buck, 1985; McDougall, 1908) is to provide amplification of the goal-directed motivation.

Many of the neurophysiological and hormonal systems involved in the experience of emotion are the same ones involved in the energization of the organism for activity. Because of this system overlap, the physiological arousal component of the emotion can add to and amplify the level of energization (see Buck, 1985, for some discussion of how this might occur). So not only is the strength of the emotional reaction a function of the strength of the initial motivation, but the strength of the resulting motivation is also a function of the strength of the emotional reaction. This amplifying function of emotions may be seen in misattribution studies, in which increased emotional arousal leads to increased goal-directed activity, but only if the emotional arousal is correctly attributed as a response to the particular goal (Coke, Batson, & McDavis, 1978; Nisbett & Schachter, 1966; Ross, Rodin, & Zimbardo, 1969; Zanna & Cooper, 1974).

Affect may also amplify motivation. In the case of affect, however, the increase is in the level of diffuse, general activity. In the case of emotion, which occurs in the context of a specific goal-directed action sequence, the increased energy is channeled into a force directed toward the attainment of the specific goal.

In sum, the distinctions I am proposing among affect, mood, and emotion emphasize the close link between each of these concepts and motivation. Basic affective reactions of pleasure and pain are crucial to the very existence of motivation. Without them, we would have no inclination to move toward or away from anything. We share some form of basic affective reaction with many other living species. Indeed, the general principle of experiential preferences that underlies affect may well be one of the defining features of life itself.

Mood and emotion both relate to more complex motivational processes, processes that involve more complex cognitions required for goal setting and goal-directed action. At a minimum, to experience mood or emotion the organism must be able to conceptualize possible states that do not exist, to compare these states with existing states to determine goals, to conceive of behavioral routes for obtaining these goals, and to assess the probability of these behaviors being effective for obtaining the goals. But moods and emotions can be distinguished. For moods, the focus is on general expectations about the occurrence of pleasurable events in the future; for emotions, the focus is on reactions to changes in one's present relationship to a given goal.

Finally, it is important to emphasize that the same event can evoke all three reactions – affect, mood, and emotion. For example, a person who succeeds at a task may feel pleasure (positive affect); in addition, if the person has worked a long time at the task and was not confident of success, he or she may feel elation and joy (positive emotions), and may perceive an increased likelihood of future positive events (good mood). Conversely, failure in this situation may lead to displeasure (negative affect), feeling sad and disappointed (negative emotions), and decreased perceived likelihood of future positive events (bad mood). All three reactions occur at once and in response to the same event, but they are psychologically distinct, because different psychological processes are involved. A blurring of these distinctions may well underlie the recent stalemate over which comes first, affect or cognition (Lazarus, 1982, 1984; Zajonc, 1980, 1984).

Toward a more differentiated view of the affect–helping relationship

Employing these two sets of distinctions – between helping and the motivation for helping, on the one hand, and among affect, mood, and emotion, on the other – one is led to consider a view of the affect–helping relationship that is more differentiated than the view provided by any of the seven explanations outlined earlier. Some of the empirical research and explanations seem to focus upon affective reactions per se, some upon moods, and some upon emotions. Often, more than one of these affective states are involved in a single research paradigm, which may be one reason for the frequent controversies among interpreters of the research. Interpreter A may focus on the affective reaction itself and invoke one motivational process to account for the relationships observed; interpreter B may focus on the mood or emotions induced and invoke a quite different process. Given that these interpreters are trying to explain the same set of data, it naturally appears that their views are in conflict. It may be, however, that they are both right, having detected quite distinct motivational processes that occur in the same situation.

Reflecting upon the existing empirical and conceptual literature in light of the distinctions proposed, I now wish to suggest some of the different motives for helping that seem to be associated with affect, mood, and emotion, respectively. My suggestions, discussed below, are summarized in Table 5.1.

Affective reactions and helping. Positive affective reactions are not, by themselves, likely to incline an organism to action; they are simply enjoyed. (Random activity may, or course, result – as when happy babies wriggle and wave their arms.) But positive affect is relative; one may imagine even more valued states, causing positive affect to be experienced as relatively negative. Moreover, once positive affect is

Table 5.1 *Different motives for helping associated with affect, mood, and emotions*

Affective state	Defining structural feature(s)	Function	Associated motives for helping
A. Affect	Valence and intensity reflecting value preference	Signal preferred states; basis for approach and avoidance motivation	1. Negative state relief via social or self-reward 1. Aversive arousal reduction via escape 3. Positive mood maintenance 4. Comparative efficacy
B. Mood	Affective state associated with temporary change in expectation of future positive or negative affect	Color expectations about likely outcome of acting on motives	No associated motives but change in probability of acting on motives
C. Emotions	Affective state associated with perceived change in position in a goal-directed action sequence	Provide information about location relative to goal and amplify motivation to reach goal	
1. Need state emotion	Emotion provoked by perception of negative discrepancy between preferred and current (impending) state	Reflect valence of current or impending state (i.e., identify goal), intensity of preference for goal, and probability of obtaining goal	1. Altruistic motivation to have other's need reduced (associated with empathic emotion) 2. Egoistic motivation to have own distress reduced (including distress evoked by threats to one's beliefs in values) 3. Egoistic motivation to reduce guilt or repair self-image 4. Egoistic motivation to avoid anticipated guilt

Affective state	Defining structural feature(s)	Function	Associated motives for helping
2. End-state (outcome) emotion	Emotion provoked by reaching or surrendering goal	Reflect valence of current or impending state (i.e., identify goal), intensity of preference for goal, and probability of obtaining goal	No direct motivational consequences; indirect consequences through resulting affect, mood, need state emotions, and means emotions
3. Means emotion	Emotion provoked by personal or situational changes toward or away from goal	Reflect valence (i.e., identify goal), intensity, and agent of change (self, other, impersonal event)	Clarification and amplification of motives associated with need state emotions

experienced, any decline in the positivity of the affect may be experienced as negative. And negative affect is likely to evoke action.

At relatively low levels of the phylogenetic or ontogenetic scale, negative affect may lead to nothing more than diffuse general activity, coupled perhaps with a habit hierarchy of learned responses: The newborn cries and wriggles. But soon specific goals emerge, and the cries for "hungry" and "wet" can be differentiated. At this and higher levels, negative affect can be contrasted with a possible preferred positive state, leading to the establishment of goals and to goal-directed action designed either to escape the situation producing the negative affect or to find a situation producing positive affect, or both.

Relating these affect-driven processes to the affect–helping literature, four of the explanations outlined earlier would seem to refer, at least in part, to processes instigated by basic affective reactions. First and most obviously, Cialdini's negative state relief model is concerned with the experience of an unpleasant affective state and with attempts to improve that affective state by finding a situation that will provide positive affect. A more positive situation may be thrust upon the individual in the form of monetary reward or praise, or the individual may seize an opportunity that is presented to gain self-rewards by helping (Cialdini et al., 1973). One key feature of this process is that it makes no difference where the negative affect came from – it could be the result of a personal failure or faux pas, of seeing someone hurt or suffering, or of remembering sad events. It is assumed that any time the person feels bad, he or she is motivated to feel better. Also, it is assumed that it makes no difference from whence the positive affect comes. If the person believes that helping can enable him or her to reach this goal, helping is likely to occur. But any other means of reaching the goal of experiencing more positive affect will do as well. Goal-directed activity is involved in this process, but the goal is relatively undifferentiated desire to feel better.

Second, the aversive arousal reduction explanation proposed by Piliavin and her colleagues (Piliavin & Piliavin, 1973; Piliavin et al., 1981) also has, among other aspects, a basic affect component. The source of the negative affect in this model is one specific subcategory of the sources considered by Cialdini – seeing someone else suffer. As in the Cialdini model, it is assumed that this bad feeling evokes motivation directed toward the general goal of feeling better. But because the source of the negative affect is more specific, a more specific set of behavioral routes are considered for reaching this goal. Rather than focusing upon the search for any source of positive affect, as does Cialdini, Piliavin and her colleagues focus specifically on escape from the stimulus causing the negative affect. One way to escape is to terminate the stimulus by ending the other's suffering (helping); another way is to terminate contact with the stimulus by leaving the field (escaping).

Third, the positive mood maintenance explanation actually seems to concern not mood but a basic affective process. Because of some experience (success, an unexpected gift or treat, reminiscing about a happy time), the person feels good. But this good feeling begins to wane (or the person anticipates that it will wane), and the person is motivated to avoid this drift into a more negative affective zone. Assuming a self-reward process like the one invoked by Cialdini, the person may perceive helping as a source of more positive affect. Alternatively and more plausibly, the person may anticipate that a failure to help could bring social or self-punishment, which would undermine the positive affect. He or she may help in order to avoid an even more rapid slide into negative affect.

Fourth, the comparative efficacy explanation proposed by Rosenhan and his colleagues seems to rest, at least in part, on basic affective reactions. Here the relative nature of affective states is emphasized. I compare my present affective state with that of those around me to determine how good or bad I am feeling. But the Rosenhan explanation diverges sharply from the previous three once the relative affective tone is established. The individual is not simply motivated to escape or avoid negative affect, as is true in the other three; instead, he or she uses the information about relative affect to determine whether a valued principle is threatened. Rosenhan and his colleagues assume that the individual values comparative equality between self and others in affective states. If such equality does not exist, a negative discrepancy is perceived, and the goal of returning to equality is established. Note that in this analysis a positive affective state is not the goal; fairness or justice in the form of equality is the goal. Affect is simply the domain in which fairness or justice is assessed. Moreover, in sharp contrast to the affect-enhancing quality of helping emphasized by Cialdini (at least for adults), Rosenhan and his colleagues assume that helping brings negative affect and therefore redresses the affective balance in favor of others, not oneself.

This difference between Cialdini and Rosenhan in the assumed affective consequence of helping may seem to involve a direct contradiction, but it does not. This is because the motivational processes underlying the affect–helping relationship in the two cases have totally different goals – negative state relief versus affective justice. Each researcher has chosen for study a form of helping that can be instrumental in reaching the specific goal he wishes to emphasize. Cialdini presents research participants with relatively low-cost opportunities to help what is clearly a good cause (e.g., phone calls to collect information from people who have already volunteered to donate specially needed rare blood types). Rosenhan presents research participants with a more onerous and less clearly virtuous opportunity to help; they are asked to answer difficult multiple-choice questions for an anonymous graduate student in education. The former type of helping has self-reward potential; the latter evokes issues of obligation and fairness. The motivational processes described by both researchers may well exist, but to consider either explanation as a general account of the negative affect–helping relationship seems misguided. It seems more useful to treat them as accounts of distinct motivational processes.

Mood and helping. The proposed definition of mood – a temporary fluctuation in general expectation for positive or negative affect in the future – is entirely consistent with the Isen et al. (1976, 1978, see also Cunningham et al., 1980) suggestion that positive mood is associated with recall of more positive aspects of past experiences and expectation of more positive results of helping (and other activities). If positive mood increases expectation of positive results of helping and other activities, then it should lead to more of these activities – which it does (see Section 5.1, as well as Batson, Coke, Chard, Smith, & Taliaferro, 1979). Conversely, and consistent with the suggestions of Hornstein (1982) and his colleagues (Hornstein et al., 1976), negative mood should by definition lead to the expectation of less positive results of helping (or any other activity), and so should lead to less helping. There is, however, some evidence that there may be an asymmetry in this process. The negative aspects of prior experiences and expectations may be less easily accessed and less extensive than the positive aspects (Isen, 1985, 1987).

According to these views, mood does not lead to the establishment of one specific goal that helping enables the person to reach; instead, mood colors the person's perceptions of the general efficacy of activity directed toward obtaining any goal. Harking back to the Gestaltists' notions of figure and ground, one might say that mood does not change the motivational figure – the specific goal and behavioral routes to this goal – it changes the ground against which this figure is perceived.

Note that the proposed relationship between negative mood and helping suggested here is exactly the opposite of the relationship between negative affect and helping proposed by Cialdini et al., by Piliavin et al., and by the so-called positive mood maintenance explanation. Negative affect should lead to increased helping (assuming that helping can be instrumental in relieving the negative affect); negative mood should lead to decreased helping. The potential helper in a negative mood should perceive less likelihood that the helping will be efficacious.

Consistent with this suggestion, at least some of the confusion and apparent contradiction concerning the negative affect–helping relationship seems to be a result of a failure to distinguish between procedures that induce negative affects and procedures that induce negative moods. Both involve feeling bad, but affect and mood seem to be related to helping through quite different psychological processes – processes that may have diametrically opposite effects on different types of helping behavior. Moreover, these processes are by no means mutually exclusive; the same experience may evoke both negative affect and negative mood, which further complicates matters.

Emotion and helping. The proposal that emotions arise in he context of goal-directed action sequences suggests the importance of identifying the goal a person is motivated to attain at the point an emotion is experienced if we are to predict the emotion–helping relationship. This suggestion applies to need-state emotions and means emotions only. It seems likely that end-state (outcome) emotions – those arising at the point of goal attainment or clear failure to attain a goal – affect motivation through their basic affective component, through a concomitant change in mood (following processes already described), or through the establishment of a new goal and resulting need state and means emotions. The prosocial effects of need state and means emotions take us beyond the previous levels of analysis that focus on affect and mood to consider the relationship to helping of more explicit goals and their associated emotions.

I shall not attempt to offer a comprehensive list of the possible explicit goals and emotions related to helping, but will suggest a few goals and associated emotions as illustrations of how a more thorough analysis might proceed. In suggsting these goals, I shall focus on those that have already been highlighted in explanations of the emotion–helping relationship.

First, there is at least the possibility that one person has a goal of increasing another's welfare; that is, that the person's motivation is truly altruistic. We might expect the existence of this goal, which is based on a perceived discrepancy between the other's current (or anticipated future) state and some valued more positive state, will evoke need state emotional reactions of sympathy, compassion, and the like, which in turn will intensify the motivation to pursue this goal. One way to reach this goal is by helping, so if other routes to the goal are not available (e.g., no one else can or will help), this emotional reaction should be associated with increased helping. There is, indeed, considerable evidence that it is (Batson et al., 1981, 1983; Toi & Batson, 1982), unless the cost of helping is so high as to evoke conflicting motives (Batson et al., 1983, study 3).

Second, various versions of the aversive arousal reduction explanation suggest a range of egoistic goals and associated emotional reactions that may motivate helping. Piliavin et al (1981; see also Batson et al., 1981, 1983; Dovidio, 1984; Hoffman, 1981) suggest that seeing someone in distress may cause the observer to feel upset, disturbed, and distressed and, as a result, to have a goal of reducing one's own distress. Although this emotional reaction and resulting goal have often been assumed to reflect nothing more than negative affect and general diffuse arousal to escape this affect, the more recent discussion by Piliavin et al. (1981) seems to assume that the distressed individual is goal directed, not just active.

In their discussion, Piliavin et al. (1981) outline a complex attributional cost–benefit analysis that intervenes between the experience of personal distress and the resulting action. Such an analysis suggests an interpretation in terms of goal-directed action and related emotion, rather than an interpretation in terms of general arousal and affect. Indeed, the movement from the earliest formulations of the Piliavin model (Piliavin, Rodin, & Piliavin, 1969) to the latest (Piliavin et al., 1981) might be characterized as a shift in level of analysis from a focus on affect to a focus on emotion. The aroused bystander is no longer thought to be made uncomfortable by any suffering; instead, his or her values about who should suffer and who should not are challenged, leading to a goal of reestablishing these values and to goal-relevant emotions (cf. Dovidio, 1984; Gaertner & Dovidio, 1977; Piliavin et al., 1981).

The variations on the aversive arousal reduction theme provided by Reykowski (1982) and Lerner (1970) certainly seem to operate at the level of goal-directed activity and emotions. Through socialization, one comes to value a certain view of the world – for example, mine is a world in which people like me do not suffer unjustly. Events that challenge this view introduce a need to see the view upheld, accompanied by appropriate need state emotions; we feel shocked, disgusted, and outraged. There are a variety of ways to repel the challenge, as Lerner (1970, 1980) has so ably demonstrated. Most basically, we can act to improve the lot of the sufferer, or we can convince ourselves that the suffering is deserved.

Third, the guilt reduction and self-image repair explanations seem to operate at the level of emotions. In this case, however, it is some action of our own (or some failure to act) that challenges our valued beliefs. Moreover, the valued beliefs are not about the way life treats or should treat people like us; the beliefs are about the kind of person we are. What has been loosely discussed as negative affect or mood resulting from a transgression seems actually to be a cluster of need state emotions associated with a threat to our self-image and the motivation to repel the threat. We feel chagrined, ashamed, embarrassed, mortified, guilty. Motivated to reach the specific goal of maintaining our positive self-image, we should prefer activities that enable us most effectively to reach this goal. These activities include repairing the damage done (i.e., helping the person harmed), justifying our action, or demonstrating to ourselves and to others that this episode is not an accurate reflection of our true nature (by, for example, helping a third party). Which of these activities will be most preferred will depend on the associated costs and the specific situation. For example, it seems likely that failures to act beneficially (sins of omission) will be easier to dismiss through justification and rationalization than acts that have caused harm (sins of commission). (See Batson, Bolen, Cross, & Neuringer-Benefiel, 1986, for some empirical evidence consistent with this view.)

In contrast to a purely affective analysis of transgression (e.g., Cialdini et al., 1973, 1981), this emotional analysis suggests that interposing a positive event such as money or praise between the transgression and the opportunity to engage in restitution, justification, or self-reaffirmation should not serve as an equally effective substitute for these image-repair activities. The interposed positive event might cause distraction and, as a result, weaken the goal directed motivation, but it should not lead to goal attainment. Although an attempt has been made to assess the distraction effects of interposing positive experiences between a transgression and opportunity to help (Cunningham et al., 1980), I do not believe that the distraction effects have been given sufficient attention (but see Batson, Griffitt, Barrientos, Brandt, & Bayly, 1989, and Cialdini, Schaller, Houlihan, Arps, Fultz, & Beaman, 1987).

To suggest that image repair following transgression is more appropriately conceived at the level of goal directed motivation and emotion rather than the level of general negative affect and negative state relief is not to suggest that the latter process can be ignored. Instead, it seems likely that both psychological processes exist.

Finally, the concept of anticipated guilt, which seems to underlie some of the Piliavin et al. (1981) discussion of "empathy costs," is closely related to guilt reduction. The major difference is that the perceived negative discrepancy that introduces the motivation for self-image repair is not between one's self-image and one's actual performance, it is between one's self-image and one's potential performance. The person is faced with the question: How am I going to feel about myself knowing that he (or she) is still suffering and I did nothing. The motives and emotions evoked by anticipated guilt, and the likely resultant behaviors, seem much the same as for guilt reduction. Past tense or future, it seems likely that failures to act beneficially may be easier to dismiss through justification and rationalization than actions that did or will cause another harm.

I have made some suggestions about the different affects, moods, and emotions experienced by subjects in several key studies in the affect–helping literature. But these suggestions are admittedly post hoc. Ultimately, the usefulness of the proposed differentiated view of the affect–helping relationship must await future research in which systematic attention is given at the design stage to the suggested qualitative differences among affect, mood, and emotion, and to the motivational and behavioral consequences of each. Such research faces a difficult challenge because, as noted, there is not a simple situational differentiation among affect, mood, and emotion as defined here. Often, a situation that evokes one type of affective state will evoke others as well. To tease apart the effects of each will require more precise conceptualization and operationalization of affective independent variables than has been true in the past. But such a requirement is not unique to research on the affect–helping relationship. Rather, it is the requirement whenever, as advocated by Lewin (1951), we shift focus from an Aristotelian classification of the co-occurrence of events to a Galilean examination of the more fundamental processes that underlie surface relationships.

Summary

I am proposing that there are a variety of different psychological processes involved in what has loosely been called the affect–altruism relationship. Some of this variety becomes clear when we distinguish between helping behavior and the motivation to help on the one hand, and among affect, mood, and emotion on the other. Helping is acting with intent to benefit, but a variety of motives can underlie this intent. Most generally, one may have an ultimte goal of increasing the welfare of the person being helped (altruistic motivation), or one may have an ultimate goal of increasing one's own welfare in one or more of a variety of ways (egoistic motivation). Affect is a very general evaluative reaction to events; it has tone (positive/negative) and intensity (strong/weak). Both mood and emotion have affective components, but each involves more as well. Mood reflects a temporary change in expectations for positive or negative affect in the future, conjoined with the present affect evoked by this change. Emotions arise in the context of goal-directed motivation; they provide information to us and others about what our goals are, and where we are in relation to these goals. In addition, emotions can add force to the energizing component of the goal-directed motive.

Employing these distinctions, I suggested that some of the conflict and controversy over the relationship between affect and helping is a result of an inappropriate comparison of the effects on helping of affect with the effects of mood or emotions. Different possible motives for helping associated with affect, mood, and emotions are summarized in Table 5.1. Negative affect may lead to general motivation to experience more positive affect, and, if the person involved perceives helping to be a source of positive affect (whether through social or self-rewards or through removing the stimulus causing the negative affect), then negative affect should lead to increased helping, as predicted by Cialdini's negative state relief model. In contrast, negative mood should lead one to focus more on possible negative outcomes of helping, and so should lead to reduced helping. Some negative emotions evoked by seeing someone suffer – disgust, distress, anxiety, envy, moral outrage – seem to reflect goal-directed motivation to see the world as a nice or fair place. These emotions may or may not be associated wiih increased helping, depending on whether helping is the most effective means of reaching this goal. Other negative emotions – sympathy, concern, compassion, tenderness – seem to reflect goal-directed motivation to see the sufferer's welfare increased (i.e., altruistic motivation). These emotions are likely to be associated with increased helping across a range of situations. Still other negative emotions – guilt, chagrin, shame, embarrassment – seem to reflect goal-directed motivation to reestablish or maintain a positive self-image. Once again, these emotions may or may not be associated with helping, depending on whether helping is the most effective means of reaching this goal.

My analysis has focused on negative affect, mood, and emotions; I have given relatively little attention to the way positive affect, mood, and emotions relate to helping because there has been less controversy and confusion on the positive side. Yet, the present analysis suggests that the consensus on the positive side may be deceptive. Because positive affect and positive mood should both lead to increased helping (so long as helping is relatively low cost and socially sanctioned), we may have overlooked some important distinctions between the underlying psychological processes. The present analysis suggests that positive affect should lead to increased helping only when one anticipates that helping can serve to maintain the positive affective state. In contrast, positive mood should lead to a more general increase in helping as a result of the changed expectation for positive outcomes of a range of activities. As yet, there is very little research on the prosocial consequences of positive emotions. When there is more, we may find that the relationship to helping of positive affect, mood, and emotion is complex as well.

Acknowledgments

Thanks to Alice M. Isen and Abe Tesser for helpful comments on an earlier draft.

References

Aderman, D. (1972). Elation, depression, and helping behavior. *Journal of Personality and Social Psychology, 24*, 91–101.

Abelson, R. P. (1983). Whatever became of consistency theory? *Personality and Social Psychology Bulletin, 9*, 37–54.

Bandura, A. (1977). *Social learning theory*. Englewood Cliffs, NJ: Prentice-Hall.

Batson, C. D. (1987). Prosocial motivation: Is it ever truly altruistic? In L. Berkowitz (Ed.), *Advances in experimental social psychology* (Vol. 20). New York: Academic.

Batson, C. D., Batson, J. G., Griffitt, C. A., Barrientos, S., Brandt, J. R., Sprengelmeyer, P., & Bayly, M. J. (1989). Negative-state relief and the empathy-altruism hypothesis. *Journal of Personality and Social Psychology, 56,* 922–933.

Batson, C. D., Bolen, M. H., Cross, J. A., & Neuringer-Benefiel, H. E. (1986). Where is the altruism in the altruistic personality? *Journal of Personality and Social Psychology, 50,* 212–220.

Batson, C. D., & Coke, J. S. (1981). Empathy: A source of altruistic motivation for helping? In J. P. Rushton & R. M. Sorrentino (Eds.), *Altruism and helping behavior: Social, personality, and developmental perspectives.* Hillsdale, NJ: Erlbaum.

Batson, C. D., Coke, J. S., Chard, F., Smith, D., & Taliaferro, A. (1979). Generality of the "glow of goodwill": Effects of mood on helping and information acquisition. *Social Psychology Quarterly, 42,* 176–179.

Batson, C. D., Duncan, B., Ackerman, P., Buckley, T., & Birch, K. (1981). Is empathic emotion a source of altruistic motivation? *Journal of Personality and Social Psychology, 40,* 290–302.

Batson, C. D., Fultz, J., & Schoenrade, P. A. (1987). Distress and empathy: Two qualitatively distinct vicarious emotions with different motivational consequences. *Journal of Personality, 55,* 19–40.

Batson, C. D., O'Quin, K., Fultz, J., Vanderplas, M., & Isen, A. (1983). Self-reported distress and empathy and egoistic versus altruistic motivation for helping. *Journal of Personality and Social Psychology, 45,* 706–718.

Berger, S. M. (1962). Conditioning through vicarious instigation. *Psychological Review, 69,* 450–466.

Berkowitz, L. (1972). Social punishments, feelings, and other factors affecting helping and altruism. In L. Berkowitz (Eds.), *Advances in experimental social psychology* (Vol. 6). New York: Academic Press.

Berkowitz, L., & Connor, W. H. (1966). Success, failure, and social responsibility. *Journal of Personality and Social Psychology, 4,* 664–669.

Berscheid, E. (1983). Emotion. In H. H. Kelley, E. Berscheid, T. L. Huston, G. Levinger, G. McClintock, A. Peplau, & D. R. Peterson. *Close relationships.* San Francisco: Freeman.

Buck, R. (1985). Prime theory: An integrated view of motivation and emotion. *Psychological Review, 92,* 389–413.

Carlsmith, J., & Gross, A. (1969). Some effects of guilt on compliance. *Journal of Personality and Social Psychology, 11,* 232–239.

Cialdini, R. B., Baumann, D. J., & Kenrick, D. T. (1981). Insights from sadness: A three-step model of the development of altruism as hedonism. *Developmental Review, 1,* 207–223.

Cialdini, R. B., Darby, B. L., & Vincent, J. E. (1973). Transgression and altruism: A case for hedonism. *Journal of Experimental Social Psychology, 9,* 502–516.

Cialdini, R. B., Kenrick, D. T. (1976). Altruism as hedonism: A social development perspective on the relationship of negative mood state and helping. *Journal of Personality and Social Psychology, 34,* 907–914.

Cialdini, R. B., Schaller, M., Houlihan, D., Arps, K., Fultz, J., & Beaman, A. (1987). Empathy-based helping: Is it selflessly or selfishly motivated? *Journal of Personality and Social Psychology, 52,* 749–758.

Clark, M. S., & Isen, A. M. (1981). Toward understanding the relationship between feeling states and social behavior. In A. H. Hastorf and A. M. Isen (Eds.), *Cognitive social psychology.* New York: Elsevier/North Holland

Clark, R. D., III, & Word, L. E. (1974). Where is the apathetic bystander? Situational characteristics of the emergency. *Journal of Personality and Social Psychology, 29,* 279–287.

Coke, J. S., Batson, C. D., & McDavis, K. (1978). Empathic mediation of helping: A two-stage model. *Journal of Personality and Social Psychology, 36,* 752–766.

Comte, I. A. (1875). *System of positive polity* (Vol. 1). London: Longmans, Green & Co. (First published, 1851).

Craig, K. D., & Lowery, J. H. (1969). Heart rate components of conditioned vicarious autonomic responses. *Journal of Personality and Social Psychology, 11,* 381–387.

Craig, K. D., & Wood, K. (1969). Psychophysiological differentiation of direct and vicarious affective arousal. *Canadian Journal of Behvioral Science, 1,* 98–105.

Cunningham, M. R. (1979). Weather, mood, and helping behavior: Quasi-experiments with the sunshine samaritan. *Journal of Personality and Social Psychology, 37,* 1947–1956.

Cunningham, M. R., Steinberg, J., & Grev, R. (1980). Wanting to and having to help: Separate motivations for positive mood and guilt-induced helping. *Journal of Personality and Social Psychology, 38,* 181–192.

Dovidio, J. F. (1984). Helping behavior and altruism: An empirical and conceptual overview. In L. Berkowitz (Ed.), *Advances in experimental social psychology* (Vol. 17). New York: Academic Press.

Epstein, S. (1984). Controversial issues in emotion theory. In P. Shaver (Ed.), *Review of personality and social psychology: Emotions, relationships, and health.* Beverly Hills: Sage Publications.

Festinger, L. (1984). *Comments on social comparison theory.* Address at the annual convention of the American Psychological Association, Toronto, August.

Freedman, J. L., Wallington, S. A., & Bless, E. (1967). Compliance without pressure: The effect of guilt. *Journal of Personality and Social Psychology, 35,* 117–124.

Gaertner, S. L., & Dovidio, J. F. (1977). The subtlety of white racism, arousal and helping behavior. *Journal of Personality and Social Psychology, 35,* 691–708.

Harris, M. B., & Huang, L. C. (1973). Helping and the attribution process. *Journal of Social Psychology, 90,* 291–297.

Hoffman, M. L. (1975). Developmental synthesis of affect and cognition and its implications for altruistic motivation. *Developmental Psychology, 11,* 607–622.

Hoffman, M. L. (1981). The development of empathy. In J. P. Ruston & R. M. Sorrentino (Eds.), *Altruism and helping behavior: Social, personality, and developmental perspectives.* Hillsdale, NJ: Erlbaum.

Hornstein, H. A. (1978). Promotive tension and prosocial behavior: A Lewinian analysis. In L. Wispé (Ed.), *Altruism, sympathy, and helping: Psychological and sociological principles.* New York: Academic Press.

Hornstein, H. A. (1982). Promotive tension: Theory and research. In V. J. Derlega & J. Grzelak (Eds.), *Cooperation and helping behavior: Theories and research.* New York: Academic Press.

Hornstein, H. A., LaKind, E., Frankel, G., & Manne, S. (1976). Effects of knowledge about remote social events on prosocial behavior, social conception, and mood. *Journal of Personality and Social Psychology, 32,* 1038–1046.

Hygge, S. (1976). Information about the model's unconditioned stimulus and response in vicarious classical conditioning. *Journal of Personality and Social Psychology, 33,* 764–771.

Isen, A. M. (1970). Success, failure, attention, and reaction to others: The warm glow of success. *Journal of Personality and Social Psychology, 15,* 294–301.

Isen, A. M. (1985). The asymmetry of happiness and sadness in effects on memory of normal college students. *Journal of Experimental Psychology: General, 114,* 388–391.

Isen, A. M. (1987). Positive affect, cognitive organization, and social behavior. In L. Berkowitz (Ed.), *Advances in experimental social psychology* (Vol. 20). New York: Academic.

Isen, A. M., Clark, M., & Schwartz, M. (1976). Duration of the effect of good mood on helping: "Footprints on the sands of time." *Journal of Personality and Social Psychology, 34*, 385–393.

Isen, A. M., Horn, N., & Rosenhan, D. C. (1973). Effects of success and failure on children's generosity. *Journal of Personality and Social Psychology, 27*, 239–247.

Isen, A. M., & Levin, P. F. (1972). Effect of feeling good on helping: Cookies and kindness. *Journal of Personality and Social Psychology, 21*, 384–388.

Isen, A. M., & Simonds, S. F. (1978). The effect of feeling good on a helping task that is incompatible with good mood. *Social Psychology, 41*, 346–349.

Isen, A. M., Shalker, T. E., Clark, M., & Karp, L. (1978). Affect, accessibility of material in memory, and behavior: A cognitive loop? *Journal of Personality and Social Psychology, 36*, 1–12.

Konecni, V. J. (1972). Some effects of guilt on compliance: A field replication. *Journal of Personality and Social Psychology, 23*, 30–32.

Krebs, D. L. (1975). Empathy and altruism. *Journal of Personality and Social Psychology, 32*, 1134–1146.

Krebs, D. L., & Miller, D. T. (1985). Altruism and aggression. In G. Lindzey & E. Aronson (Eds.), *The handbook of social psychology* (Vol.2). Hillsdale, NJ: Erlbaum.

Lazarus, R. S. (1982). Thoughts on the relations between emotion and cognition. *American Psychologist, 37*, 1019–1024.

Lazarus, R. S. (1984). On the primacy of cognition. *American Psychologist, 39*, 124–129.

Lazarus, R., Opton, E. M., Nomikos, M. S., & Rankin, N. O. (1965). The principle of short-circuiting of threat: Further evidence. *Journal of Personality, 33*, 622–635.

Lerner, M. J. (1970). Desire for justice and reactions to victims. In J. Macauley & L. Berkowitz (Eds.), *Altruism and helping behavior*. New York: Academic Press.

Lerner, M. J. (1980). *The belief in a just world: A fundamental delusion*. New York: Plenum.

Leventhal, H. (1980). Toward a comprehensive theory of emotion. In L. Berkowitz (Ed.), *Advances in experimental social psychology* (Vol. 13). New York: Academic Press.

Levin, P. F., & Isen, A. M. (1975). Further studies on the effect of feeling good on helping. *Sociometry, 38*, 141–147.

Lewin, K. (1951). *Field theory in social science*. New York: Harper.

MacIntyre, A. (1967). Egoism and altruism. In P. Edwards (Ed.), *The encyclopedia of philosophy* (Vol. 2). New York: Macmillan.

Mandler, G. (1975). *Mind and Emotion*. New York: Wiley.

Manucia, G. K., Baumann, D. J., & Cialdini, R B. (1984). Mood influences in helping: Direct effects or side effects? *Journal of Personality and Social Psychology, 46*, 357–364.

McDougall, W. (1908). *Introduction to social psychology*. London: Methuen.

McMillen, D. L., Sanders, D. Y., & Solomon, G. S. (1977). Self-esteem, attentiveness, and helping behavior. *Personality and Social Psychology Bulletin, 3*, 257–261.

Mischel, W. (1973). Toward a cognitive social learning reconceptualization of personality. *Psychological Review, 30*, 252–283.

Moore, B. S., Underwood, B., & Rosenhan, D. L. (1973). Affect and altruism. *Developmental Psychology, 8,* 99–104.

Nisbett, R. E., & Schachter, S. (1966). Cognitive manipulation of pain. *Journal of Experimental Social Psychology, 2,* 227–236.

Piliavin, J. A., Dovidio, J. F., Gaertner, S. L., & Clark, R. D. III. (1981). *Emergency intervention.* New York: Academic Press.

Piliavin, J. A., & Piliavin, I. M. (1973). *The good samaritan: Why does he help?* Unpublished manuscript, Department of Sociology, University of Wisconsin.

Piliavin, I. M., Rodin, J., & Piliavin, J. (1969). Good samaritanism: An underground phenomenon? *Journal of Personality and Social Psychology, 13,* 289–299.

Rawlings, E. I. (1968). Witnessing harm to another: A reassessment of the role of guilt in altruistic behavior. *Journal of Personality and Social Psychology, 10,* 377–380.

Regan, J. (1971). Guilt, perceived injustice, and altruistic behavior. *Journal of Personality and Social Psychology, 18,* 124–132.

Reykowski, J. (1982). Motivation of prosocial behavior. In V. J. Derlega & J. Grzelak (Eds.), *Cooperation and helping behavior: Theories and research.* New York: Academic Press.

Rogers, M., Miller, N., Mayer, F. S., & Duval, S. (1982). Personal responsibility and salience of the request for help: Determinants of the relation between negative affect and helping behavior. *Journal of Personality and Social Psychology, 43,* 956–970.

Rosenhan, D. L., Salovey, P., & Hargis, K. (1981a). The joys of helping: Focus of attention mediates the impact of positive affect on altruism. *Journal of Personality and Social Psychology, 40,* 899–905.

Rosenhan, D. L., Salovey, P., Karylowski, J., & Hargis, K. (1981b). Emotion and altruism. In J. P. Rushton & R. M. Sorrentino (Eds.), *Altruism and helping behavior: Social, personality, and developmental perspectives.* Hillsdale, NJ: Erlbaum.

Rosenhan, D. L., Underwood, B., & Moore, B. (1974). Affect moderates self-gratification and altruism. *Journal of Personality and Social Psychology, 30,* 546–552.

Roseman, I. J. (1984). Cognitive determinants of emotion: A structural theory. In P. Shaver (Ed.), *Review of personality and social psychology: Emotions, relationships, and health.* Beverly Hills: Sage Publications.

Ross, L., Rodin, J., & Zimbardo, P. G. (1969). Toward an attribution therapy: The reduction of fear through induced cognitive-emotional misattribution. *Journal of Personality and Social Psychology, 12,* 279–288.

Rushton, J. P., & Littlefield, C. (1979). The effects of age, amount of modeling, and a success experience on seven- to eleven-year-old children's generosity. *Journal of Moral Education, 9,* 55–56.

Schachter, S. (1964). The interaction of cognitive and physiological determinants of emotional state. In L. Berkowitz (Ed.), *Advances in experimental social psychology* (Vol. 1). New York: Academic Press.

Scherer, K. R. (1984). Emotion as a multicomponent process: A model and some cross-cultural data. In P. Shaver (Ed.), *Review of personality and social psychology: Emotions, relationships, and health.* Beverly Hills: Sage Publications.

Smith, C. A., & Ellsworth, P. C. (1985). Patterns of cognitive appraisal in emotion. *Journal of Personality and Social Psychology, 48,* 813–838.

Stotland, E. (1969). Exploratory studies of empathy. In L. Berkowitz (Ed.), *Advances in experimental social psychology* (Vol. 4). New York: Academic Press.

Thompson, W. C., Cowan, C. L., & Rosenhan, D. L. (1980). Focus of attention mediates the impact of negative affect on altruism. *Journal of Personality and Social Psychology, 38,* 291–300.

Toi, M., & Batson, C. D. (1982). More evidence that empathy is a source of altruistic motivation. *Journal of Personality and Social Psychology, 43,* 281–292.

Vaughn, K. B., & Lanzetta, J. T. (1980). Vicarious instigation and conditioning of facial expressive and autonomic responses to a model's expressive display of pain. *Journal of Personality and Social Psychology, 38,* 909–923.

Wallington, S. A. (1973). Consequences of transgression: Self-punishment and depression. *Journal of Personality and Social Psychology, 28,* 1–7.

Weyant, J. M. (1978). Effects of mood states, costs, and benefits on helping. *Journal of Personality and Social Psychology, 36,* 1169–1176.

Wispé, L. (1986). The distinction between sympathy and empathy: To call forth a concept, a word is needed. *Journal of Personality and Social Psychology, 50,* 314–321.

Zajonc, R. B. (1980). Feeling and thinking: Preferences need no inferences. *American Psychologist, 35,* 151–175.

Zajonc, R. B. (1984). On the primacy of affect. *American Psychologist, 39,* 117–123.

Zanna, M. B., & Cooper, J. (1974). Dissonance and the pill: An attribution approach to studying the arousal properties of dissonance. *Journal of Personality and Social Psychology, 29,* 703–709.

6. Passionate love in intimate relationships

ELAINE HATFIELD AND RICHARD L. RAPSON

Social psychologists interested in emotion initially began their work by attempting to develop a taxonomy of the basic emotions and to describe their cognitive and neuroanatomical/neurophysiological characteristics. This research has been singularly productive (see Darwin, 1872; Davitz, 1969; Ekman, 1982; Izard, 1972; Kemper, 1978; Levi, 1975; Plutchik & Kellerman, 1980). Now social psychologists may well be ready to begin an even more difficult task: to acknowledge that the "basic" emotions – such as love and hate, joy and despair, anxiety and relief, anger and fear, and jealousy – are complicated phenomena with complicated interlinkages. Scientists must now set out to discover how such complex emotions interact. They must begin to determine how intimates can best deal with the complicated and contradictory feelings they experience in love relationships. In this paper, we will begin to do that.

6.1. Kinds of love: passionate and companionate

For most people, love is the sine qua non of an intimate relationship (Berscheid & Peplau, 1983). Love, however, comes in a variety of forms. Hatfield and Walster (1978) distinguish between two forms of love, passionate love and companionate love. They define passionate love, (sometimes labeled puppy love, a crush, lovesickness, obsessive love, infatuation, or being in love) as follows: "A state of intense longing for union with another. Reciprocated love (union with the other) is associated with fulfillment and ecstacy. Unrequited love (separation) with emptiness, anxiety, or despair. A state of profound physiological arousal" (p. 9).

The Passionate Love Scale (PLS) has been designed to measure this emotion (see Appendix). It assesses the following cognitive, emotional, and behavioral indicants of "longing for union":

126

Cognitive Components

1. Intrusive thoughts about or preoccupation with the partner. (In Appendix, items 5, 19, and 21 tap this component.)
2. Idealization of the other or of the relationship. (Items 7, 9, and 15 measure this component.)
3. Desire to know the other and be known. (Item 10 measures the desire to know. Item 22 measures the desire to be known.)

Emotional Components

1. Attraction to other, especially sexual attraction. Positive feelings when things go well. (See Items 16, 18, and 29.)
2. Negative feelings when things go awry. (See Items 1, 2, 8, 20, 28, and 30.)
3. Longing for reciprocity. Passionate lovers not only love but want to be loved in return. (Item 14.)
4. Desire for complete and permanent union. (Items 11, 12, 23, and 27.)
5. Physiological arousal. (Items 3, 13, 17, and 26.)

Behavioral Components

1. Actions toward determining the other's feelings. (Item 24.)
2. Studying the other person (Item 4.)
3. Service to the other (Items 6 and 25.)

The authors of the PLS had hoped to include some items designed to measure lovers' efforts to get physically close to the other, but the lovers did not endorse such items, and they were dropped from the final version of the scale. In sum, passionate love has cognitive, emotional, and behavioral components (see Hatfield & Sprecher, 1986; Easton, 1985; Hatfield and Rapson, 1987; and Sullivan, 1985, for information on the reliability and validity of the PLS).

Companionate love (sometimes called true love or conjugal love) is a far less intense emotion. It combines feelings of deep attachment and friendly affection. Hatfield & Walster (1978) define it as "the affection we feel for those with whom our lives are deeply entwined" (p. 9). Rubin (1970) argues that this type of love (which he terms romantic love) includes such elements as responsibility for the other, tenderness, self-disclosure, and exclusivity. Rubin has developed an excellent scale to measure companionate love. Other scientists who have distinguished between the various forms of love are Burgess (1926), Cunningham and Antill (1981), Kelley (1979), Lee (1977), Maslow (1954), and Sternberg (1985).

6.2. The nature of love

For centuries, theorists have bitterly disagreed over the nature of passionate love. Is it an intensely pleasurable experience, a painful one, or both? Early researchers took the position that passionate love is a thoroughly positive experience. Such a vision is often depicted in contemporary films. For example, in Diane Kurys's *Cocktail Molotov*, 17-year-old Anne falls head over heels in love with Frederic after he declares his love for her. Scenes of their wild, exhuberant, coltish love portray the delights of passion.

Theorists such as Kendrick and Cialdini (1977) have argued that passionate love can easily be explained by the reinforcement principle. They believe passionate feelings are fueled by positive reinforcements and dampened by negative ones. Byrne (1971) reported a series of carefully crafted studies demonstrating that people love/like those who reward them and hate/dislike those who punish them (see Berscheid & Hatfield, 1969, for a review of this research.)

Passionate love: a more complicated vision

In the 1980s, social psychologists began to develop a far more complicated concept of love. Sometimes passionate love *is* a joyously exciting experience, sparked by exciting fantasies and rewarding encounters with the loved one. But that is only part of the story.

Passionate love is like any other form of excitement. By its very nature, excitement involves a continuous interplay between elation and despair, thrills and terror. Think, for example, of the mixed and rushed feelings that novice skiers experience. Their hearts begin to pound as they wait to catch the ski lift. When they realize they have made it, they are elated. On the easy ride to the top, they are still a bit unnerved; their hands shake and their knees still tremble, but they begin to relax. Moments later they look ahead and realize it is time to jump off the lift. The landing looks icy. Their rush quickly turns to panic. They cannot turn back. They struggle to get their feelings under control. They jump off the lift, elated and panicky; it is hard to tell which. Then they start to ski downhill, experiencing as they go a wild jumble of powerful emotions. Eventually, they arrive at the bottom of the hill, elated, relieved. Perhaps they feel like crying. Sometimes, they are so tired they are flooded with a wave of depression, but usually they get up, ready to try again. Passionate lovers experience the same roller coaster of feelings – euphoria, happiness, vulnerability, anxiety, panic, despair. The risks of love merely add fuel to the fire.

Sometimes men and women become entangled in love affairs where the delight is brief, and pain, uncertainty, jealousy, misery, anxiety, and despair are abundant. Some instances that we encountered follow: One teenage girl we interviewed was a stunning actress in a local production company. She had a crush on her 18-year-old costar. She spent hours each day lying on her bed dreaming about him. She spent an equal amount of time obsessively worrying about what she should say to him; the more she obsessed, the more terrified she became that she would sound awkward and stupid. The whole process was so painful that eventually she came to wish fervently that he would move away, so that she could relax.

Another interviewee, a pilot, insisted on loving a woman who had no interest whatever in him. Despite trying every ploy imaginable, he failed to interest her in even talking to him on the phone. When it became clear that his suit was hopeless, he decided that one possibility remained: He tried to kill himself by carving her name on his wrist. If he did not die, he thought, surely she would recognize the depth of his love and come around. He did not die; she did not come around. We were surprised at how many years he could continue to remain desperately in love, enduring rejection after rejection. It was hard to see how his love had been "dampened by pain" or "muted by negative reinforcements."

Other men and women discover they love their mates, but their discovery comes too late. They realize their love when their partners have finally found someone else or after they have died. In the cases we have described, passionate love seems to be fueled by a sprinkling of hope and a large dollop of anxiety, loneliness, mourning, jealousy, and terror. In fact, in a few cases, it seems as if these men and women love others not in spite of the pain they experience, but because of it. Recent social psychological research explores how passionate love, which thrives on anxiety and excitement, may be linked to a variety of strong related emotions, both positive and negative (see Hatfield & Walster, 1978).

6.3. The genesis of passionate love

Evolutionary theorists such as Plutchik (1980) argue we can best understand all emotions – be it love, hate, anger or fear – if we think of them in their evolutionary context. (We agree.) The reason the primary, prototypic emotions developed in the first place, were shaped and reshaped over the millenea, and continued to survive, was because they were adaptive. Our prehistoric ancestors were forced to deal with certain situations again and again. They had to seek out prey and escape predators. Adults had to mate and nurture their offspring. Infants had to cling tightly to their parent(s) until the infants were old enough to survive on their own. The basic emotions, then, are wired in. They are "neural packages" that predispose people to think, feel, and act in certain ways that were once adaptive, when in these prototypic situations. These emotional packages developed because they once helped the species survive and reproduce.

Rosenblum (1985) points out that primates, far below humankind on the phylogenetic scale, seem to experience something very much like passionate love. In infancy, primates are prewired to cling to their mothers. For an infant primate, separation can be deadly. If mother and child are separated, the infant is unlikely to find another caretaker. Therefore, to ensure survival, the "desire for union" is necessarily wired into all primates. As long as mother and child are in close proximity, all goes well. When a brief separation occurs, the primate quickly becomes desperate. He howls and rushes frantically about, searching for Mother. If she returns, the infant is joyous. He clings to his mother or jumps around in excitement. If she does not return, and his frantic efforts to find her fail, eventually he will abandon all hope of contact, despair, and probably die. The experience Rosenblum describes certainly sounds much like passionate love's "desire for union" – and its accompanying lows and highs. This, we thought, is the groundwork for passionate attachments.

Ainsworth and her colleagues (1978) and Bowlby (1973) describe a comparable experience of attachment, separation, and loss in children. Hatfield and her colleagues (1988 and 1989), too, find that children as young as four years old are capable of feeling passionate love. As you might expect, they find that anxious children and adolescents or children and adolescents under stress are particularly susceptible to falling passionately in love.

We see then that there is an evolutionary reason why passionate love might be tightly linked to both joy (when there is union) and anxiety (when people are especially anxious about themselves, their relationships, or the worlds they inhabit) as well as to a variety of other related emotions: jealousy, fear, depression, and so forth.

Scientists have collected a great deal of information as to the thoughts, physiological reactions, and behavioral reactions associated with passionate love. They make it clear that in passionate love, relief and anxiety, euphoria and pain, are often intermingled. These interact to produce the bittersweet experience that is passionate love.

Cognitive factors

The experience of passionate love is generally described as being a mixture of positive and negative emotions. Tennov (1979) interviewed more than 500 passionate lovers. Almost all the lovers took it for granted that passionate love (which Tennov labels "limerence") is a bittersweet experience. Liebowitz (1983) provides an almost lyrical description of the mixed nature of passionate love:

> Love and romance seems [*sic*] to be one, if not the most powerful activator of our pleasure centers. . . . Both tend to be very exciting emotionally. Being with the person or even just thinking of him or her is highly stimulating. . . . Love is, by definition, the strongest positive feeling we can have. . . . Other things – stimulant drugs, passionate causes, manic states – can induce powerful changes in our brains, but none so reliably, so enduringly, or so delightfully as that "right" other person. . . . If the relationship is not established or is uncertain, anxiety or other displeasure centers may be quite active as well, producing a situation of great emotional turmoil as the lover swings between hope and torment. [pp. 48–49]

It is clear, then, that people assume it is appropriate to use the term "passionate love" to label any "intense longing for union with another" regardless of whether that longing is reciprocated (and thus a source of fulfillment and ecstacy) or is uncertain or unrequited (and thus is a source of emptiness, anxiety, or despair).

The physiological component of love

Recently, psychologists have assembled information from neuroanatomical and neurophysiological investigations, ablation experiments, pharmacologic explorations, clinical investigations, and behavioral research as to the nature of love. This research, too, documents the contention that passionate love is a far more complicated phenomenon than it had at first seemed (see Kaplan's 1979 discussion of the neuroanatomy and neurophysiology of sexual desire and Liebowitz's 1983 discussion of the chemistry of passionate love, for a lengthy review of this research).

The anatomy of love

According to Kaplan (1979), the anatomy of passionate love and sexual desire is relatively well understood. The brain's sexual center consists of a network of neural centers and circuits. These are centered within the limbic system, with nuclei in the hypothalamus and in the preoptic region. The limbic system is located in the limbus or rim of the brain. In primitive vertebrates, this system controls emotion and motivation; it ensures that animals will act for their own survival and that of their species. In humans, this archaic system remains essentially unchanged. It is here that men's and women's most powerful emotions are generated, and that their behavior is most powerfully driven. In the sexual centers, scientists have identified both activating and inhibitory centers.

The sexual system has extensive neural connections with other parts of the brain. For example, it has significant connections, both neural and chemical, with the brain's pleasure and pain centers. All behavior is shaped by the seeking of pleasure (i.e., seeking stimulation of the pleasure center) and the avoidance of pain (i.e., avoiding stimulation of the pain center.)

The pleasure centers. Chemical receptor sites, located on the neurons of the pleasure centers, respond to a chemical that is produced by the brain cells. This has been tagged an "endorphin" because it resembles morphine chemically and physiologically (i.e., it causes euphoria and alleviates pain.) Kaplan (1979) observes: "It may be speculated that eating and sex and being in love, i.e., behaviors which are experienced as pleasurable, produce this sensation by stimulation of the pleasure centers, electrically, or by causing the release of endorphins, or by both mechanisms" (p. 11).

The pain centers. Sexual desire is also anatomically and/or chemically connected with the pain centers. If sexual partners or experiences are associated with pain, they will cease to evoke sexual desire. A chemical mediator for pain, analogous to endorphin, may exist. Our brains are organized so that pain takes priority over pleasure. This, of course, makes sense from an evolutionary point of view.

Kaplan acknowledges that cognitive factors have a profound impact on sexual desire. Thus, the cortex (that part of the brain that analyzes complex perceptions and stores and retrieves memories) must have extensive neural connections with the sexual center.

The chemistry of love

Psychologists are beginning to learn more about the chemistry of passionate love and a pot pourri of related emotions. They are also learning more about the way that various emotions, positive and negative, interact. Liebowitz (1983) has been the most willing to speculate about the chemistry of love. He argues that passionate love brings on a giddy feeling, comparable to an amphetamine high. It is phenylethylamine, an amphetamine-related compound, that produces the mood-lifting and energizing effects of romantic love. He observes that "love addicts" and drug addicts have a lot in common: The craving for romance is merely the craving for a particular kind of high. The fact that most romances lose some of their intensity with time may well be due to normal biological processes. The crash that follows a breakup is much like amphetamine withdrawal. Liebowitz speculates that there may be a chemical counteractant to lovesickness: Monoamine oxidase inhibitors may inhibit the breakdown of phenylethylamine, thereby "stabilizing" the lovesick.

Liebowitz also offers some speculations about the chemistry of the emotions that crisscross lovers' consciousness as they plunge from the highs to the lows of love. The highs include euphoria, excitement, relaxation, spiritual feelings, and relief. The lows include anxiety, terrifying panic attacks, the pain of separation, and the fear of punishment. His speculations are based on the assumption that nondrug and drug highs and lows operate via similar changes in brain chemistry.

Excitement. Liebowitz proposes that naturally occurring brain chemicals similar to stimulants such as amphetamine and cocaine produce the "rush" lovers feel. Passionate love is surely tightly tied to these chemical reactions.

A variety of other emotions, and other chemical reactions, may contribute to the subtle shadings of passionate love. Liebowitz articulates some of the chemical reactions that may be threaded through the passionate experience.

Relaxation. Chemicals related to the narcotics (such as heroin, opium, and morphine), tranquillizers (such as Librium and Valium), sedatives (such as barbiturates, Quaaludes, and other "downers"), alcohol (which acts chemically much like the sedatives), and marijuana and other cannabis derivatives, produce a mellow state and wipe out anxiety, loneliness, panic attacks, and depression.

Spiritual peak experiences. Chemicals similar to the psychedelics (such as lysergic acid diethylamide, mescaline, and psilocybin) produce a sense of beauty, meaningfulness, and timelessness.

Separation anxiety, panic attacks, and depression. Physiologists do not usually try to produce separation anxiety, panic attacks, or depression, but such painful feelings may arise from two sources: (1) withdrawal from the chemicals that produce the highs and (2) chemicals that in and of themselves produce anxiety, pain, or depression.

Research has not yet established whether or not Liebowitz's speculations as to the chemistry of love are correct.

Sexual desire. Kaplan (1979) provides some information as to the chemistry of sexual desire. In both men and women, testosterone (and perhaps LH-RF) are the libido hormones. Dopamine may act as a stimulant, serotonin or 5-HT as an inhibitor, to the sexual centers of the brain. Kaplan observes:

> When we are in love, libido is high. Every contact is sensuous, thoughts turn to Eros, and the sexual reflexes work rapidly and well. The presence of the beloved is an aphrodisiac; the smell, sight, sound, and touch of the love – especially when he/she is excited – are powerful stimuli to sexual desire. In physiologic terms, this may exert a direct physical effect on the neurophysiologic system in the brain which regulates sexual desire. . . . But again, there is no sexual stimulant so powerful, even love, that it cannot be inhibited by fear and pain [p. 14]

Kaplan ends by observing that a wide array of cognitive and physiological factors shape desire.

Similarity among emotions. Finally, although passionate love and the related emotions we have described may be associated with specific chemical neurotransmitters (or with chemicals that increase or decrease the receptors' sensitivity), most emotions have more similarities than differences. Finck (1891) made the interesting observation that "love can only be excited by strong and vivid emotion, and it is almost immaterial whether these emotions are agreeable or disagreeable" (p. 240). Negative emotions, he thought, could enhance, if not incite, the positive emotion of love. Chemically, intense emotions do have much in common. Kaplan reminds us that in chemical terms, love, joy, sexual desire, and excitement, as well as anger, fear, jealousy, and hate, have much in common: They are all intensely arousing. They all produce a sympathetic response in the nervous system. This is evidenced by the symptoms associated with all these emotions – a flushed face, sweaty palms, weak knees, butterflies in the stomach, dizziness, a pounding heart, trembling hands, and accelerated breathing. The exact *pattern* of reaction, however, aries from person to person (see Lacey, 1967).

Recent neuroanatomical/neurophysiological research suggests that the various emotions probably have tighter links than psychologists once thought. This is consistent with the recognition that in a passionately exciting encounter, people can move from elation, through terror, to the depths of despair, and back again in a matter of seconds. Excitement may be confusing, but at least its arousing. Such observations led Hatfield and Walster (1978) to conclude that passion can be ignited by pleasure and/or pain; by delight in the other's presence or pain at the other's loss. Recently, other researchers have begun to examine the exact nature of these interlinkages (see, for example, Zillman, 1984).

6.4 "Cross magnification" – what makes passionate love so powerful?

When people are passionately in love they often act in ways that sometimes seem insane to those of us who are not so besotted. People may know that an affair is not in their best interest, but when they are passionately in love, nothing else matters. They will not be deterred. How can we account for the passion of passionate love? Why should elation and anxiety add up to such a potent combination?

Hatfield (1971a and b; Hatfield & Carlson, in press) argued that the various emotions are more tightly linked than psychologists have thought. Generally, psychologists talk about emotions as if they usually exist in a pure form. People are happy *or* sad; passionately in love *or* angry. In fact, in real life, people's emotional lives are far more complex than that. In family life, mixed emotions are the norm.

Hatfield argued that sometimes people have trouble knowing just what they feel. Perhaps we feel vaguely neglected by our mates. Is the appropriate label for that feeling "love"? Resentment? Indignation? Embarrassment? Anger? Sometimes, it is difficult to unravel the tangle of one's emotions.

When we try to describe our physiological reactions, things get even muddier. Sometimes it is easy to identify an emotion with its accompanying physiological correlates. For example, certain emotions link up with very specific facial muscle movements. (We recognize that furrowed *corrugator* muscle, those squinting eyes. That is the look of self-righteous anger.) Sometimes, however, two or more emotions link up with the same physiological correlates. (Being startled, for example, produces a shower of catacholamines. But so do anger, joy, passion, and other emotions.) Sometimes we don't know whether we want to laugh or cry. What about the feeling that we are about to cry – the heavy breathing, tight chest, shaking hands? Is that hurt or anger? It is hard to tell. Perhaps we are simply getting a cold!

When we move to the skeletal-muscular system, things are equally difficult. For example, either joy or fury may spark the same kind of outsize sweeping movements.

There is yet another problem in describing our inner lives. Many emotional reactions are nonconscious. Conscious awareness is a precious commodity. Miller (1956) has argued that people can be aware of only seven or so things at a time. Thus, much cognitive and emotional processing must be run off automatically in other parts of the brain. For example, if a given perceptual-behavioral sequence is replayed again and again, it will soon become automatic. We offer an opinion, our mother cries or gets angry, we get angry or frightened; in return, we apologize and comfort her; things return to normal. The same sequence runs off again and again. Soon the complex actions and reactions begin to happen automatically. We lose consciousness of our own feelings. Instead, as soon as we begin to speak, incipient anxiety, well below the level of consciousness, begins to stir. Without even thinking of it, our hand reaches out and pats our mother's shoulder. Our precious consciousness can be devoted entirely to the conversation; other parts of the brain can reel out the appropriate emotional coordination sequences.

If we try, often we can replay such sequences, and retrieve our feelings; at the very least we can focus attention on our feelings, and "catch" them the next time the inevitable sequence happens. Usually, however, such self-conscious regulation is unnecessary. Consciousness is too valuable to be wasted on the routine. If we are not even conscious then, of many of the emotions that flicker across our minds, it certainly makes it difficult to know just what emotions are interacting at a given time.

Of course, in real life things are even more complicated than that. Time does not stand still. Emotions are labile. People can move from elation, through terror, to the shoals of despair . . . and back again . . . in a matter of seconds. Passionate love often involves just such a complicated interplay. Joy and pain often crisscross consciousness.

These observations led Hatfield to argue that psychologists must study not just pure emotions, but must devote some attention to analyzing how emotions interact. Logically, emotions should be able to interact in three major ways: (1) Sometimes, when one is experiencing several emotions, one may be able to identify the ebb and flow of separate emotions. One would experience a series of distinct emotions, or emotional blends. (2) Sometimes, however, it should be possible for contradictory emotions to cancel each other out. (3) Generally, however, Hatfield proposed, one will get *emotional spillover* (sometimes called *cross magnification*) effects. A given emotional experience can be intensified by emotions that briefly precede, coexist, or follow the target emotion.

For example, once one of your authors was literally dancing with joy because her first article had been accepted by the *Journal of Personality and Social Psychology*. Just then, her cat, hurtling across the room after a smaller cat, knocked into her. Just in time she caught herself. In a matter of milliseconds, her joy had turned to fury. She was poised to smack the cat; something she would normally never be tempted to do. Somehow, her extravagant happiness had turned into equally extravagant anger. The two emotional states had somehow "summed." Once you become aware of the concept of "emotional spillover," you begin to notice examples of this process everywhere. We find ourselves responding rudely to a friend and remind ourselves to settle down, that we are simply overwrought from having to rush around all day. We dissolve in a fit of giggling when we trip on the stairs and barely save ourselves from hurtling down the stairs.

Hatfield argued that in life such emotional spillover effects can have powerful consequences. Most intense emotional experiences involve blends of emotions. Perhaps this is not a coincidence. Perhaps, emotions (especially positive emotions) have a better chance to rise to a fever pitch when several emotional units are activated.

There is considerable evidence that cross-magnification processes do exist. Let us now turn to her evidence that, under the right conditions, either pleasure or anxiety and pain (or a combination of both) can fuel passion.

6.5. Behavioral evidence that both pleasure and pain may fuel emotion

Passionate love is risky. Success sparks delight; failure invites despair. We get some indication of the strength of our passion by the intensity of our delight or despair. Of course, trying to calibrate emotions is an elusive business. Sometimes it is difficult to tell to what extent your lover is responsible for the delight you feel and to what extent the highs you are experiencing are due to the fact that you are ready for romance:

The day is a glorious one, and you are simply feeling good. It is also difficult to tell to what extent your lover's coolness is responsible for your misery. To what extent is it due to the fact that you are lonely? That you are afraid to go off on your own? Your period is about to begin? Or you are simply low? Often it is hard to tell. In any case, there is an abundance of evidence to support the contention that, under the right conditions, a variety of intensely positive experiences, intensely negative ones, or neutral but energizing experiences, can add to the passion of passion.

Passion and the positive emotions

In our definition of love we stated that *"reciprocated love (union with the other) is associated with fulfillment and ecstacy."* No one doubts that love is a delightful experience in its own right: It is such a "high" that the joys of love generally spill over and add sparkle to everything else in life. What *has* been of interest to psychologists is the converse of this proposition: that the "adrenalin" associated with a wide variety of highs can spill over and make passion more passionate.

A number of carefully crafted studies make it clear that a variety of positive emotions – listening to a comedy routine (White, Fishbein, & Rutstein, 1981), sexual fantasizing (Stephan, Berscheid, & Hatfield, 1971), erotic excitement (Istvan & Griffitt, 1978), or general excitement (Zuckerman, 1979) – can intensify passion. In one investigation, for example, Istvan, Griffitt, and Weider (1983) caused some men to become aroused by showing them pictures of men and women engaged in sexual activities. Other men were shown nonarousing, neutral fare. Then they asked the men to evaluate the appeal of beautiful and unappealing women. When the woman was pretty, the aroused men rated her as more attractive than did the nonaroused men. When the woman was unattractive, the aroused men rated her as less attractive than did the nonaroused men. It seems as if the men's sexual arousal spilled over and intensified whatever it was they would otherwise have felt for the woman – for good or ill. Similar results have been secured with women. Sexually aroused women find handsome men unusually appealing, homely men less appealing, than do nonaroused women.

Passion and the negative emotions

In defining passionate love we observed that *"unrequited love (separation) is associated with emptiness, anxiety, or despair."* Psychologists have long understood that the failure to acquire or sustain love is an extraordinarily painful experience. Theorists such as Bowlby (1973), Peplau and Perlman (1982), and Weiss (1973) describe the panic, despair, and eventual detachment that both children and adults feel at the loss of someone they love.

Psychologists have amassed considerable evidence that people are especially vulnerable to love when their lives are turbulent. Passion can be intensified by the spillover of feeling from one realm to another. A variety of negative experiences have been found to deepen desire. For example, Dutton and Aron (1974), in a duo of studies, discovered a close link between fear and sexual attraction.

In one experiment, the researchers invited men and women to participate in a learning experiment. When the men showed up, they found that their partner was a strikingly beautiful woman. They also discovered that by signing up for the experiment they had gotten into more than they had bargained for. The experimenter was studying the effects of electric shock on learning. Sometimes the experimenter quickly went on to reassure the men that they had been assigned to a control group and would be receiving only a barely perceptible tingle of a shock. At other times, the experimenter tried to terrify the men: He warned them that they would be getting some quite painful electric shocks.

Before the supposed experiment was to begin, the experimenter approached each man privately and asked how he felt about the beautiful coed who "happened to be" his partner. He asked the men to tell him, in confidence, how attracted he was to her (e.g., how much he would like to ask her out for a date, how much he would like to kiss her). The investigators predicted that fear would facilitate attraction. And it did. The terrified men found the women a lot sexier than did the calm and cool men.

In another study, the investigators compared reactions of young men crossing two bridges in North Vancouver. The first bridge, the Capilano Canyon Suspension Bridge, is a 450-foot-long, 5-foot-wide span that tilts, sways, and wobbles over a 230-foot drop to rocks and shallow rapids below. The other bridge, a bit further upstream, is a solid, safe structure. As each young man crossed the bridge, a good-looking college woman approached him. She explained that she was doing a class project and asked if he would fill out a questionnaire for her. When the man had finished, the woman offered to explain her project in greater detail. She wrote her telephone number on a small piece of paper, so the man could call her if the wanted more information. Which men called?

Nine of the 33 men on the suspension bridge called her; only two of the men on the solid bridge called.

This single study could, of course, be interpreted several ways. Perhaps the men who called really were interested in ecology. Perhaps the adventurous men were most likely to cross dangerous bridges and call dangerous women. Perhaps it was not fear but relief at having survived the climb that stimulated desire. It is always possible to find alternative explanations for any one study.

But by now there is a great deal of experimental and correlational evidence for the more intriguing contention that, under the right conditions, a variety of awkward and painful experiences can deepen passion. Some of these are anxiety and fear (Aron, 1970; Brehm et al., 1978; Dienstbier, 1979; Dutton & Aron, 1974; Hoon, Wincze, & Hoon, 1977; Riordan & Tedeschi, 1983), embarrassment (Byrne, Przybyla, & Infantino, 1981), the discomfort of seeing others involved in conflict (Dutton, 1979), jealousy (Clanton & Smith, 1977), loneliness (Peplau & Perlman, 1982), anger (Barclay, 1969); anger at parental attempts to break up an affair (Driscoll, Davis, & Lipsetz, 1972), grisly stories of a mob mutilating and killing a missionary while his family watched (White et al., 1981), or even grief.

Passion and emotionally neutral arousal

In fact, recent laboratory research indicates that passion can be stirred by "excitation transfer" from such emotionally neutral but arousing experiences as riding an exercise bicycle (Cantor, Zillman, & Bryant, 1975) or jogging (White, Fishbein, & Rutstein, 1981).

White et al. (1981) conducted a series of elegant studies to demonstrate that passion can be intensified by any intense experience. In one experiment, some men (those in the high-arousal group) were required to engage in strenuous physical exercise (they ran in place for 120 seconds). Other men (those in the low-arousal group) ran in place for only 15 seconds. Although the men's moods were not effected by exertion, a variety of self-report questions and heart rate measures established that these two groups varied greatly in arousal.

Men then watched a videotaped interview with a woman they expected soon to meet. In half of the interviews, the woman was attractive; in half, unattractive. After the interview, the men gave their first impression of the woman; they estimated her attractiveness and sexiness. They also indicated how attracted they felt to her; how much they wanted to kiss and date her.

The authors predicted that exertion-induced arousal would intensify men's reactions to the woman – positively or negatively. Aroused subjects would be more attracted to the attractive confederate and more repulsed by the unattractive confederate than would subjects with lower levels of arousal. The authors found just that. If the woman was beautiful, the men who were aroused via exertion judged her to be unusually appealing. If the woman was unattractive, the men who were aroused via exertion judged her to be unusually unappealing. The effect of arousal, then, was to intensify a person's initial "intrinsic" attractiveness. Arousal enhanced the appeal of the pretty woman as much as it enhanced the lack of appeal of the homely one (see Zillman, 1984, for a review of this research on excitation transfer). The evidence suggests that adrenalin makes the heart grow fonder. Delight is one stimulant of passionate love, yet anxiety and fear, or simply high arousal, can often play a part.

Each new discovery, of course, generates more questions. What is needed now is a theoretical framework to guide us in predicting when powerful emotions such as anxiety, anger, and fear will stimulate passionate attraction and when they will destroy it. As yet, no one has begun to answer this important question.

6.6 Implications for intimate relationships

In the previous section, we traced the history of social psychological research on emotion. We discovered that basic laboratory research has led psychologists to recognize that passionate love is a far more complicated phenomenon than had originally been thought. At the same time, clinical psychologists have been conducting research on love and intimate relationships that has leaned heavily on clinical studies. They, too, by a very different route, have come to recognize that passionate, intimate relationships are far more complicated than they had originally believed. Clinicians started out thinking of family relationships as relatively straightforward, capable of rigorous control. They now recognize that relationships are as muddy and mixed as life itself. This recognition has caused marital and family therapists to devise new strategies for dealing with intimate encounters.

In the 1940s, the 1950s, and through the 1960s, clinicians, especially those with a behaviorist bent, tended to think of passionate love and intimate relationships in fairly simple ways. It was believed that love and intimacy would thrive best on a steady diet of pleasant interactions.

Unpleasantness was to be avoided at all costs. This vision shaped the advice early behaviorists gave couples.

The performing mode and the intimate mode

In social situations, people have a choice as to which of two very different strategies they will adopt. They can act as performers or as intimates. In some situations – when one is acting in a theatre company, interviewing for a job as a salesperson, or dealing with people whom one has little reason to trust – one must give a performance. One tries to look one's best (or worst), act confidently (or shyly), be rewarding (or punishing). Scales such as Christie's Mach II (see Christie & Geis, 1970) or Snyder's Self-Monitoring Scale (see Snyder, 1974; Lennox & Wolfe, 1984; or Gangestad & Snyder, 1985), measure such manipulative abilities.

In other situations, such as dealing with intimate lovers, family members, and friends, one wants to be as relaxed and honest as possible. Scales such as Schaefer and Olson's (1984) Intimacy Scale or Miller's Intimacy Measure (Miller & Lefocurt, 1982) measure such intimacy skills. In most real-life encounters, one engages in a balancing act between performing and intimacy.

In the 1950s, behavioristically oriented clinicians concentrated on teaching men and women how to reward their mates for acting as they wished them to (see Patterson, 1971; Jacobson & Margolin, 1949; Berscheid & Hatfield, 1969). Popular authors such as Andelin (1971) advised women to be at the door with a cold martini when their husbands came home. They should have the house spotlessly clean and the children snugly tucked in. Such advise had two shortcomings: (1) the husband may have been delighted with all the positive reinforcements he was receiving, but women were getting madder and madder at the inequity and (2) such relationships were singularly lacking in intimacy. Couples were giving a performance. (It is interesting in this regard that the reward Andelin promised wives in return for all their work was not intimacy, but a new stove and refrigerator.) Sometimes putting on a show is necessary. It is profitable to be able to hold your tongue, to slow things down when that is what is called for. But that is not enough. A relationship that is all acting is no relationship at all.

Recently, the pendulum has begun to shift. Cognitive psychologists (Tavris, 1982; Paolino & McCrady, 1978), family therapists (Guerin, 1976; Napier & Whitaker, 1978), existential humanists (Yalom, 1980), gestalt therapists (Polster & Polster, 1973), eclectic therapists (Offit, 1977; Pope et al., 1980), and social psychologists (Brehm, 1985; Duck & Gilmour, 1980–84) have begun to shape the way people think about relationships. Clinicians now take it for granted that love and intimate relationships are extraordinarily complex phenomena. One person, the performer, just cannot manipulate a relationship into perfection. It takes two; and even then things are difficult. In relationships, there are rarely blacks and whites. Real existence inhabits the area between, the multi-fold shades of gray. One simply has to recognize that life is muddy, and to try to enjoy, as best as possible, slopping around in it. Increasingly, clinicians are involved in teaching their clients intimacy skills. These are fundamental to the relationship. Manipulation is a more limited talent, to be used when a special intractable problem arises.

Intimacy: what is it?

The word "intimacy" is derived from the Latin "intimus," meaning inner or inmost. In a wide variety of languages, the word intimate refers to a person's innermost qualities. For example, the French *"intime"* signifies secret, deep, fervent, and ardent. The Italian *"intimo"* conveys the sense of close in friendship. In Spanish, *"intimo"* means private, close, and innermost. To be intimate means to be close to another. Hatfield (1984) defines intimacy as a "process in which people attempt to get close to another; to explore similarities (and differences) in the way they think, feel, and behave" (p. 208). Intimate relationships can be described in terms of cognitive, emotional, and behavioral characteristics.

Cognitive. Intimates are willing to reveal themselves to one another. They disclose information about themselves and listen to their partner's confidences. In deeply intimate relationships, friends and lovers feel free to reveal most facets of themselves. They reveal their complexities and contradictions. As a result, intimates share profound information about one another's histories, values, strengths, weaknesses, idiosyncracies, hopes, and fears (Altman & Taylor, 1973; Huesmann & Levinger, 1976; Jourard, 1964).

Emotional. Intimates care deeply about one another. It is in intimate relationships that people feel most intensely. People generally feel more intense love for intimates than for anyone else. Yet because intimates care so much about one another, they have the power to elicit intense pain as well. The dark side of love is jealousy, loneliness, depression, and anger. It is this powerful interplay of conflicting emotions that gives vibrancy to the most intimate of relationships (see Berscheid, 1979, 1983; Hatfield & Walster, 1978). Basic to all intimate relationships, of course, is trust.

Behavioral. Intimates are comfortable in close physical proximity. They gaze at one another (Argyle, 1967), lean on one another (Galton, 1884; Hatfield, Roberts, & Schmidt, 1980), stand close to one another (Allgeier & Byrne, 1973), and perhaps touch.

A prescription for intimacy

Nearly everyone needs a warm, intimate relationship. At the same time, one must recognize that in every social encounter there are some risks. What, then, is the solution? Social psychological research and clinical experience give us some hints. A basic theoretical assumption provides the framework we use in teaching people how to be intimate with others. People must be capable of independence in order to be intimate with others. Independence and intimacy are not opposite personality traits but interrelated skills. People who lack the ability to be independent, can never really be intimate. Lovers who are dependent on their mates, who cannot get along in life without the other, are precisely those least likely to reveal their fears, irritations, and anxieties to the other lest the partner leave the relationship. They are walking on eggshells, anxious not to upset or anger their mate with their darker, interior concerns. They dare not risk intimacy. Independent persons, on the other hand, who know they can make it on their own, are in a position to be brave about insisting on intimacy. They are not willing to settle for mates who do not care and cannot listen. They can afford to be unusually brave about sharing their innermost lives with their mates.

American culture has come to recognize that most young college-educated women crave both careers and marriage. But the broader implications of that discovery, which are not yet widely understood, are that most men want exactly the same thing, and that many of them know that means they must be closer to their wives and their children than were their fathers. There may be an instinctive awareness among growing numbers of people that independence and intimacy are not only connected, but greatly to be desired.

What we set out to do in therapy, then, is to make people comfortable with the notion that they are separate people, with separate ideas and feelings, who can sometimes come profoundly close to others. According to theorists, one of the most difficult tasks people face is to learn how to maintain their own identity and integrity while engaging in deeply intimate relationships. (for a fuller discussion of this point, see Hatfield, 1984).

In a few situations in life, the only thing one can do is to play out a stereotyped role. In most situations, one has to be at least tactful. In a few situations, downright manipulation may be called for if one is to survive. But on those occasions when real intimacy is possible, independent men and women can recognize its promise, seize the opportunities, and take chances. As relationships and families decompose and recompose themselves in the years ahead, the goals for recomposition are likely to focus on the extent to which both independence and intimacy are reconcilable and may be maximized (see Rapson, 1978). Already we live in creatively explosive times in which there is a rapid emergence of new shapes in relationships and new kinds of families. In these new families, members both wish to be themselves and wish not to be alone; they are forming kinds of connections barely imaginable a generation ago. It is not unreasonable to expect that there will be a great deal more of this kind of experimentation in the years ahead (see Argyle, 1967, and Hatfield, 1984, for more detailed information on teaching people to be more intimate in their love relationships).

Appendix: passionate love scale

In this section of the questionnaire you will be asked to describe how you feel when you are passionately in love. Some common terms for this feeling are passionate love, infatuation, love sickness, or obsessive love.

Please think of the person whom you love most passionately *right now*. If you are not in love right now, please think of the last person you loved passionately. If you have never been in love, think of the person whom you came closest to caring for in that way. Keep this person in mind as you complete this section of the questionnaire. (The person you choose should be of the opposite sex if you are heterosexual or of the same sex if you are homosexual.) Try to tell us how you felt at the time when your feelings were the most intense.

All of your answers will be strictly confidential.

    1. Since I've been involved with _____ , my emotions have been on a roller coaster.
* 2. I would feel deep despair if _____ left me.
    3. Sometimes my body trembles with excitement at the sight of _____ .
    4. I take delight in studying the movements and angles of _____ 's body.
* 5. Sometimes I feel I can't control my thoughts; they are obsessively on _____ .
* 6. I feel happy when I am doing something to make _____ happy.
* 7. I would rather be with _____ than anyone else.
* 8. I'd get jealous if I thought _____ were falling in love with some else.
    9. No one else could love _____ like I do.
*10. I yearn to know all about _____ .
*11. I want _____ – physically, emotionally, mentally.
 12. I will over _____ forever.
 13. I melt when looking deeply into _____ 's eyes.
*14. I have an endless appetite for affection from _____ .
*15. For me, _____ is the perfect romantic partner.
 16. _____ is the person who can make me feel the happiest.
*17. I sense my body responding when _____ touches me.
 18. I feel tender toward _____ .
*19. _____ always seems to be on my mind.
 20. If I were separated from _____ for a long time, I would feel intensely lonely.
 21. I sometimes find it difficult to concentrate on work because thoughts of _____ occupy my mind.
*22. I want _____ to know me – my thoughts, my fears, and my hopes.
 23. Knowing that _____ cares about me makes me feel complete.
*24. I eagerly look for signs indicating _____ 's desire for me.
 25. If _____ were going through a difficult time, I would put away my own concerns to help him/her out.
 26. _____ can make me feel effervescent and bubbly.
 27. In the presence of _____ , I yearn to touch and be touched.
 28. An existence without _____ would be dark and dismal.

*29. I possess a powerful attraction for _____ .
*30. I get extremely depressed when things don't go right in my relationship with _____ .

Possible responses to each item range from:

1	2	3	4	5	6	7	8	9

Not at all   Moderately   Definitely
true   true   true

Note: The asterisk indicates items selected for a short version of the PLS.

REFERENCES

Ainsworth, M. D. S., Blehar, M. C., Waters, E., & Walls, S. (1978) *Patterns of attachment: Assessed in the strange situation and at home.* Hillsdale, NJ: Lawrence Erlbaum.

Allgeier, A. R., & Byrne, D. (1973). Attraction toward the opposite sex as a determinant of physical proximity. *Journal of Social Psychology, 90,* 213–219.

Altman, I., & Taylor, D. A. (1973). *Social penetration: The development of interpersonal relationships.* New York: Holt.

Andelin, H. B. (1971). *Fascinating womanhood.* Santa Barbara, CA: Pacific Press.

Argyle, M. (1967). *The psychology of interpersonal behavior.* Baltimore, MD: Penguin Books.

Aron, A. (1970). *Relationship variables in human heterosexual attraction.* Unpublished doctoral dissertation. Department of Psychology. University of Toronto. Toronto, Canada.

Aron, A., & Dutton, D. G. (1985). *Arousal, attraction and strong attractions.* Unpublished manuscript. Maharishi International University. Fairfield, IA.

Averill, J. R. (1969). Autonomic response patterns during sadness and mirth. *Psychophysiology, 5,* 399–414.

Ax, A. F. (1953). The physiological differentiation between fear and anger in humans. *Psychosomatic Medicine, 15,* 433–442.

Barclay, A. M. (1969). The effect of hostility on physiological and fantasy responses. *Journal of Personality, 37,* 651–667.

Berscheid, E. (1979). *Affect in close relationships.* Unpublished manuscript. Dept. of Psychology. University of Minnesota. Minneapolis, MN.

Berscheid, E. (1983). Emotion. In H. H. Kelley, E. Berscheid, A. Christensen, J. H. Harvey, T. L. Huston, G. Levinger, E. Mc Clintock, L. A. Peplau, & D. R. Peterson (Eds.), *Close relationships.* New York: Freeman.

Berscheid, E., & Hatfield (Walster), E. (1969). *Interpersonal attraction.* Reading, MA: Addison-Wesley.

Berscheid, E., & Peplau, L. A. (1983). The emerging science of relationships. In H. H. Kelley et al. (Eds.), *Close relationships.* New York: Freeman.

Bowlby, J. (1973). Affectional bonds: Their nature and origin. In R. W. Weiss (Ed.), *Loneliness: The experience of emotional and social isolation.* Cambridge, MA: MIT Press.

Brehm, J. W., Gatz, M., Goethals, G., McCrimmon, J., & Ward, L. (1978). Psychological arousal and interpersonal attraction. *JSAS Catalogue of Selected Documents in Psychology, 8,* 63(ms. 1724).

Brehm, S. (1985). *Intimate relationships.* New York: Random House.

Burgess, E. W. (1926). The romantic impulse and family disorganization. *Survey, 57,* 290–294.

Byrne, D. (1971). *The attraction paradigm.* New York: Academic Press.

Byrne, D., Przybyla, D. P. J., & Infantino, A. (1981). The influence of social threat on subsequent romantic attraction. Paper presented at the meeting of the Eastern Psychological Association, New York City, April.

Cannon, W. B. (1929). *Bodily changes in pain, hunger, fear and rage* (2nd ed.). New York: Appleton.

Cantor, J., Zillman, D., & Bryant, J. (1975). Enhancement of experienced sexual arousal in response to erotic stimuli through misattribution of unrelated residual excitation. *Journal of Personality and Social Psychology, 32,* 69–75.

Christie, R., & Geis, F. L. (1970). *Studies in Machiavellianism.* New York: Academic Press.

Clanton, G., & Smith, L. G. (Eds.) (1977). *Jealousy*. Englewood Cliffs, NJ: Prentice-Hall.

Cunningham, J. D., & Antill, J. K. (1981). Love in developing romantic relationships. In S. Duck & R. Gilmour (Eds.), *Personal relationships 2. Developing personal relationships*. New York: Academic Press.

Darwin, C. (1872). *The expression of the emotions in man and animals*. London: John Murray.

Davitz, J. R. (1969). *The language of emotion*. New York: Academic Press.

Dienstbier, R. A. (1979). Emotion-attribution theory: Establishing roots and exploring future perspectives. In H. E. Howe & R. A. Dienstbier (Eds.), *Nebraska Symposium on Motivation, 26*. Lincoln: University of Nebraska Press.

Driscoll, R., Davis, K., E. & Lipsetz, M. E. (1972). Parental interference and romantic love: The Romeo and Juliet effect. *Journal of Personality and Social Psychology, 24*, 1–10.

Duck, S. & Gilmour, R. (Eds.) (1981–1984). *Personal relationships*. (Vols. 1–5). New York: Academic Press.

Duffy, E. (1962). *Activation and behavior*. New York: Wiley.

Dutton, D. (1979). *The arousal-attraction link in the absence of negative reinforcement*. Canadian Psychological Association. Toronto, Canada

Dutton, D., & Aron, A. (1974). Some evidence for heightened sexual attraction under conditions of high anxiety. *Journal of Personality and Social Psychology, 30*, 510–517.

Easton, M. (1985). *Love and intimacy in a multi-ethnic setting*. Dept. of Psychology. Unpublished doctoral dissertation. University of Hawaii at Manoa, Honolulu.

Easton, M. J., Hatfield, E., & Synodinos, N. (1984). *Development of the juvenile love scale*. Unpublished manuscript. Dept. of Psychology University of Hawaii, Honolulu, HI.

Ekman, P. (Ed.). (1982). *Emotion in the human face*. London: Cambridge University Press.

Finck, H. T. (1891) *Romantic love and personal beauty: Their development, causal relations, historic and national peculiarities*. London: Macmillan.

Funkenstein, D. H., King, S. H., & Drolette, M. (1953). *The experimental evocation of stress*. Symposium on stress, March 16–18, 1953. Washington, DC: U.S. Government Printing Office.

Galton, F. (1884). Measurement of character. *Fortnightly Review, 36*, 179–185.

Gangestad, S., & Snyder, M. (1985). To carve nature at its joints: On the existence of discrete classes in personality. *Psychological Review, 92* (3), 1–90.

Guerin, P. J. (Ed.) (1976). *Family therapy: Theory and practice*. New York: Gardner Press.

Hatfield (Walster), E. (1971a). Passionate love. In B. I. Murstein (Ed.), *Theories of love and attraction*. New York: Springer.

Hatfield, E. (1984). The dangers of intimacy. In V. Deriaga (Ed.), *Communication, intimacy, and close relationships*. New York: Academic Press.

Hatfield (Walster), E. (1971b) Studies testing a theory of positive affect. Proposal for National Science Foundation Grant 30822 X. Washington, D.C.

Hatfield, E., Brinton, C., & Cornelius, J. Anxiety and children's feelings of passionate love. Submitted to *Motivation and emotion*.

Hatfield, E. & Carlson, J. G. (in press). *The psychology of emotions*. Monterey, CA: Brooks-Cole.

Hatfield, E., & Rapson, E. (1987). Passionate love: New directions in research. In D. Perlman & W. Jones (Eds.) *Advances in Personal Relationships, 1*, 109–139.

Hatfield, E., Roberts, D., & Schmidt, L. (1980). The impact of sex and physical attractiveness on an initial social encounter. *Recherches de psychologic sociale*, 2, 27–40.

Hatfield, E., Schmitz, E., Cornelius, J., & Rapson, R. L. (1988) Passionate love: How early does it begin? *Journal of Psychology and Human Sexuality*, 1, 35–52.

Hatfield, E., & Sprecher, S. (1986). *Measuring passionate love in intimate relations. Journal of Adolescence*, 9, 383–410.

Hatfield, E., & Walster, G. W. (1978). *A new look at love*. Lantham, MA: University Press of America.

Hoon, P. W., Wincze, J. P., & Hoon, E. F. (1977). A test of reciprocal inhibition: Are anxiety and sexual arousal in women mutually inhibitory? *Journal of Abnormal Psychology*, 86 (1), 65–74.

Huesmann, L. R., & Levinger, G. (1976). Incremental exchange theory: A Forman model for progression in dyadic social interaction. In L. Berkowitz & E. Hatfield (Eds.), *Equity theory: Toward a general theory of social interaction*. New York: Academic Press, 9, 192–230.

Istvan, J., & Griffitt, W. (1978). *Emotional arousal and sexual attraction*. Unpublished manuscript, Dept. of Psychology Kansas State University, Manhattan.

Istvan, S., Griffitt, W., & Weider, G. (1983) Sexual arousal and the polarization of perceived sexual attractiveness. *Basic and Applied Social Psychology*, 4, 307–318.

Izard, C. (1972). *Patterns of emotions*. New York: Academic Press.

Jacobson, N. S., & Margolin, G. (1949). *Marital therapy: Strategies based on social learning and behavior exchange principles*. New York: Brunner/Mazel.

Jourard, S. M. (1964). *The transparent self*. Princeton, NJ: Van Nostrand.

Kaplan, H. S. (1979). *Disorders of sexual desire*. New York: Simon and Schuster.

Kelley, H. H. (1979). *Personal relationships: Their structures and processes*. Hillsdale, NJ: Erlbaum.

Kemper, T. (1978). *A social interaction theory of emotions*. New York: Wiley.

Kendrick, D. T., & Cialdini, R. B. (1977). Romantic attraction: Misattribution vs. reinforcement explanations. *Journal of Personality and Social Psychology*, 35, 381–391.

Lacey, J. I. ((1967). Somatic response patterning and stress: Some revisions of activation theory. In M. H. Appley & R. Trumbull (Eds.), *Psychological stress*. New York: Appleton.

Lee, J. A. (1977). *The colors of love*. New York: Bantam.

Lennox, R. D., & Wolfe, R. N. (1984). Revision of the self-monitoring scale. *Journal of Personality and Social Psychology*, 46 (6) 1349–1364.

Leventhal, H. (1980). *Toward a comprehensive theory of emotion*. Unpublished manuscript. Dept of Psychology. University of Wisconsin. Madison, WI.

Levi, L. (Ed) (1975). *Emotions: Their parameters and measurement*. New York: Raven Press.

Liebowitz, M. R. (1983). *The chemistry of love*. Boston: Little, Brown, and Co.

Lindsley, D. B. (1950). Emotions and the electroencephalogram. In M. R. Reymert (Ed.), *Feelings and emotions: The Moosehearet symposium*. New York: McGraw Hill.

Maslow, A. H. (1954). *Motivation and personality*. New York: Harper and Row.

Mesulam, M. M., & Perry, J. The diagnosis of love sickness: Experimental physiology without the polygraph. Cited in Liebowitz, M. R. (1983). *The chemistry of love*. N.Y.: Little Brown.

Miller, G. A. (1956). The magical number seven, plus or minus two: some limits on our capacity for processing information. *Psychological Review*, 63, 81–97.

Miller, R. S., & Lefocurt, H. M. (1982). *The assessment of social intimacy*. Unpublished manuscript. Department of Psychology, University of Waterloo; Waterloo, Ontario, Canada.

Napier, A., & Whitaker, C. (1978). *The family crucible*. New York: Harper and Row.

Offit, A. K. (1977). *The Sexual Self*. New York: Congdon & Weed, Paolino, T. J., & McCrady, B. S. (1978). *Marriage and marital therapy*. New York: Brunner/ Mazel

Patterson, G. R. (1971). *Families: Applications of social learning to family life.* Champaign, IL: Research Press.

Peplau, L. A., & Perlman, D. (1982). *Loneliness.* New York: Wiley.

Plutchik, R. (1980). *Emotion: A psychoevolutionary synthesis.* New York: Harper and Row.

Plutchik, R., & Kellerman, H. (1980). *Emotion: Theory, research and experience,* 1: *Theories of emotion.* New York: Academic Press.

Polster, E., & Polster, M. (1973). *Gestalt therapy integrated.* New York: Vintage.

Pope, K. S., & Associates. (Eds.) (1980). *On love and loving.* San Francisco: Jossey-Bass.

Rapson, R. L. (1978). *Denials of doubt.* Washington, DC: University Press of America.

Riordan, C. A., & Tedeschi, J. T. (1983). Attraction in aversive environments: Some evidence for classical conditioning and negative reinforcement. *Journal of Personality and Social Psychology, 44,* 683–692.

Rosenblum, L. A. (Sept. 18, 1985) Discussant: Passionate love and the nonhuman primate. Paper presented at the International Academy of Sex Research meetings. Seattle, WA.

Rubin, Z. (1970). Measurement of romantic love. *Journal of Personality and Social Psychology, 16,* 265–273.

Schachter, S. (1964). The interaction of cognitive and physiological determinants of emotional state. In L. Berkowitz (Ed.), *Advances in Experimental Social Psychology.* New York: Academic Press.

Schaefer, M. T., & Olson, D. H. (1984). *Diagnosing Intimacy: The PAIR inventory.* Family Social Science, 290 Mc Neal Hall, University of Minnesota, St. Paul, 55108.

Snyder, M. (1974). Self-monitoring of expressive behavior. *Journal of Personality and Social Psychology, 30,* (4), 526–537.

Stephan, W., Berscheid, E., & Hatfield (Walster), E. (1971). Sexual arousal and heterosexual perception. *Journal of Personality and Social Psychology, 20,* 93– 101.

Sullivan, B. O. (1985). *Passionate love: A factor analytic study.* Honolulu: University of Hawaii.

Sternberg, R. J. (1988). Triangulating love. In R. J. Sternberg & M. L. Barnes (Eds.), *The psychology of love.* (pp. 119–138) New Haven: Yale University Press.

Tavris, C. (1982). *Anger: The misunderstood emotion.* New York: Simon and Schuster.

Tennov, D. (1979). *Love and limerence.* New York: Stein and Day.

Weiss, R. S. (1973) *Loneliness: The experience of emotional and social isolation.* Cambridge, MA: MIT Press.

White, G. L., Fishbein, S., & Rutstein, J. (1981). Passionate love and the misattribution of arousal. *Journal of Personality and Social Psychology, 41,* 56–62.

Yalom, I. (1980). *Existential psychotherapy.* New York: Basic Books.

Zillman, D. (1984). *Connections between sex and aggression.* Hillsdale, NJ: Erlbaum.

Zuckerman, M. (1979). *Sensation seeking: Beyond the optimal level of arousal.* Hillsdale, NJ: Erlbaum.

7. Attitude, affect, and consumer behavior

JOEL B. COHEN

This chapter provides an overview of the factors leading researchers in consumer behavior to focus on affective states and processes and indicates why it might be useful to distinguish more carefully between attitudinal and affective concepts in this research tradition. A framework for doing so is presented and current research in consumer behavior is looked at from this standpoint.

An increasingly active research program has sought to understand the nature, causes, and consequences of consumers' affective reactions to the goods and services offered for sale in the marketplace. This interest stems in part from the pervasiveness and economic significance of the resulting behavior. Wilkie (1986) reports that consumers in the United States spend about $2.7 trillion per year out of a total gross national product of $4 trillion, truly a staggering sum.

On a more micro level, consumers' responses to the offerings of any given firm will determine not only its profitability but the ability of the firm to stay in business and provide jobs for its employees. It is little wonder, then, that marketers are not only keenly interested in understanding the nature of consumers' wants and preferences so that their offerings can be better tailored to them but also anxious to know how to assess the success of their marketing efforts, preferably well in advance of the bottom-line marketplace judgement. This had led, first, to a long-standing interest in finding and measuring intervening variables that are predictive of purchase behavior, and second, to the recognition that a more adequate conceptualization of consumers' decision processes (i.e., the stages leading up to purchase), and particularly the information-processing aspects of this process, is vital.

Preparation of this chapter was supported by the Center for Consumer Research at the University of Florida, Gainesville.

7.1. Learning and attitudes: two traditions at work

The search for intervening variables that would both predict consumers' behavior and serve as a proxy for behavior in evaluating alternative marketing executions has led to some exotic excursions into motivation research (see Packard, 1957; Dichter, 1960, 1964; Bartos, 1977), as well as to an unending series of attempts to divide consumers into relatively homogeneous clusters using a variety of person descriptors, from overt behavior and socioeconomic variables to personality traits and values.[1] Inevitably, the trail led back to "attitude," which in various visits assumed the guise of a rather unsophisticated single-item evaluative scale (ideal for survey research), to sets of internally consistent items presumed to load on an underlying evaluative factor, and finally to attitude measures based on various combinatorial rules involving brand-attribute beliefs and their evulations.[2] It is important to note, however, that the major purpose in most of this activity was to locate an intervening variable that would convincingly "sum up" all the personal and marketplace influences at work and that would stand in a direct line causally to behavior.

Let us retrace our steps just a bit. Those having a day-to-day working interest in getting their brands established in the marketplace and consumer researchers interested in the dynamics of consumer purchase and repeat purchase behavior had gone down a somewhat different road. Even a very good static brand assessment measure (and locating individuals who were prone to purchase) could provide only a snapshot, and these practitioners and researchers were more interested in the purchase process and how to affect it. In addition to trying to determine what specific needs and wants served as the "springs of action," the early efforts to come to grips with the acquisition and reacquisition of a brand conceived of consumer behavior as a learning process. Accordingly, conceptual frameworks loosely derived from stimulus–response (S–R) views of motivated behavior found their way into research on consumer behavior (e.g., Howard, 1965; Krugman, 1962; Sheth, 1968). Classical as well as instrumental conditioning principles continue to guide research on consumer decision making in general and consumers' responses to marketing tactics (e.g., coupons, price promotions, advertising) in particular (e.g., Nord & Peter, 1980; McSweeney & Bierley, 1984). The heritage of this tradition can best be seen, however, in the burgeoning consumer information-processing literature.[3] To take one notable example, throughout the time the field has been preoccupied with attitudes (e.g., their relationship to behavior, the brand evaluation process leading to attitude formation), a smaller group of researchers have consistently argued that much of consumer behavior is based on habit and that consumer learning is a low-involvement process (e.g., Krugman, 1965; Ray, 1982; Greenwald & Leavitt, 1984; Kassarjian, 1978). In other words, both what was learned and how it was learned had more to do with principles of association and conditioning than with models of high-involvement evaluation and decision making. With the coming of the information-processing revolution, such ideas (suitably modernized, of course) became more popular and began to receive more systematic study.

Somewhat lost in the shuffle, however, were the key "noncognitive" aspects of this group's original interest (e.g., specific buying motives, feeling regarding brand use/ownership, drive strength). Learning about a product is not nearly as important as acquiring an action tendency toward the product. Unfortunately, the majority of process-oriented academic consumer researchers had, by the mid-1970s, become sufficiently intrigued by the cognitive revolution to put lingering thoughts of motivational variables aside. Advertising practitioners, by contrast, have probably always "known" that more was going on than a simple and hopefully convincing transmission of brand information and evaluation followed by memory storage, retrieval, and so on. It had been earlier speculated that perhaps this "extra effect" involved classical conditioning, with aspects of the ad (e.g., well-chosen symbols and other valenced people and objects) all serving as the unconditioned stimulus (see Staats, 1968; Lott & Lott, 1968; Kroeber-Riel, 1984b). In some way or other one had to account for the increased motivation to attain products that were successfully advertised. Only someone exclusively pursuing the innerworkings of consumers' cognitive processes could fail to note that those who were most likely to buy a particular product had something other than better developed product schemata (or less uncertainty): They seemed to *want* the product more and sometimes even displayed considerable emotion (e.g., joy, frustration, pride, anger) at various stages of the process. Early advertising-oriented "models" of the process often included a term like "desire" to describe a stage higher up the hierarchy of purchase likelihood than mere receipt of brand information. These early models assumed a fixed order in which thinking led to feeling and (if all went well) to doing.

7.2. The multi-attribute model: a hoped-for integration

The earlier response of many of those in the attitude tradition to the obvious need to go beyond attitude–behavior correlations in an effort to understand purchase behavior was to try to refine their ideas regarding the nature of consumer attitudes and their relationship to behavior. Both to explain better how marketing and advertising works and to provide a better description of the consumer decision process, the multi-attribute attitude model was used as a convenient representation of how consumers first come to like, then to prefer (i.e., by comparing alternatives either on their overall attitudes or various attribute-based decision rules), then to intend to buy, and finally to purchase a particular product. It was all perfectly sensible: Brands that were perceived to provide or possess more of the features that consumers evaluated positively would themselves come to be evaluated more highly (e.g., Lutz, 1975; Holbrook, 1978). So, for a great many students of consumer behavior, evaluation, attitude, and affect became linked, and each was used to describe the judged favorability of a brand without explicit consideration of any motivational state.[4]

Even within the attitude tradition, however, many of those having a particular interest in communication and attitude change found this streamlined and paramorphic account of the process inadequate. One important impetus toward a more accurate description was the finding that cognitive responses to an advertisement were more decisive for subsequent judgments than was the comprehension of message-based brand-attribute associations. This led to much greater interest in the state of mind of the consumer during information transmission. Research of this type proved to be important in shifting the field away from measures of attitudinal outcomes to richer accounts of the process (e.g., Wright, 1973; Olson, Toy, & Dover, 1982; Petty, Cacioppo, & Schumann, 1983; Park & Young, 1983; Batra & Ray, 1986). In a related vein other researchers put forth the view that perhaps the consumer's response to an advertisement was an amalgam of two attitudes: an attitude toward the brand advertised and an attitude toward the ad (see Mitchell & Olson, 1981; Shimp, 1981; Lutz, McKenzie, & Belch, 1983). The latter might even be influenced by background features such as sunsets and smiling babies. The consumer's overall attitude, then, would be a function of each, though early research raised many more questions than it answered regarding a possible integration or transfer mechanism (e.g., Under what conditions and through what mechanisms does exposure to smiling babies lead consumers to become more positively predisposed to the product advertised?).

7.3. Disentangling attitude and affect in consumer behavior

Through all of this research several things have become clear. First, the field of consumer behavior will continue to benefit from systematic research both on evaluative judgments (e.g., attitude, preference, choice) and the nature and structure of product-based cognitions and on response-predisposing states (e.g., motivation to purchase, positive feelings instilled by an advertisement, feelings of satisfaction after a purchase). Second, there exists a good deal of semantic confusion as to whether a particular study is attempting to manipulate or measure one's evaluation of a product or how product-related stimuli make one feel. Part of the blame for this state of affairs is undoubtedly due to the blurring of the distinction between attitude (which, I submit, belongs in the first camp) and affect (which, I will argue, is best reserved for the second). As it stands now, the terms "affect" and "attitude" appear to be intertwined to the extent that no clear meaning for "affect" emerges. This should hardly be surprising given the prominent history of attitude research in social psychology and the tendency of most attitude researchers to incorporate affect within their models of attitude. The definitional ambiguity surrounding the term "affect" undoubtedly goes back to the tripartite division of the mind and the subsequent partitioning of emphasis that placed stress on one domain and tended to interpret activities in the others in that light (see Hilgard, 1980, and Isen & Hastorf, 1982, for a more detailed historical treatment of this issue).

An important premise of this paper is that both evaluation (along with its cognitive representation, i.e., attitude) and affect are of great significance to the study of consumer behavior (see also Batra & Ray, 1986). Inconsistent or ambiguous treatment of these concepts, therefore, is hardly optimal. While greater definitional clarity could be achieved in a variety of ways, this chapter presents one such resolution of the difficulty and then offers a framework within which research on both topics can be brought together and assessed.

Affect and affective traces

In contemporary treatments of consumer behavior, attitude is almost always thought of in terms of an evaluation (e.g., bipolar scales such as like–dislike, good–bad). Implied, therefore, is a cognitive element that results, deliberately or not, from some type of object identification (i.e., as a member of an evaluative category) or comparison with a criterion (e.g., some personal goal, norm, frame of reference). "Affect," on the other hand, has some unique properties that have tended to be obscured when it is viewed either as a component of attitude or as synonymous with attitude (cf. Batra & Ray 1983). First, it is a response that is intimately linked to a state of arousal. Second, its status in the cognitive domain is as a tag, or marker, used to both label and record the aforementioned state.[5] In this sense, then, it is a trace of an emotional response to an entity with which we have come into psychological contact (Bower, 1981). The necessary antecedent is an affective state strong enough to leave a cognitive trace.

While the affect itself may be short-lived, it is often possible to retrieve the memory of that experience after a considerable length of time. In general, an attitude is likely to be more enduring, possibly as a function of more elaborate encoding processes and greater functional relevance (thus producing more retrieval opportunities that should strengthen connections to other concepts).

An argument against lumping evaluative cognitions and affective traces together (and perhaps referring to both as affect) is that many, if not most, evaluative cognitions are "cold" things; outcomes of object/person assessment processes (e.g., Ajzen & Fishbein, 1980), remembrances of things learned. Affective traces, on the other hand, are often the residue of highly involving and emotional states. When the term "affective trace" is restricted to cognitive elements that serve as tags for experienced states of affect, their instantiation implies more than mere retrieval of information. In particular, the memory of such an episode frequently has the capacity to elicit a similar feeling or emotion (though not always to the same degree). One of the most frequently used mood induction techniques is simply to ask people to bring to mind such a recollection. Retrieval of evaluative cognitions associated with some person, object, or event, on the other hand, is little different from the retrieval of any other kind of information. We would lose too much by ignoring the distinction between mental representations of affective states and evaluations, regardless of any similarities in representational code that might exist. While there may be no compelling reason to tamper with the general synonymy in the use of the terms "affect" and "affective state," I think it is useful to refer to the cognitive representation of a feeling state as an "affective trace."

This convention will be adopted thoughout the remainder of the chapter.

How the variables interact

To see how these definitions apply to consumer behavior, let us work through an example. Imagine that a consumer goes to a large department store to look for a television set. In the store the consumer notices many products enroute to the department selling television sets. But the television set purchase dominates the consumer's mind, and so (even though the names of the other products could probably be retrieved from memory subsequently) the likelihood of an affective response to any of these products is low. Not only is no affect created, but in the absence of any reason to evaluate these products there is probably no change in any preexisting attitude toward any of them.

Now suppose that the store has made some changes since the consumer's last visit. The lighting has been made softer, pleasant music added, displays made a little less cluttered. While hurrying to look at televisions, the consumer experiences positive feelings in response to the surroundings and may even be vaguely aware of that. When the television salesman introduces himself, the consumer finds herself smiling and makes a cheerful remark. Later, over dinner, she recalls feeling good in the store and attributes those feelings to a plausible object (e.g., the store rather than the time of day). The resulting inference is that it is a good store to shop at, and she forms the intention to go back there to look for a new coffee maker.

According to our usage of terms, we would say that the consumer's experience in the store influenced her mood state, thus creating positive affect. Further, through a coding process that probably requires little conscious processing (see Bargh, 1984; Mandler, 1982), an affective (episodic memory) trace resulting from the mood state would then exist, though in the absence of a greater amount of thought, there might well be no attitude change toward the store. This might be the case until an evaluative frame of reference was subsequently applied to the store and the affective trace was retrieved. One is aware, at that moment, of having had a favorable feeling toward the store. This "informational aspect" of the affective trace can produce an effect similar to that of retrieving positive evaluations of the store. In addition, however, since the retrieved affective trace represents "pure feeling" (i.e., it lacks an evaluative or judgmental basis), the individual may attempt to infer "reasons" for being able to recall a positive feeling toward the store, perhaps because she desires to explain or understand why she feels this way. Finally, if the retrieved affective trace is sufficiently positive (or negative), the person may actually reexperience some of the same feelings. Should this occur an even stronger and more highly valenced attitude is likely to result. Of course, if the consumer attributes this retrieved affective trace and any resulting affect to some dispositional factor, there may be no attitude change toward the store at all. Although the creation of an affective state of any intensity will usually produce its own affective trace, only a strong associative bonding to something present at the time or further inferential processes will definitely lead to the formation or change of an attitude toward some object.

Clearly, a very direct route to attitude formation and change is through evaluative cognitions that result from judgments made regarding the strengths and weaknesses of particular objects with respect to one's needs and goals. So, any and all aspects of the department store that were important to the person might have been assessed, evaluative cognitions formed, and some overall attitudinal judgment made. Similarly, the mere observation of store features that are regarded positively or negatively might culminate in attitude formation or change, either through an integration of feature-associated evaluative cognitions or by means of assignment of the store to some evaluatively regarded category (see Cohen & Basu, 1987). In none of the above cases, however, must affect either lead to or result from such cognitive operations, which represent an evaluative rather than an affective process.

A personal experience from long ago that is still quite vivid to me provides another illustration of the distinctions we are drawing between affect and attitude, especially as concerns the "transfer" of affect to a product. When I was growing up, a bunch of us used to play a serious game of baseball in the sweltering summer's heat. There happened to be a gas station with a Coke machine near the ball field that kept the Coca Cola at what must have been the perfect temperature. There could not have been a better Coca Cola anywhere in the world! When we were thoroughly exhausted, we would head for the gas station and put our money in that marvelous machine. Halfway through the game, I would begin to imagine the taste of that Coke. My cognitive response to drinking the Coke was very direct and very primitive. Though the affective trace and the affect itself seem almost indistinguishable, I can be prompted to recall my feeling state (i.e., affective trace) without actually experiencing the affective state. One may, I suppose, speculate as to the larger functional significance of such affective traces: Are they "markers" for the specific "purpose" of helping us identify the source of our satisfaction (to aid us in finding our way back to it)? In any event the surest way to evoke that affect was for me to begin to experience situational cues similar to those surrounding the behavior in the first place. Yet if there was anything like a more general effect on my attitude toward Coca Cola, it was not very powerful. Rather, my affect seemed to reflect the totality of that particular experience. Either there was no strong associative bonding uniquely to Coca Cola (or possibly too much interference with other aspects of the situation) or the more deliberative and conscious thought processes one engages in when inferring causes would not favor that product attribution. One reason habits such as cigarette smoking or craving food may be so difficult to break is that feeling states involving them may produce affective traces, whereas many attempts to change such behavior involve the modification of attitudes. These two cognitive elements (i.e., affective traces and attitudes) may well interact, but one is not reducible to the other such that the former would be cancelled out by the latter.

Affective processes are of great interest to people in the field of consumer behavior who are interested in how advertising works. A typical television commercial might use music and other "peripheral" factors to create a positive feeling state (undoubtedly the state would be more complex than this emotionally), often without demanding the degree of attention likely to cause more active processing of the information in the commercial. The positive affective state is then thought to produce a heightened and favorable reaction to other elements in the commercial, possibily through mechanisms similar to those discussed above. In addition, consumers may like the commercial (i.e., have a positive attitude toward it, evalute it favorably), and this may impact directly on their attitude toward the product, almost as if this were an additional product attribute or reason to like the product. Merely knowing that a consumer "likes" a commercial is not very diagnostic as to whether the underlying process is primarily affective or attitudinal, and yet these processes are quite different both in concept and in implications. A consumer may "like" a commercial perceived to be factual and informative and may come to hold a more favorable attitude toward the advertised product as a result of this. Seeing a commercial in which a senior citizen goes to work for McDonald's and proves that he can still make a contribution may or may not produce the above effect on product attitudes, but it has the potential to generate a great deal more affect. The latter case seems far more complex, in part because of the affective response, but also because of the difficulty in specifying the relationship between the resulting affective trace, relevant evaluative cognitions, and subsequent information-processing activities (e.g., inferential mechanisms, retrieval cues).

7.4. A framework for research on affect in consumer behavior

Overview

Although a great deal of research in consumer behavior touches upon affect, the term is used so broadly (and inconsistently) that researchers are often talking about very different things. In an attempt to bring some order to an otherwise largely disconnected literature, I have adopted the three-part framework shown in Figure 7.1. The figure assumes a flow from the manipulated or measured antecedent variables to the set of cognitive and behavioral consequences and provides illustrative lists of variables that have drawn research attention. Arrows are used to specify research paths that, in this view, encompass affect. Before these relationships are discussed, however, mention should be made of paths that, in the interest of simplicity, are not specified in the figure.

A great deal of research in marketing seeks to establish the equivalent of dose–response relationships between marketing stimuli and purchase behavior. This could be illustrated by a path directly from stimulus factors to behavior. Research that relates consumer characteristics (e.g., personality, product knowledge, purchase objectives) directly to behavior could be displayed in a similar fashion. Such research has been quite important for market segmentation purposes (Wilkie & Cohen, 1977; Wilkie, 1986, chapter 11).

In the remainder of the chapter we shall examine research that specifically focuses on cognitive structure/processes and that looks at affect in one of two ways: (1) as an evaluative cognition or component of attitude, or (2) as a valanced feeling state that generates affective traces. The first of these conceptualizations can be illustrated via a path from the set of antecedent variables to cognitive structure/processes on the outcome side; work of this type will be described next. Such research has been among the most prolific in the field of consumer behavior, and so rather than enumerate a long list of similar studies I have chosen instead to focus on particular exemplars of research that treats affect as an evaluative cognition.

The final section of the chapter looks at research that examines the

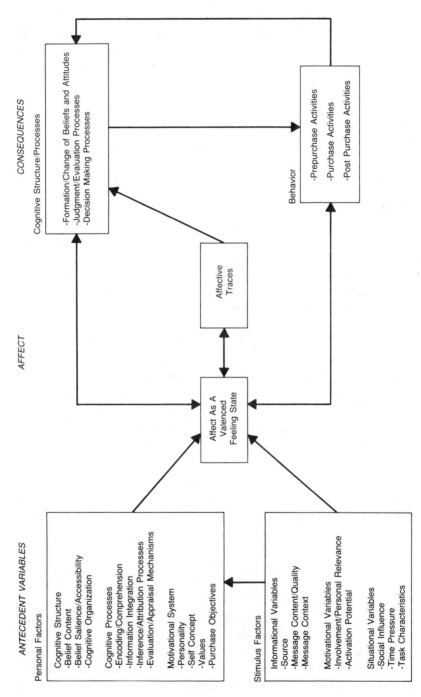

Figure 7.1 Research on affect in consumer behavior.

relationships identified in the figure. By and large this work is more recent, and it does not approach the previous research stream in quantity. Nor have all the relationships portrayed in the figure been examined. Relationships illustrated with bidirectional arrows are to be thought of as dynamic in that the potential for mutual influence over a short period of time is assumed to be high. Note that this conceptualization allows affective traces to be influenced directly only through affective states; however, these respond directly to all antecedent variables as well as cognitive and behavioral consequences. The latter variables are linked via a feedback loop so that, for example, behavior during the prepurchase stage can affect both cognitive structure and processes leading to subsequent behavior. Finally, while affective states can impact directly on both cognitive and behavioral outcomes, affective traces must first be interpreted by the cognitive system before they can influence subsequent behavior.[6]

Most of the attention to antecedent variables has been to situationally induced (usually by advertising) moods rather than more enduring motivational factors and stronger emotional states. In part this is due to the growing consensus about both the nature and the limits of advertising: There appear to be plenty of "warm" effects, but the ability of advertising to generate more intense drivelike states seems quite limited. The ability of purchase settings, consumption experiences, and want satisfaction episodes to influence affectively charged states is just beginning to come under systematic study. Relationships among affective states, affective traces, and subsequent cognitive elements and processes are as yet poorly understood. One example of an underresearched relationship is that between affective traces and subsequent behavior when the consumer comes into contact with the product (or perhaps with a brand or company name). To what extent, for example, is the probability of an impulse purchase or the intensity of immediate postpurchase enthusiasm enhanced by the incremental contribution of affect beyond that of favorable attitudes (Weinberg & Gottwald, 1982)? The ability of retrieval cues at the point of purchase to evoke originally associated feeling states and thereby increase the likelihood of a purchase is assumed by some practitioners, but empirical evidence is lacking. There is a greater measure of support for the ability of overall favorable affect to bias retrieval of favorable information about features (e.g., Isen, 1984b).

This section was intended to introduce the conceptual framework and to provide an overview of the kinds of research issues that are addressed in the field of consumer behavior when affect is treated as an evaluative cognition, on the one hand, and as a valenced feeling state, on the other. Now we will take a more systematic look at research of both types.

7.5. Affect as an evaluative cognition

As a rule studies in this category make no real distinction between affect and attitude, often using the terms interchangeably. The focus is on how brand, advertisement, or store evaluations are shaped by both within-consumer and external/marketplace factors and, in turn, are related to subsequent information processing and choice behavior.

An emphasis on cognitive structure

Consumer research during the 1970s was dominated by multi-attribute models of attitude. These models were used for predictive purposes, but more importantly for understanding the formation and change of brand attitudes and preferences. Fishbein's (1967) conceptualization provided the major theoretical rationale for the latter thrust, and in this context attitude and affect were treated as essentially equivalent. Lutz (1975) provides a classic example of research in this category. Attention is paid to external antecedent variables having both informationally and motivationally relevant aspects by identifying need-related product attributes and assessing their affective values (i.e., evaluative ratings). In separate studies Lutz manipulated belief content and attribute evaluations, via external communications, and tracked the impact of these manipulations on both cognitive structure and brand attitudes. A considerable amount of research during the period went into evaluating the adequacy of various multi-attribute models, particularly Fishbein's attitude and behavioral intention models (e.g., Wilkie & Pessemier, 1973; Mazis, Ahtola, & Klippel, 1975; Ryan & Bonfield, 1975; Lutz & Bettman, 1977; Burnkrant & Page, 1982; Miniard & Cohen, 1981; Ryan, 1982). In addition, the contribution to overall attitudes of such internal factors as confidence (Bennett & Harrell, 1975), the number and kinds of beliefs brought together in such a model (Oliver & Berger, 1979), and mechanisms of information integration (Bettman, Capon, & Lutz, 1975; Troutman & Shanteau, 1976) were explored in considerable depth. In keeping with recent interest in heuristic processes in reasoning and judgment, there has been some development of less mechanistic and analytical approaches to attitude formation and (to a lesser extent) change. One view is that people sometimes categorize and evaluate objects on the basis of overall similarity to previously evaluated instances.[7]

The impact of stimulus factors

Effects of a range of stimulus factors on attitudes have been studied, the majority dealing with informational stimuli important in advertising. Holbrook (1978) looked at the effects of a message content dimension termed "factualness/evaluativeness" (the first referring to some combination of content and presentation objectivity and the second to subjectivity) on subjects' beliefs about and reactions to the message as well as a scaled measure of affect (i.e., liking the product). Other message characteristics within the communication research tradition have come under close scrutiny (e.g., Sternthal & Craig, 1974; Brooker, 1971; Baker & Churchill, 1977; Atkin & Block, 1983; Golden, 1979; Gorn & Weinberg, 1984). Belch (1983), for example, examined modality (i.e., print vs. television) in the context of one- and two-sided advertising messages, using a number of belief items related to message acceptance as well as semantic differential types of attitude measures. Percy and Rossiter (1983) were among several groups of researchers to study characteristics of pictures in regard to the formation and change of beliefs and attitudes in advertising (e.g., Edell & Staelin, 1983; Childers & Houston, 1984). Operationalizing brand attitude on a variety of scales (e.g., socially acceptable-socially unacceptable, expensive-cheap) and affect using dimensions such as good-bad and unpleasant-pleasant, Percy and Rossiter examined such factors as color versus black and white and picture size in print advertising. Loken (1983) found that providing negative purchase information (e.g., about a store) might have little bearing on a consumer's attitude toward a product sold at the store, but it could have a substantial impact on one's attitude toward purchasing the product (i.e., Fishbein's A_{act}).

Attention to cognitive processes

One of the important developments in the attitude stream of research was the increased emphasis on information processing, per se, instead of exclusive concentration on measures of cognitive structure (and sometimes attempting to make inferences about aspects of the attitude formation/change process by relying entirely on input–output designs). Wright (1973), for example, utilized verbal protocols (assigning these to support argument, counterargument, or source derogation categories) to examine the relationship between cognitive responses to advertising and message acceptance. The latter was assessed both through beliefs about the advertising message and self-reports of how people "felt" about the product (along a degree-of-liking dimension). Both capacity for different types of cognitive responses and motivation were identified as important factors. The development of this so-called cognitive response paradigm (e.g., Calder, 1978; Wright, 1980; Belch, 1982) led to a richer conceptualization of the relationship between informational stimuli and overall attitudes. Olson et al. (1982) found that the three categories of cognitive responses mediated the effect of advertising content on the traditional measures of cognitive structure (i.e., brand beliefs, attitudes, purchase intentions), though it did not do so for all message execution effects. Establishing the appropriate cognitive response categories, developing noninvasive procedures to tap ongoing mental activity adequately, and determining the causal/temporal flow between message elements, preexisting beliefs, and cognitive responses were some issues that troubled researchers in this area. Interestingly, difficulties such as these proved to be a spur to the use of more sophisticated methods of identifying aspects of cognitive activity important to the study of consumer information processing and decision making (see Bettman, 1986; and Cohen & Chakravarti, 1990, for a more comprehensive review of consumer psychology).

Central and peripheral aspects of the stimulus

Research on consumers' cognitive responses to advertising combined with long-held views regarding the low-involvement nature of television advertising (Krugman, 1965; Ray, 1982) was also important in directing attention to nonproduct aspects of the message. This has led to the concept of "attitude toward the ad" and more generally to a more systematic study of central and peripheral factors in the formation and change of attitudes (e.g., Mitchell & Olson, 1981; Lutz et al., 1983; Gardner, 1985b; Mitchell, 1986; Petty et al., 1983; Chaiken, 1980). Mitchell & Olson (1981) were interested in whether the nonverbal content of advertising might have important effects on consumers' behavior that would not be mediated by the standard evaluative scales used to measure attitude toward the product. Specifically, in their study product-attribute beliefs (as part of a multi-attribute attitude model) failed to pick up a significant amount of variance that was captured by evaluative scales (e.g., good-bad, like-dislike) designed to measure attitude toward the advertisement itself (and that the authors attribute to "affect-laden" properties of the picture). Subsequent research indicates that the relationships among measures of product-attribute beliefs, overall attitude toward the product, and attitude toward the advertisement are more complex. Mitchell (1986) for example, found that pictures differing in their evaluative ratings (sunsets, wildcats, an aerial view of a closely cropped field) influenced both of these overall attitudes without seemingly working through the beliefs thought to underlie attitude toward the product (defined to be strictly aspects of the product itself). This crossover effect of advertising execution elements on brand attitudes is likely to be more substantial than a distraction/interference (Edell & Staelin, 1983) phenomenon; though a potential "reporting bias" (i.e., subjects restricting their reported evaluative product judgments to those based on product features because they believe this is what is intended) may be a serious source of confounding.

The research of Lutz et al., (1983) implicates the role of both prior product knowledge and involvement, suggesting that a broader consideration of advertising execution factors within the context of alternative routes to persuasion (Petty et al., 1983) may be most useful. The latter's "elaboration likelihood model" requires that both motivation and ability to process information content must achieve a requisite level in order for issue-relevant thinking to have a substantial impact on attitudes (the "central route" to persuasion). Any factors in the persuasion setting that reduce one's motivation or ability to engage in thoughtful evaluation of message content (e.g., low involvement, distraction, low prior knowledge) will reduce the likelihood that information contained in the message will be "elaborated." Therefore, more peripheral aspects of the message (i.e., cues regarding message quality, such as communicator characteristics, number of arguments, and affective responses to the message) should play a more significant role. This framework is consistent with a good deal of the attitude research carried out in social psychology (Petty & Cacioppo, 1981) and is proving to be quite useful in examining the relationships among important external factors (e.g., source, message, situational context), cognitive processes, and attitudes in consumer behavior (e.g., Yalch & Elmore-Yalch, 1984; Moore, Hausknecht, & Thamodaran, 1986).

Involvement-mediated consequences

As indicated above, the elaboration likelihood model assigns an important role to a motivational variable. This can be operationalized simply in terms of high- versus low-importance outcomes or personal relevance of a message; however, viewer involvement can be a far more complex variable (Greenwald & Leavitt, 1984; Mitchell, 1981; Cohen, 1983). To the extent involvement is conceived to be merely a surrogate for interest in a product or product importance, it reduces to a fairly straightforward individual difference factor similar to those used to delineate market segments. Within the consumer attitude tradition, segments have often been defined in terms of desired product attributes and benefits (e.g., Haley 1968, 1983; Calantone & Sawyer, 1978). "Highly involved" consumers, in this view, are such because they perceive that a given product provides a great number of important benefits. The marketer, having described the motivational system of the consumer in terms of relevant needs and wants, manipulates external factors (most importantly product characteristics, but also advertising appeals, price, service, etc.) to enhance the likelihood of a match to these needs and a resulting favorable attitude about (and ultimate purchase of) the product. Consumers are more likely to be attracted to informational stimuli that are consistent with their self-system, broadly defined, both in terms of content and execution.

Views of involvement that stress information-processing implications as a joint function of personal and stimulus factors, such as advertising content, execution, and placement, are more actively motivational (Greenwald & Leavitt, 1984; Burnkrant & Sawyer, 1983; Batra & Ray, 1983). Park and Young (1983) distinguished between cognitive and affective involvement, the former operationalized by directing attention to performance aspects of a shampoo being advertised and the latter by asking subjects to focus on "emotional" and self-image associations to the advertised product. A smaller proportion of the variance in attitude toward the brand was explained as a combined function of a brand-attribute–based model and attitude toward the ad under "affective involvement," leading the authors to suggest that the type of nonanalytical categorization process discussed by Cohen (1982) might be generating the favorable brand attitudes. Conceptualizing involvement as a state of activation having both direction and intensity (Mitchell, 1981; Cohen, 1983) is likely to implicate affective responses directly, bringing greater research attention to relationships involving affect as a valanced feeling state; but more will be said about this later.

Motivational factors

By and large research involving motivational variables and their effect on attitudes and behavior has proceeded from a rather static analysis of consumer needs and wants (as reflected in product attributes and benefits) to an examination of various attempts to link brands to consumer needs and wants or alter their importance or relevance. Nonproduct reinforcers (e.g., advertising execution variables, attitude toward the ad, store surroundings, product promotions) have been manipulated to see what impact they might have, either through product attitudes or directly, on behavior.[8]

On the consequences side of the figure, we see that postpurchase activities can involve both evaluative and affective factors. A reflection of the former is the literature dealing with the subject of consumer satisfaction/dissatisfaction. Oliver (1980) proposes a model of consumer satisfaction in which prepurchase expectations provide an adaptation level that is then compared to product experience to determine subsequent evaluations (and a revised adaptation level). There seems little doubt that satisfaction mediates revisions in both attitudes and behavior, though the extent of previous "loyalty" to the brand appears to moderate this effect (LaBarbera & Mazursky, 1983). Woodruff, Cadotte, and Jenkins (1983) have proposed modifications in the basic structure of the model to incorporate norms (for the class of products) rather than merely single brand expectations and to suggest the possibility of a true emotional response to outcomes that are considerably at variance with the norm (see Kahneman & Miller, 1986, for an insightful discussion of related issues).

Whereas any number of factors may produce increased liking for chosen products following purchase (e.g., favorable product performance, success in mastering more complex products, greater appreciation of attributes not easily observable prior to purchase), a true spread of attitudes involving both the chosen and unchosen brands may indicate the operation of "decision justification" processes (Cummings & Venkatesan, 1976; Cohen & Goldberg, 1970). Cohen and Moore (1988) differentiate between cognitive effects of selecting a particular product (e.g., inferential reasoning) and motivational effects (e.g., pressures toward cognitive consistency, defense of the self-concept). The latter are quite likely to involve affective states as well as subsequent cognitive processes.

Attitude–behavior relationships

A great deal of the research on consumer attitudes as evaluative cognitions has emphasized the role of attitudes in determining intentions to buy and ultimately leading to purchase behavior (e.g., Axelrod, 1968;

Shimp & Kavas, 1984) and has, since the mid-1970s, relied heavily on the work of Fishbein and Ajzen (1975). The early focus on attitude–behavior relationships has continued to flourish, with increasing interest both in what types of attitudes seem to be most predictive of subsequent behavior and in cognitive processes (e.g., organization and retrieval of information) that intervene subsequent to the formation or change of attitude. This research tradition appears to have been injected with renewed vigor with the publication of a number of influential papers in the social psychology literature (see especially Fazio & Zanna, 1981, and the edited collection by Zanna, Higgins, & Herman, 1982). Though it is possible to derive a number of research propositions from this work that highlight relationships conveyed in Figure 7.1, at least five are worth mentioning here.

Strength and salience of the attitude. Strong as opposed to weakly formed attitudes (e.g., those constructed on the spot) and attitudes that are likely to be salient at the time of behavior should have a greater impact on behavior. As for the strength of an attitude, those that serve more important needs and that are more central to the individual's values will have greater potential strength, though such strength may at times be inversely correlated with salience (i.e., "deeper" attitudes may be less salient).

Attitude relevance and implicativeness. If an attitude is highly relevant to the behavior, it should have a greater impact on the behavior than would other less relevant attitudes. Further, to the extent that an attitude directly implies engaging in one particular behavior rather than alternative behaviors, it is not only relevant but prescriptive.

Attitude conflict. To the extent that a behavior is multiply determined by a person's attitudes (e.g., more than one attitude is relevant), the less conflict there is among the behavioral implications of the set of attitudes the more likely one is to engage in a specific behavior. Note, however, that when little conflict exists among a set of attitudes, behavior is overdetermined, so predictions based upon an individual's standing on any one of the relevant attitudes may appear to be weak (i.e., people both high and low on that attitude engage in the behavior).

Attitude and situational conflict. To the extent that a behavior is multiply determined by a person's attitude and situational factors (e.g., it being culturally prescribed, subject to rewards or sanctions, constrained by conditions), the less conflict there is among the behavioral implications of the attitudinal and situational forces the more likely one is to engage in a specific behavior. Note again, however, that when little conflict exists, behavior is overdetermined, so predictions based upon an individual's score on some attitude scale may appear to be weak (i.e., most people will engage in the behavior regardless of their attitude score).

Internal structure of an attitude. A person's attitude toward an object is a function of the beliefs that become salient at a given time. Differential belief salience at two points in time can, therefore, cause attitude–behavior inconsistency. The likelihood of differential belief salience for a given person should be directly related to the unidimensionality of that person's attitude structure (see Schlegel & DiTecco, 1982). The more unidimensional one's attitude structure is, the less differentiated one's attitude is toward the object, and hence the less impact differential belief salience should have. Given consumer researchers' interest in multiattribute models as representations of product belief structure, one might anticipate a number of attempts to build indices of attribute dimentionality, possibly in relationship to variance accounted for in the overall attitude. The smaller the number of attributes needed to account for a criterion level of variance in attitude, the lower the dimensionality, and the less the potential effect of fluctuations in salience.

Attitude accessibility

Some research conducted in consumer behavior to explore factors likely to produce greater attitude accessibility (for example, direct personal experience with a product rather than learning about a product indirectly) is consistent with Fazio's model (see Fazio, 1986). Smith and Swinyard (1983), for example, observed that attitudes based on product trials were more predictive of subsequent behavior than were attitudes based on advertising. Whether accessibility will prove to be a sufficient explanation of such effects is a separate question. For one thing, a number of important factors tend to covary with accessibility (e.g., attitude content, polarity, certainty, internal consistency) and may be difficult to unconfound. More fundamentally, accessibility may itself prove to be an important by-product of more basic factors that affect attitude formation and internal organization (e.g., amount of exposure to information, opportunity to elaborate, personal involvement) and that are more deserving of center stage. Building on accessibility,

Kisielius and Sternthal (1986) present an "availability valence" explanation of a series of studies designed to explore differential picture word persuasiveness in advertising. In their view stimulus factors, such as vividness, by themselves cannot account for differences in attitudinal judgments since both positive valence of the information content and its accessibility at the time of judgment are necessary for favorable evaluations. A discussion of some implications of accessibility for consumer choice can be found in Biehal and Chakravarti (1983).

7.6. Affect as a valenced feeling state

We turn now to consumer research that examines affect as a valenced feeling state. The creation of affect has long been regarded as important to marketing success. Indeed, many accounts in the history of marketing and advertising's view of the consumer point out that as far back as the 1930s (based largely on psychoanalytic theories) emotional appeals became, "the order of the day, reflecting a new view of consumers as emotional beings" (Robertson, Zielinski & Ward, 1984, p. 13). The emotional appeal of various background factors of the purchase setting is frequently referred to in the marketing literature. For example, Kotler (1974) has advocated that considerable attention be paid to the ambient environment within which products are purchased in the conviction that variations in overall design and "atmospherics" can play a major role in shaping attitudes and behavior. Still, systematic research on the effects of feeling states (induced or otherwise) in consumer behavior was almost nonexistent until quite recently.

The in-store context

As indicated above, one external factor believed to have the ability to impact on both affective states and related evaluative outcomes is the context in which purchase decisions are made. Donovan and Rossiter (1982), using interviewers to assess the affective tone of a set of stores, found that they provided more favorable self-reported purchase intentions when they also rated the environment as both pleasant and arousing. As Gardner (1985a) points out, some bias may be created by obtaining both sets of subjective assessments from the same people. It would seem that shopping environments are a particularly fertile setting in which to study both mood/affect generation and its consequences. Gardner and Siomkos (1986) attempted to simulate store atmospherics using written descriptions high in both detail and evaluative tone (e.g., dirty, dingy) and then asked subjects to imagine either themselves or others in either a high- or low-image store. Store descriptions elicited consistent evaluative ratings. Hirschman and Holbrook (1982) raise the provocative notion of "hedonic consumption," according to which the goal of experiencing emotive stimulation becomes an important end state for consumers, quite apart from enjoyment of the product purchased. Thus, shopping environments that are made more enjoyable, exciting, and multi-sensory may not only become more desirable for their own sake but also inject positive affect into the product evaluation and decision-making process. Esthetic aspects of products, advertisements, and so on and sensory experience itself, with its varied emotional texture, are advocated topics for study. Research carried out in other contexts (e.g., Isen & Shalker, 1982; Isen, Means, Patrick & Nowicki, 1982; Carson & Adams, 1980) strongly implicates the moderating effect of similar states on expectations, judgments of risk, and evaluations.

In a recent study (Sherman & Smith, 1987), the moods of 89 shoppers at different clothing and specialty stores were assessed using the Mehrabian–Russell scale. Factor analysis identified three distinct factors – pleasure-displeasure, arousal/excitement, and alertness – that were significantly correlated with ratings of store image, number of items purchased, amount of money spent, and time spent shopping. Since the results are correlational we do not know to what extent mood "caused" such effects or, on the other hand, is a reflection of a favorable shopping experience. Nevertheless, the results are interesting and indicate that this is a potentially promising area for further research.

The precise effects of different affective tones and mechanisms of affect induction (e.g., background variables, store displays, salesperson's behavior) in shopping environments may have widely divergent consequences depending, in part, on the extent and nature of consumers' attributional processes. If, for example, consumers are well aware of the attempt and attribute it to a manipulative purpose, the outcome could well be the reverse of that intended. Ethical issues may be involved at the other end of the spectrum if, for example, as a result of background manipulations, consumers are induced to alter their deliberative processes, spend more money, and so on. There is almost no published research in consumer contexts to draw on in addressing these and related issues, but one exception is the work by Milliman (1982, 1986). In the first study, supermarket shoppers over a 2-month period were exposed to either no music, music at 60 beats per minute, or music at 108 beats per minute (with a wide variation of musical selections in each condition). All were played at the level of background music, and awareness was consistently low over treatments. However, walking speed was 17 percent faster with the fast music than it was with the slow (with no music shoppers midway between these speeds), and the slower walkers spent about 38 percent more money! Milliman (1986) also found that playing slow-tempo background music in a restaurant led customers to stay longer and consume more alcoholic beverages. They did not consume more food, possibly because after the food order had been taken people did not wish to violate social norms by either changing their orders or eating food served to others!

Defining impulse buying in terms of a combination of a high level of activation, a low level of intellectual control, and largely automatic behavior actuated by the situation, Weinberg and Gottwald (1982) obtained a nonreactive record of mimical expressions as well as a subsequent self-report of emotional content, strength, and direction on the part of consumers secretly filmed as they were shopping for decals. These filmed sequences of 15 selected buyers and nonbuyers (who subsequently gave their consent for the filming and were interviewed) were shown to 35 subjects who were uninformed as to whether or not a purchase had been made by each. Emotional qualities (e.g., surprise, boredom, anger, enthusiasm, doubt) together with strength (e.g., stimulating, exciting) and direction (e.g., pleasant, inspiring) were assessed by both observers and participants using scale items, and a comparable factor structure emerged. The buyers assessed themselves as more amused, delighted, and enthusiastic than nonbuyers and as less astonished and indifferent; in general the naive observers agreed with these assessments. With regard to activation, the authors concluded, on the basis of both self-assessments and observed behavior, that the buyers were significantly more emotional. Linking these results to impulsive behavior, however is problematic since the relationship between particular scale items and the concept of impulsiveness per se is not particularly clear. In addition, the study does not allow us to determine when these emotional states were experienced, and many of the results are consistent with postpurchase emotions.

Gardner (1985a) speculates that despite the well-documented and consistent general effects of positive mood, particularly when combined with moderate arousal, such effects should not dominate either when they are inconsistent with objective features of the context (i.e., little ambiguity is present) or when situational factors stress the importance of objectivity and precision. While this may be a very reasonable position to take at this time, it is not sufficiently grounded in directly applicable evidence (i.e., with respect to both the typicality of the above description of the setting and the outcomes). A consumer survey by Westbrook (1980) examines the moderating role of both generalized attitudes (e.g., overall life satisfaction, optimism) and transient affective states (e.g., elation–depression) coincident with product experience on ratings of product satisfaction. Some support for the role of the former (but not the latter) factors was obtained.

Affective responses to advertising

The most frequently studied of the external factors thought to affect the consumer's cognitive and motivational systems is, of course, advertising. In this research domain affective feeling states are thought to result from both the advertisement (i.e., its appeal and execution) and the program context (e.g., television program, magazine) in which it is embedded. The consumer's cognitive structure and the degree to which the advertisement matches prior expectations together may play an important role in determining affective response. Little work has been done to examine the impact of departures from expectations in this context, although the notion of an "optimum stimulation level" (Raju, 1980) had been suggested. Zinkhan and Martin (1983) assessed consumers' cognitive complexity with respect to calculators and exposed them to ads differing in the clarity of their internal structure (as assessed by individuals' ability to provide deleted words). Using self-report scales to tap "affective response" (e.g., enjoyment, likeability) the authors found that the more cognitively complex the viewer was the more the complex ad was preferred (i.e., the content of the ad would then appear to become more predictable). They suggest that the advice often given to "keep it simple" in advertising might not always be sound.

Program context. Affective responses to the advertisement are also a function of the affective state consumers bring into the situation and the expectations and predispositions that are likely to play some role in their comprehending and interpreting the advertising. A survey study by Schultz (1979) involving the marketing managers and media directors of leading advertising companies and agencies suggests that such context effects are of growing concern to practitioners. Conventional wisdom suggests that both the affect induced by the program context and its consistency with the affective tone of the advertisement should be important, but this has been a matter of some disagreement within advertising circles (e.g., Yuspeh, 1979). Many practitioners are leery of programmatic material that is too arousing, that would create negative feelings or outlooks, or that would encourage too critical a response orientation. Instead they would rather have consumers feeling generally positive, both about themselves and others.

An early and frequently cited study by Axelrod (1963) supports this point of view, though the programmatic material (documentary footage of Nazi war crimes) is certainly stronger stuff than most advertisers would use. The film was successful in inducing the expected mood, and it also influenced viewers' beliefs that the use of various products would prompt a similar affective state (e.g., depression), thus leading attitudes toward the products to shift in a consistent manner. Whether such product beliefs generally would be formed (i.e., in the absence of an attempt to assess them) while the consumers were in such a strong affective state is very much an open question.

More recently, Goldberg and Gorn (1987) manipulated program valence (happy vs. sad) and type of appeal (informational vs. emotional) by pretesting actual broadcast ads and program segments. The ads were then embedded within each program to resemble real commercial spots. It was hypothesized that the affective context generated by the programs would influence subjects' (1) ratings of product effectiveness, (2) purchase intentions, (3) recall, and (4) cognitive responses in an affect-congruent direction through processes described by Isen (1984b). These effects were postulated to be more pronounced for emotional ads. Although the hypothesized interaction was not observed, significant program effects were obtained for the perceived effectiveness and cognitive response measures. A subsequent experiment demonstrated superior recall for subjects in the happy program condition.

Singh and Churchill (1987) provide a general theoretical interpretation of context effects with their "excitation transfer" explanation. Here, arousal (defined as energy that enhances psychological and motor activity), is implicated as a mediating variable. The excitation transfer hypothesis centers on Schachter and Singer's (1962) notion of the misattribution of arousal, by which individuals are thought to misattribute the arousal generated by television programming to the embedded advertisements, thus producing attitudinal effects. Although this interpretation has some general intuitive appeal, the conditions that would lead people to misattribute such arousal are not obvious, and the relevance of this explanation for advertising context effects needs to be established.

Getting through versus being liked. Robertson et al. (1984, p. 229) report that advertisers, in general, operate with two conflicting theories about the affective aspects of messages. The first, which they term the "law of extremes," is that whether consumers like or dislike an advertisement is less important than the intensity with which they perceive it. In the second, the "superiority of the pleasant" view, pleasant stimuli are thought to be more effective than unpleasant stimuli. The latter hypothesis is loosely modeled after various conditioning principles; the former takes particular account of the importance of getting through the clutter of competing advertisements and registering the strongest possible associations between the product category and a brand's name and key features (some support for this view can be found in a study by Silk & Vavra, 1974). There is also some belief that the affective tone of the message and the content of the message may become disassociated in consumers' minds with the passage of time (a type of "sleeper effect"; see Moore & Hutchinson, 1985, for a particularly relevant discussion). It is conceivable, in addition, that certain negative affective states (whether created by elements of the message or the surrounding context) may, if they are not overly threatening, promote greater attention to and interest in the product (e.g., fear- and anxiety-based increases in sensitivity to the problem the product is attempting to remedy). More generally, however, advertisers seek to create positive moods that they hope will somehow rub off onto their products and either persist until purchase or be reintroduced by similar cues at the point of purchase (Shimp, 1981).

Affect and attitude toward the ad. Increasingly, models offered to explain this effect have involved affective as well as cognitive responses to the ad. Lutz (1988) offers a conceptualization in which a consumer's attitude toward the ad is seen as a consequence of both cognitive and affective antecedents. Attitude toward the ad is defined in predispositional terms as "an affective reaction to the ad generated at the time of exposure." Indeed, Lutz argues that a strong attitude toward the ad, although situationally bound, can have not only a direct effect on immediate consumer responses (e.g., toward the brand advertised) but a continuing indirect effect on the consumer's behavior. Cognitive antecedents of attitude toward the ad include perceived credibility, beliefs regarding advertising execution (along dimensions such as informativeness,

entertainment, and vigor), and more general attitudes toward the advertiser and advertising. Affect enters the model separately, primarily as a
result of the consumer's mood at the time of exposure. This is further
thought to result from both personal factors and the context into which
the ad has been placed (e.g., program material, number of ads presented). Lutz's analysis treats mood as a largely peripheral factor within
the framework of the elaboration likelihood model. In this view the
transfer of affect from the advertisement to the product is most likely
when the consumer's involvement is low and little cognitive capacity is
being directed to the ad. Though this is an intriguing conceptualization,
and it has the decided virtue of directly addressing the role of affect
apart from evaluation, it may be too restrictive in relegating affect to
low-involvement status. Even executional aspects of ads may generate
considerable attention and affect, and we simply know very little about
the fate of the affective traces from that point on. The thorny issue of
exactly how affect transfers from the ad to the brand will no doubt
plague the field for some time.

Affect and classical conditioning

One explanation for this type of affect transfer has been classical conditioning (McSweeney & Bierley, 1984; Gresham & Shimp, 1985; Kroeber-Riel, 1984b). The general acceptance of the idea that classical conditioning is responsible for many such effects in advertising is well
documented by Allen and Madden (1985). Careful research on the
nature of this process within the advertising context has only recently
begun to appear in the literature, although higher-order classical conditioning of both evaluative meaning and affect has been studied for
some time in the attitude research area (e.g., Zanna, Kiesler, & Pilkonis,
1970). One problem has always been the difficulty of ruling out an
"experimenter demand" interpretation of the results both because the
hypothesis under study is frequently easy to grasp and because subjects
may understand that it is their task to comply with these expectations.
Indeed, in some studies only subjects who are aware of both the contingencies and the demands show evidence of conditioning. Procedures
used by Zanna et al., however, appear to overcome some of the usual
criticisms and demonstrate not only heightened arousal and altered
evaluations of the conditioned words but also generalization to semantically related words. Yet demonstrating that this is truly an automatic
and unconscious process presents vast difficulties.

Gorn (1982) has done much to spark interest in classical conditioning in consumer behavior. By pairing slides of one of two colors of the same pen with either liked or disliked music (ostensibly to be used in a commercial for a pen) he found that subjects' pen preferences – indeed choices – could be influenced. Further, this conditioning effect required only one trial, a fact that has led some to question whether or not classical conditioning was responsible for the effect (even with a strong unconditioned stimulus a number of trials are often needed). Bierley, McSweeney, and Vannieuwkerk (1985) also argue that a "true" classical conditioning procedure must establish that increased familiarity coupled with contiguity of stimuli does not produce the effect: Rather, subjects exposed to the conditioned stimulus (e.g., the pen) followed by the unconditioned stimulus (e.g., the music) should demonstrate superiority over subjects who are presented the two stimuli randomly in time. The established "predictiveness" of the conditioned stimulus, in this view, is necessary to differentiate classical conditioning from simpler familiarity effects (McSweeney & Bierley, 1984). Gorn believes that his use of disliked music (in one condition) provides a sufficient check on the possibility that familiarity might have been responsible for the effect on subjects' pen choices.

Replicating Gorn's use of colors and music, Bierley, et al. (1985) used a predictiveness design (with a random-order control group) in which each noncontrol subject was exposed to a set of 84 red, blue, and yellow geometric figures, each followed or not by music from the movie *Star Wars*. (For red predictiveness subjects, every red figure was followed by music, half of the blue figures were followed by music, and yellow figures were never followed by music.) Instructions to subjects included, it should be noted, asking them to attempt to predict the onset of music. After separating out basic color preference differences, reliable but small combined conditioning effects were found in subjects' ratings of the set of conditioned stimuli (in the above case, excitatory/positive for red and inhibitory/negative for yellow). A very weak generalization effect to new geometric forms of the same colors was observed. In general, though, the results were somewhat discouraging in their applicability to the noisy reality of advertising since 28 consecutive predictive trials were needed to establish even a weak effect. The authors note, however, that only mild affect may have been produced by the unconditioned stimulus, severely limiting the strength of the conditioning. Finally, though the authors made some attempt to rule out an awareness demand explanation (by asking subjects about the basis for their music predictions and their understanding of the purpose of the experiment), they unnecessarily complicated this issue by, in fact, making subjects aware of the predictive link between the slides and the music. Level of awareness, adequacy of awareness assessment procedures, and potential self-report biases, therefore, are troublesome issues for this study.

Allen and Madden's (1985) careful review of this topic leads them to regard the conditioning of evaluative meaning as quite different from the conditioning of affect. The latter, they also argue, may be less susceptible to criticism on "awareness" grounds since "as the cognitive complexity of the conditioned response increases, one might anticipate more confounding from conscious, deliberate mental processes" (p. 303). In a partial replication and extension of Gorn's (1982) study, Allen and Madden exposed subjects to humorous program segments that had received widely divergent ratings on a set of evaluative scales while they were viewing a slide for one of two pens differing only in color. In what was described as a test of different "styles of humor" being considered for a radio advertising campaign for the pen, subjects next rated the comic material (just as Gorn's subjects evaluated the music), provided a retrospective thought listing, and then were encouraged to take one pen from a box filled with a mixture of both colors (recorded after subjects left the room). Whereas Gorn's subjects had been run in large groups, and hence choices made were visible to other subjects, Allen and Madden processed their subjects individually to minimize the possibility of social influence. Allen and Madden's subjects did not display the anticipated conditioning effect: Roughly two-thirds picked the color pen displayed on the slide regardless of whether it was paired with the pleasant or unpleasant comic material. The data suggest, however, that the manipulation designed to create an unpleasant program segment was not successful. Further, the stimuli may well vary along other dimensions that produce unwanted effects.

In a series of four experiments, Stuart, Shimp, and Engle (1987) present the most comprehensive investigation of classical conditioning yet carried out using advertising stimuli. Their research employs sophisticated control procedures (i.e., random presentation and conditioned-stimulus-only control groups) in an effort to rule out "mere exposure" effects (Zajonc, 1980) and to assess the effects of forward, simultaneous, and backward pairing of the unconditioned and conditioned stimuli. The stimuli were slides of fictitious brands for various products (CS) and slides of outdoor scenes (US) determined to be affectively positive or neutral in pretests. The number of learning trials was manipulated at 1, 3, 10, and 20. Significant conditioning effects were obtained for various attitudinal measures in all contiguous conditions, but there was only a slight (and nonsignificant) enhancement as a function of the number of trials. The implication was that a substantial amount of conditioning occurred after just one trial. The authors demonstrate latent inhibition by producing more modest conditioning effects when the conditioned stimulus was presented alone several times before the conditioning trials began and backward conditioning by yielding small but significant effects when the conditioned stimulus followed the unconditioned stimulus in the trials.

In evaluating this study, one must be concerned, as always, with possible demand effects. Although the authors combined filler trials involving dummy brands and affectively neutral outdoor slides with irrelevant questionnaire items to alleviate such influences, their direct assessment of these effects involved only an open-ended questionnnaire item asking subjects what they thought the experiment was about. Though 48 percent of the subjects seemed generally aware of the CS–US contingency, an analysis of the data for the remaining subjects continued to support the hypotheses, and an analysis of variance using awareness as a factor suggested that it played only a minor role. However, the depth of the awareness probe can be questioned. Such concerns point to a need for the development of a middle-range awareness assessment tool for future research.

Allen and Janiszewski (1989) focus specifically on awareness as a causal factor in the conditioning process. They also wished to impede hypothesis guessing while adhering to recognized conditioning principles. The latter objective was achieved through an ingenious paradigm influenced by the work of McSweeney and Bierley (1984). The cover story described the experiment as an attempt to identify the kinds of foreign words susceptible to "spurious meaning development." Subjects played a game that involved the unscrambling of a series of letters to determine if previously learned Norwegian words could be spelled from them. This task was made virtually impossible by the restriction of exposure to the letter string to 3 seconds. Following a manipulation employed by Isen, Shalker, Clark, and Karp (1978), differential success rates (US) accompanied each word (CS). The success rate of each word differed between groups, allowing for both a within- and between-groups test for conditioning effects. The dependent measures of interest were word evaluations and ratings of the word as a cologne brand name.

Contingency and demand (i.e., hypothesis) awareness were assessed through a battery of 10 questions, ranging from an open-ended item to an item that stated the hypothesis interrogatively and asked for a yes/no response. Even when subjects coded as being "demand aware" were removed from the analysis, the results supported a conditioning hypothesis. Further evidence against a demand explanation is found in the result that the trials produced an effect only for the word evaluation measures. One would expect hypothesis guessers to show an effect for brand name ratings also. Perhaps even more interesting is the finding that no effects were obtained for subjects classified as being completely unaware. This suggests that contingency awareness may play a critical role in the conditioning process.

A second experiment was conducted to provide stronger evidence for contingency awareness as a causal factor. Here contingency and demand awareness were manipulated experimentally through pretrial instructions to subjects. The 10-question assessment tool provided evidence that these manipulations were successful. The results were exactly as expected. Subjects in the unaware (no directions) condition exhibited no conditioning effect for either dependent variable; those in the contingent aware condition exhibited conditioning effects only for the word evaluations, and the demand aware subjects showed conditioning effects for both word evaluations and brand name ratings. This study thus provides strong evidence for contingency awareness as a causal factor in the conditioning process.

Gorn (1982) had also investigated the moderating effects of purchase involvement by having half of his subjects in a second experiment devote thought to a choice between a three-pen packet (displayed in conjunction with the well-liked music) and its differently colored equivalent (for which a planned informational commercial was described). After a delay of an hour, all subjects were allowed to choose a pen, and a strong reversal was obtained: Subjects selected the pen for which product information was presented when choice was salient at the time of exposure but selected the pen associated with well-liked music in the nonchoice condition. Allen and Madden (1985) chose to examine the issue of active cognitive evaluation through the use of a postchoice buy-back measure in which subjects were offered the option to sell the pen back ("Our sponsor would also like to get some idea of what you think a pen like this is worth"). Somewhat surprisingly (given their weak choice results) subjects in the pleasant humor condition *were* less inclined to sell the pens back. A conditioning explanation for this in the absence of an effect on choice is problematic. The authors speculate that subjects placed into a pleasant mood might generate more positive thoughts about the pens, making them more resistant to a buy-back attempt, but given the lack of such an effect on choice, why this should occur is not obvious.

The classical conditioning explanation for the transfer of affect from some aspect of an advertisement to a product, at this juncture at least, faces some formidable obstacles. Applying the underlying process to domains this far beyond the traditionally studied autonomic and skeletal nervous systems has proved troublesome. Nonautomatic and conscious mechanisms may well be implicated despite every methodological precaution. If one departs from a rigorous theoretical treatment of conditioning to deal with the complex advertising domain (e.g., nonneutral and informationally rich products as conditioned stimuli, informationally and affectively complex unconditioned stimuli), one may merely be proposing basic association concepts. Rossiter and Percy (1980), for example, had earlier sought to conceptualize any increase in evaluation of a product as an outcome of associating unconditioned (i.e., favorably regarded) product attributes as well as visual and auditory imagery with it, thus leading to a positive emotional response to the product.

Allen and Madden (1985) recommend further research on two competing positions, affective conditioning and mood. The former is assumed to operate by a "direct or noncognitively mediated transfer of pleasant (or unpleasant) feelings" (p. 312) from the advertisement to the brand and the latter through "prompting and biasing cognitive activity" rather than some automatic transfer of affect. Although the first position does not appear to contain a compelling explanation of the process, it seems to be equated with the operational stricture of finding no evidence of cognitive mediation. This is a subtle point as cognitive mediation may occur at different stages: first, awareness of the unconditioned stimulus and, second, linking the unconditioned stimulus to the conditioned stimulus (see Allen and Janiszewski, 1989).[9] The authors go on to suggest that these two processes might be unravelled through the use of noncognitive measures (e.g., choice, amount consumed). Although such measures may be useful in reducing demand-like effects (depending on the study's design), the processes producing overt behavior of this type cannot be assumed to be carried out in the absence of considerable cognitive activity, as the authors suggest, unless there is literally nothing to be learned, no other connections to be strengthened, and no inferences to be drawn from increasing familiarity (see, for example,

Alba & Marmorstein, 1987). Some of the cognitive activity involved in both conditioning and mood explanations appears to be preattentive and nondeliberative (e.g., hypothesized "automatic" biasing effects of positive mood; see Isen, 1984a.). The point at which the cognitive and noncognitive distinction is to be drawn seems, at this stage at least, to be more a matter of judgment than something more conceptually rigorous.

We have, it seems, almost returned to the point at which we began in attempting to understand the affect transfer process. The phenomenon has virtually become its own explanation. Allen and Madden (1985) may, however, be on the right track in thinking that we should approach the problem by delineating possible mechanisms (i.e., antecedent variables, processes) leading to affect formation and to subsequent evaluatively based judgments and behavior. Adopting a pluralistic orientation in order to reduce unexplained variation at the level of the phenomenon may be the best way to attack the problem. Learning more about each mechanism (i.e., when it occurs, its limits) is something we can do, and if some are more difficult than others to tie down it may still not mean that the account is wrong.

Repeated exposure

Though there has been almost no hard evidence brought to bear on this issue in consumer behavior, a number of papers have dealt with the possibility that affect as well as positive or negative evaluations may simply arise out of repeated exposures to products and advertising.[10] In their *Journal of Consumer Research* paper, Zajonc and Markus (1982) distinguish between preferences as combined utilities (resulting from components or features of products) and preferences resulting from "affective supports," which appear to include such things as parental reinforcement and social identification. In the latter case, so argue Zajonc and Markus, not only affective reactions but also preferences may precede cognitive appraisal. With respect to how these terms are used in consumer behavior, the general view would probably be that preferences go beyond mere liking for a product and are not precognitive, since they imply a type of comparison process related either to some criterion or other products or both. Obermiller (1985), manipulating the number of exposures to melodies, reports no evidence for the notion that affective responses occurred independently of cognitive mediation. Evaluation, using bipolar adjective scales, constituted the key dependent measure. Repeated exposures, he argues, may reduce uncertainty as well as provide additional opportunities for the development of positive associations. As noted in a comment to Zajonc and Markus (1982), the precise point at which cognition enters the picture in any affective process depends to a considerable extent on what one includes in a definition of cognition (Tsal, 1985). The position adopted in this chapter is consistent with Tsal's view: The generation of an affective trace is often an unconscious process resulting from some motivational or mood state (of which we may be aware), and the attribution of such affect or its trace to a causal agent or property of a stimulus is a secondary process (see also the discussions in Allen & Madden, 1985, and Allen & Janiszewski, 1989). We would add that the latter process belongs to the domain of evaluative judgment. Though there is much seeming controversy here, modifying Zajonc and Markus's discussion to suggest that affective reactions and their subsequent cognitive traces may arise out of somewhat different but largely nonconscious and nondeliberative processes may provide a basis for more widespread agreement (Cohen & Basu, 1987).

Assessing affective responses to advertising

Research to identify factors that contribute to the formation of favorable affective states toward products (rather than mere favorable attitudes) is just beginning to emerge as a solid research stream. Over the years, there have been a number of attempts to simply measure emotional reactions, particularly to advertising, using various self-report techniques (e.g., Leavitt, 1970; Schlinger, 1979; Moore & Hutchinson, 1983; Batra & Ray, 1986). Advertising agencies have relied on the types of measures exemplified by the Viewer Response Profile (Schlinger, 1979; see also Aaker & Bruzzone, 1981). In the development of this type of instrument, a large number of statements from people who have been exposed to various television commercials were accumulated and then reduced (e.g., using factor analysis) to underlying response themes. Many of these recurrent themes have emotional content and are used to construct self-report scale items to be used in assessing subsequent commercials. For example, Gresham and Shimp (1985) measured emotional responses to advertisements using seven item dimensions (e.g., happy, affectionate, sad). Retrospective response protocols have become popular in this tradition as a way of overcoming the intrusiveness and reactivity thought to be associated with concurrent protocols (either written or verbal). Hill and Mazis (1986), for example, exposed subjects to either emotional or factual advertising inserted during breaks in a television movie. They attempted to match two versions of three commercials on length and other aspects. After the commercials were viewed, written protocols were obtained and coded into several categories including positive affect (e.g., feeling good) and negative affect (e.g., feeling angry). In addition, subjects rated each commercial using 45 adjectives taken from Leavitt's (1970) factor analysis of responses to television commercials (e.g., amusing, sensual, dislike). The authors found that emotional advertisements produced more affective comments, but no clear pattern emerged in counterarguments or source-bolstering statements. Whereas scales used to report overall evaluation of the ads (e.g., good-bad, like-dislike) did not discriminate between the factual and emotional ads, the execution-related adjectives (e.g., sensual, energetic) did somewhat better. Individual differences in execution almost certainly differ so widely that the two categories used (i.e., factual and emotional) are far too broad.

Batra and Ray (1986) distinguish between affective and cognitive responses to advertising on the basis that the former are not evaluative but reflect advertising-evoked moods and feelings. They review previous work on affect typologies and develop a nine-category coding scheme for cognitive responses, six of which are primarily cognitive (e.g., support arguments, execution discounting) and three of which are considered affective response categories: surgency/elation; deactivation (e.g., soothing, relaxing); social affection (e.g., warm, tender). After exposing subjects to a variety of affective and rational ad executions under conditions designed to produce high variance (e.g., involvement level, prior knowledge, response opportunity), the authors encouraged self-reports of both thoughts and feelings (not "play back" but such things as statements about agreement-disagreement, what the ad reminded them of, how it made them feel). Satisfactory interjudge agreement in coding was obtained, and roughly 12 percent of the responses were placed into one of the three affective categories. There was a significant, though small, incremental impact of these responses in predicting attitudes toward the ad. The authors also suggest that the process their measures allow them to study is apparently quite open to conscious awareness, and therefore, is different from the affect transfer mechanisms thought to be linked to classical conditioning.

Holbrook and Batra (1987) examine the manner in which intervening emotional reactions mediate the relationship between advertising content and attitudes toward the ad or brand. Each set of variables (e.g., advertising content, emotional reactions) was determined by judges' ratings of each ad along selected inventories of items (i.e., 66 advertising content items and 94 items representing 29 emotional indexes). A separate set of judges was used to rate the ads on each set of variables. Principal component analysis with a varimax rotation reduced the 66 ad content items to emotional, threatening, mundane, sexy, cerebral, and personal dimensions. The 93 emotional response items were reduced to pleasure, arousal, and domination dimensions. These latter three dimensions are consistent with previous taxonomies of emotion (Mehrabian & Russell, 1974; Russell, 1978, 1980). Interjudge reliability for the emotional response ratings was quite low (.52), suggesting that conceiving emotional responses to be invariant properties of the stimulus may be inappropriate. Many individual content dimensions seemed to be correlated with their emotional dimension counterparts. The causal flow of the model through attitude toward the ad was generally supported, with the emotional dimensions mediating the effect of the content dimensions. The relationship of these variables to attitude toward the brand seems somewhat more complex.

Edell and Burke (1987) distinguish between the way consumers describe an ad and the feelings that the ad generates in them. They build upon the Puto and Wells (1984) characterization of ads as being informational or transformational. Ads defined as being in the latter category connect the experience of the ad so tightly to the brand that feelings evoked by the ad invariably come to mind when the brand is considered. Feelings, then, were hypothesized to be more important (relative to semantic judgments) for ads that were high in transformation (as opposed to information). A 69-item inventory of feelings was factor analyzed to form scales described as upbeat feelings, negative feelings, and warm feelings. When combined with three semantic judgment scales (evaluation, activity, gentleness) in a regression, feelings were found to contribute significantly to predictions of both attitude toward the ad and attitude toward the brand, though no consistent results were obtained for the two different types of ads (i.e., transformational and informational). A second study again demonstrated that the self-rated feelings/reactions to the ad contributed significantly to relevant attitudes and judgments about the ad and brand when these were unfamiliar to subjects. One can, of course, question whether the gain in prediction came about because of the addition of a separate class of variables (i.e., feelings) or, more simply, a set of different dimensions of judgment.

As one might imagine, therefore, there is far from a consensus that verbal protocols (and the instructional sets used to gather them), scaled self-reports, and the like represent an adequate system of measurement for affective responses. At a theoretical level, it is not clear that these measures successfully isolate affect from evaluation and inference processes. At a more applied level, one concern is that, being essentially cognitive, these measurement approaches may fail to tap more immediate and transitory, as well as less easily verbalizable, feeling states. A second concern is that they might not be sufficiently diagnostic, representing more a summary report of feelings than a device to pinpoint affect generation and relate it back to executional and content elements. As Aaker, Stayman, and Hagerty (1986) point out, however, physiological measures not only are difficult to administer but cannot be easily linked to specific feeling states (and they may not tap "warm," mood-like states as successfully as "hot," emotional responses). Several concurrent dial-turning methodologies have been employed in advertising research, and although these have the advantage of more precise tracking of the onset of feeling states, they have had only a bidirectional orientation (i.e., positive-negative) and may also confound feeling and evaluation. Aaker et al. (1986) have developed a "warmth monitor," essentially a paper and pencil instrument in which respondents move down the paper at a constant rate of speed while viewing a commercial and indicate the absence of warmth by moving the pencil to the left and progressively greater warmth (i.e., warmhearted/tender, emotional/moist eyes) by moving it to the right. Some evidence for the reliability and convergent validity of the instrument (with respect to postexposure scale ratings) was obtained. In addition, subjects viewing several commercials produced warmth monitor scores that were significantly correlated with a standard measure of skin resistance for ads judged by a different sample to be warm but not for ads judged to be humorous, informative, or irritating (although some evidence that subjects may tend to assign higher warmth monitor scores to more generally positive executions was obtained in a subsequent study). Trends both between ads (of same vs. different warmth) and within ads (of varying warmth segments) were generally consistent with predictions (including contrast and adaptation effects), and warmth monitor scores were also correlated with attitude toward the ad and purchase likelihood. The authors suggest that similar instruments might be developed to tap other feeling states, although the methodology seems to be limited to one dimension at a time.

In general, the measurement difficulties involved in assessing feeling states are extreme. Neither an adequate taxonomy nor an adequate understanding of the relationships among moods, emotions, arousal, and generalized affect can be said to exist. This is further complicated by the differing levels of analysis (i.e., physiological to attributional) at which research on these constructs is being conducted. There may also be important effects of more diffuse feeling states that are at a reduced level of awareness and for which no target (or causal agent) is clearly perceived. Finally, the proverbial chicken and egg problem is likely to plague this measurement area for a long time, since it is almost impossible to separate out initial affective responses from more cognitively determined ones in the effort to explain higher-order cognitive outcomes (c.f. Coyne, 1982).

At a conceptual level, Hoffman (1986) makes a useful distinction between a temporal view of affective processes and a view that stresses primacy (i.e., strength) of impact. Though direct affective responses to physical/sensory aspects of a stimulus are likely to be primary in the sense of generating an initial response (and possibly biasing later responses), subsequent affective responses to the meaning of a stimulus (particularly as the outcome of comparative and appraisal processes involving the self-system) are likely to modify earlier responses and have greater impact. Although some consumer contexts may exert an impact at a more direct, almost sensory level (e.g., shopping environments), the large majority of controlling affective responses are likely to be more accessible (and measurable) – indeed, more cognitively implicated. This does not mean, however, that their status is "reduced" to that of evaluative cognitions, since they may well retain affective properties that can impact on a range of cognitive and behavioral outcomes.

Thinking versus emotional advertising

Friestad and Thorson (1986), in addressing this distinction, produced both long-term memory and positive evaluative effects through a one-time exposure to emotional ads. The authors define an emotional message as "a vehicle that creates over-time flow of feelings that people report as emotional experience" (p. 111). This is a departure from earlier definitions that emphasized either the type of information/appeal being used, the viewer's mood, or judgments of liking for the ad. A key premise of the authors' approach is that an experience that occurs in the presence of emotional arousal leaves much stronger episodic traces that may or may not become integrated into product-related semantic memory. Such integration is much more likely under higher involvement, personal relevance, and "on-line" (i.e., same time) judgment conditions. Subjects either were instructed to watch and evaluate promotional messages as to personal relevance (in the semantic processing condition) or were simply asked to watch the material carefully (episodic conditions). They were each exposed to five emotional and five neutral commercials embedded in several program segments. Two months later subjects were telephoned, and the emotional messages generated a higher level of free recall (number of messages, brand names, executional elements), with episodic instructions providing a weak but consistent advantage. In contrast to Golden and Johnson (1983), who found that emotional ads in four product categories were not as well liked as ads relying on objective (i.e., "thinking") appeals, the emotional messages were significantly better liked and had a higher perceived influence. (Golden and Johnson's [1983] emotional ads tended to rely on music and dramatic display to create a mood, and hence may have been different in several respects.)

While Friestad and Thorson acknowledge the difficulty of establishing the equivalence of emotional and neutral messages on other dimensions that could make the latter less accessible, more work needs to be done on this if we are to understand better the process that is producing these effects. For example, is the emotional aspect more responsible for the recall differences than the potentially greater distinctiveness of those messages? Also, while episodic and semantic memory differences may be involved, the semantic memory instructions introduced an additional task that may have drawn subjects' attention away from the message elements themselves and toward an evaluation of them. Nevertheless, the conceptualization and results are very interesting and provide a strong challenge to the conventional wisdom that "feeling" ads are likely to fare badly in recall tests (the standard of the copy-testing industry being day-after recall), possibily because "thinking" ads and recall may both emphasize left-brain activity (Zielski, 1982; Puto & Wells, 1984).

With respect to the kinds of external, stimulus properties likely to generate an affective response, we have seen that emotional ads often give a dominant role to music and pictures (e.g., Kroeber-Riel, 1984a; Mitchell, 1986). In the Puto and Wells (1984) twofold classification system, informational ads are perceived to present factual, relevant information in a verifiable format. Transformational advertising, on the other hand, associates the experience of using the product with a unique set of psychological charcteristics. Thus, the experience of using the product is likely to be made "richer, warmer, more exciting, and/or more enjoyable" (p. 638) than it would otherwise be by the advertisement.

The authors see this "transformational" designation as comparable to "affect-based," but they also require such ads to cause consumers to relate such affective properties to the experience of owning or using the product. Further, they advance the proposition that the "generalized emotion" resulting from transformational advertising will have a number of selective effects on recall (e.g., recall of similar feelings) and experience generation (e.g., producing similar feelings). Any advertisement may represent a combination of informational and transformational approaches. The latter type of ad is thought to be at some initial disadvantage in standard recall tests. The authors report initial work to develop an inventory composed of informational and transformational scale items that can be used in assigning ads to these categories or rating their adequacy on each dimension.

Role of affect on cognitive processes

There is now an emerging research thrust in the field of consumer behavior to examine the impact of affective states on both cognitive processes and outcomes (e.g., evaluations, inferences). Srull (1983) induced either positive or negative moods by asking subjects to recall everything possible from an appropriately affectively toned event in their lives. Subjects then read either two positive, two negative, or two neutral ads, all of which were unfamiliar and informationally complex but varied in presenting valenced attribute evaluations. After an irrelevant task they were asked to recall as much information as possible. In one study intense moods, regardless of valence, were found to lead to better recall, and mood-incongruent ads were, unexpectedly, better recalled. In a second study, ratings of the products advertised were found to be more favorable if subjects were in a positive mood and less favorable if subjects were in a negative mood, but only if mood was consistent with the evaluative implications of the ad. In a third study subjects returned after 24 hours and were randomly put into a positive, negative, or neutral mood for a second time. Unexpectedly, there were assimilation effects on product ratings at encoding but contrast effects (only for mood-incongruent ads) at the time of judgment. A fourth experiment provided some insight into the process that may have produced these results. Subjects in a positive mood at retrieval were found to be better able to retrieve negative than positive attributes. However, subjects in a negative mood at retrieval were more likely to retrieve positive attributes. No such differences were found for mood state at encoding, and there were no significant recognition memory differences across conditions. Srull speculates that mood at retrieval may cue a large number of additional (and irrelevant) cue-consistent events. Such a "set size" effect might undermine the cue's effectiveness in retrieving the specific mood-consistent attributes of the product relative to the more distinctive cue-inconsistent attributes. He cautions, however, that such cue overload effects may even reverse over time with lower levels of recall since some cue-consistent retrieval may still be likely.

Lawson (1985) presents data that are more consistent with a mood-congruent retrieval effect and argues that mood at retrieval may be able to prime mood-congruent information in memory. Using a mood induction procedure similar to Srull's (1983), Lawson found that sad subjects recalled more negative than positive attributes and happy subjects recalled roughly equal amounts of both, though there was no tendency for either group to retrieve more of the information from reports differing in the proportion of positive and negative attributes included. Subjects were required to rate a set of products twice in terms of desirability, and their post–mood induction ratings revealed a change in the direction of mood-consistent evaluations. This type of procedure may, however, sensitize subjects to expected consequences of mood states, though Lawson reports little apparent subject awareness as a result of his debriefing session. The author suggests that mood effects on recall are likely to be modest at best. This may, in part, be a function of the deliberativeness of internal information search as well as the nature and extent of processing during encoding.

Srull (1984) differentiates between evaluations resulting from a retrieval process (i.e., bringing to mind overall judgments formed earlier) and those resulting from a computational process (i.e., bringing to mind information, probably at the attribute level, and combining it into an overall judgment). The person's goals or processing objectives during encoding (i.e., evaluation vs. comprehension/incidental learning) will likely determine whether or not an overall evaluation is formed at that time and is subsequently available in memory. One implication of this conceptualization is that the relationship between the overall evaluation of a product and recall of evaluative attribute information may not always be very strong (e.g., when overall evaluations were based on information that is no longer easily accessible).

A second implication is that affective states during encoding should have an effect on overall evaluations if these are formed at the time of encoding but not if such evaluations are computed at a subsequent time. These effects were found in a study using a mood induction procedure similar to that of Srull (1983) but varying subjects' processing objectives at the time of exposure to a complex informational advertisement. Thus, some subjects formed an evaluation of the product on-line and others rated the advertisement on product-neutral factors (e.g., how grammatical it was). No effects on attribute recall were found; however, the correlations between recall and judgment were higher when the judgments were made after a short delay rather than on-line (since presumably retrieval of the preformed judgment in the latter condition is independent of attribute recall). Affective states influenced product judgments for those subjects whose evaluations were formed at the time of encoding but not for those who "computed" them later. The effect was shown for both positive and negative moods.

In a series of three experiments, Calder and Gruder (1988) manipulated both positive and negative emotional states (anger, satisfaction, fear, and disgust) using hypnotic induction as well as subjects' retrieval of strong emotional experiences. These induced emotional states were shown to influence subjects' selection/use of associated objective information (from a larger set of positive and negative items contained in a restaurant review), such that subsequent attitudes toward the object became more highly valenced and there was some enhancement in subjects' recall of information having similar affective content. One interesting finding was that attitudes became more negative when the activated emotional state and the information content were similar (i.e., manipulated anger and reported anger in the restaurant script) than when they were different (i.e., a combination of anger and disgust). More complex relationships among emotions were suggested by the data: Disgust seems to be more strongly associated with anger than the reverse, and fear may inhibit anger, producing a less negative evaluative response to an object. The authors interpret their work in terms of network models (Bower & Cohen, 1982) and production rules, even though this research does not constitute a strong test of any particular conceptualization of memory. It is, however, very consistent with the model set forth in Figure 7.1 and represents one of the few studies that chart the interaction among affective states, affective traces, and subsequent cognitive and evaluative processes.

Srull (1987) demonstrated that subjects placed into a positive mood at retrieval (all subjects were in a neutral mood during exposure to product information 48 hours earlier) provided more favorable product evaluations when they had not formed a product evaluation earlier but instead computed their evaluation on the basis of information from memory.

Apparently, mood at retrieval colored their evaluations, though the precise mechanism is unclear (e.g., selective retrieval, selective attention, or weighting of features). Srull also suggests that this type of effect is more likely for consumers who are less familiar with a product since they would be more apt to form an evaluation at the time of retrieval than to rely on already existing evaluations.

Looking at the expert–novice distinction in greater depth, Srull (1987) found that mood at the time of encoding had a stronger effect on the judgments of self-designated automobile "nonexperts" that it did on those of "experts." He suggests that these effects may be due to novices' searching for an algorithm to combine the information contained in an advertisement while experts may have well-developed computational rules. Presumably, mood states exert greater influence in the former case. It is also true, however, that experts are likely to be considerably more certain of what their evaluations of the automobile advertised should be, and therefore could be less sensitive to *any* influence attempts (i.e., informational or mood based). Nonexperts might be more inclined to respond to any situational cue and possibly to be more susceptible to demand effects as a result. A caution (see also Srull, 1987) may apply to studies manipulating mood and requesting judgments at about the same time. It is possible that mood will influence how subjects use evaluative scales quite apart from the separate question of mood effects on substantive evaluative processes and judgments. This is an important distinction and deserves careful treatment in this type of research.

Mitchell (1986) calls into question the robustness of the on-line only mood effect, believing that affective traces should become linked to the product during encoding regardless of whether a brand attitude is formed at the same time. Such traces would then be available in memory and retrieved at a time of subsequent judgment.

Srull (1987), however, presents additional evidence that only subjects asked to form a product evaluation on-line benefited from the effects of the mood state at encoding. Why the presumably favorable mood state associations had little or no impact some 48 hours later for subjects who were *only then* asked to evaluate the product (and who were put into a neutral mood at the time) is not entirely clear. Is there some initial difference in encoding between affective traces and other cognitive traces that results in weakened or less accessible memory links for the former? A further possibility is that experiencing a different mood at retrieval could create a response competition or interference effect.

With the greater difficulty of the delayed recall and evaluation task, this may also tend to involve a more deliberate and analytic product evaluation, one in which peripheral factors such as mood play a smaller role. Given the plausibility of Mitchell's (1986) basic presumption that these affective traces should be available, we need to understand under what conditions they either are made less accessible or fail to have a noticeable impact.

Though the effect is elusive at best, we probably should not dismiss the possibility that a comparable mood state at the time of judgment might be more likely to cue the earlier encoded affective trace if the ad generated a strikingly similar mood at encoding. Cue overload, however, is likely to be sufficiently high in the affective domain to render such state-dependent effects of marginal significance.

Specifying the mechanisms through which mood at retrieval influences recall of information will require a great deal of further research. When viewed as a relatively undifferentiated affective state, mood should not constitute a strong retrieval cue, especially for semantically unrelated items. Thus, even for product attributes that are positive in evaluation, why should a positive feeling state add significantly to the likelihood of recalling these items? Such a positive mood may have stronger links to positive episodic traces than to more neutral items. Yet because our life histories are filled with positive episodic traces, such cues are hardly likely to benefit from having unique associations, unless, of course, something more than mere directionality of affect is involved (cf. Isen, 1984b).

The evidence is not compelling that categories of differing valences exist that might merely be primed by equivalently valenced feeling states. If this were the case, items could simply be sampled from within the appropriately primed category, partially transforming the recall task into an easier recognition task in which item familiarity (after category-based sampling) could play a vital role. This depiction raises a methodological concern. We need to be aware that a demand effect, in which individuals become aware that the instigation of a particular mood bears some relationship to the recall task they are about to undertake, could be a rival explanation. This awareness could lead to the ad hoc construction of a category of similarly valenced items (perhaps those that have been recently experienced). Then, the aforementioned recognition or familiarity test could be applied to the items generated by the category prime. Unless experiments are cleverly designed, it may be difficult to eliminate this type of problem-solving mechanism on the part of subjects. Its implications could be serious in that affective category formation and priming might have far greater weight in such experimental settings than they would in the large majority of contexts in which mood should not play such an active role.

Evidence that supports the beneficial effect of positive mood states on retrieval of not only positive but evaluately neutral items would not be as readily explainable through the above mechanisms. This is particularly intriguing since it may imply the existence of more generally facilitating effects of positive feeling states and dispositions on cognitive processes themselves, with resulting effects on creativity, risk taking, and evaluative judgments (see Isen, 1984a; Isen et al., 1978; Isen, Daubman, & Nowicki, 1987). If research continues to support the motivational processes Isen (1984b) refers to as mood maintenance (for positive moods) and mood repair (for negative moods), these active (as opposed to automatic) processes may prove to be among the most important affective processes identified in the literature. This should be an especially fertile area for research, involving not only memory and related cognitive processes but consumer decision making. Hill and Gardner (1987) suggest that it might be quite productive to carry out an ambitious research program of this type in consumer behavior. As a way of organizing this type of endeavor, they suggest looking at the impact of affect on the several stages through which a consumer is assumed to proceed in purchasing a product: need recognition, product evaluation, product purchase, product consumption, and post consumption (which completes our journey through the variables depicted in Figure 7.1).

7.7. Affect and consumer behavior: Be fruitful and multiply

Although the field of consumer behavior has engaged in the systematic study of attitudes and evaluative judgment for many years, the study of affective processes is only now starting to receive careful attention. The importance of motivational variables, desire, and feelings have long been recognized, but until recently most attempts to actually examine such factors have involved the use of measures intended to locate individuals on various content or predispositional dimensions. This chapter has sought to clarify the use of evaluative and affective concepts and to suggest the vital role each plays in consumer behavior. A framework has been provided to structure the consumer research literature involving both of these concepts and to suggest relatively unexplored relationships. Consumer behavior, as is true in a number of fields, appears to be at a point of development at which a better integration of affective, cognitive, evaluative, and behavioral domains is likely to be particularly productive. There may be a particular willingness to start with a problem focus that not only encourages a broader within-individual orientation but also recognizes the importance of the context within which the problem is set. The field of consumer behavior is an especially fertile laboratory in which to study the interactions among these domains. Such interactions arise in the normal course of daily life. They run the gamut from the most trivial to some of the most involving activities, from events of very short duration to plans and behaviors that span months, that are internally driven or externally instigated and that, in short, allow us to explore almost any facet of human behavior.

Acknowledgments

Appreciation is expressed to Prakash Nedungadi, Darrel Miller, Ajay Sirsi, Charles Areni, and especially Jhinuk Chowdhury for their help in compiling and organizing the extensive list of references on which the chapter is based.

1.   The attempt to divide consumers into relatively homogeneous clusters has been the focus of a stream of research known as segmentation research (see Smith, 1956; Frank, Massy, & Wind, 1972; Wilkie & Cohen, 1977; and Kahle, 1986).
2.   Research on multi-attribute models dominated the marketing literature in the 1970s. For a review of multi-attribute models, see Wilkie and Pessemier, 1973, and Lutz & Bettman, 1977. The most widely used form stems from SEU models of economic utility theory, with a considerable amount of research based on the attitude models of Fishbein (Fishbein & Ajzen, 1975; Ajzen & Fishbein, 1980) and, to a lesser extent, Rosenberg (Rosenberg, 1956).
3.   Useful discussions and assessments of these research literatures can be found in Bettman, 1979, 1986, Alba and Hutchinson, 1987, Cohen and Chakravarti, 1990, and Kassarjian and Robertson, 1990.
4.   The extent to which this was intentional (e.g., to simplify things a bit by focusing on evaluation, per se) or simply inadvertent (i.e., those within the attitude tradition tending to subsume affect as either a part of or synonymous with attitude) is not always easy to determine.
5.   See Hoffman (1986) for an extended discussion of conditions influencing affect arousal and Schachter and Singer (1962) and Weiner (1986) for additional accounts of the process of assigning meaning to such states.
6.   In a review of the literature on mood states Gardner (1985) groups effects into three categories – behavior, evaluation, and recall – as a function of the following types of marketing execution; service encounters, point-of-purchase stimuli, and communications. Hoffman (1986) has recently proposed a framework in which there are three types of affective response to a

stimulus; (1) direct affective responses to physical/sensory aspects of a stimulus, (2) affective responses to the match between physical/sensory aspects and an internal representation or schema, and (3) affective responses to the meaning of a stimulus (particularly its causes, consequences, and implications for the self).

7. Discussions of alternative categorization approaches and their relationship to affective concepts can be found in Cohen (1982), Cohen and Basu (1987), Fiske (1982), and Fiske and Pavelchak (1986).

8. The use of incentives and modeling to attract, "shape," stimulate, and reinforce behavior (i.e., create brand loyalty) has come under greater examination (by marketing academics) in recent years. See Kassarjian and Robertson, 1990) for a discussion and further references.

9. For subjects to actually think about the *purpose* of the US–CS pairing creates an interpretational nightmare. Merely presenting stimuli such as music or colors to subjects in the guise of an advertising study may be problematic in this regard. Subjects may assume (in some studies this is made explicit) that if they (often in the role of judges) like the stimulus the "advertiser is intending to use" (e.g., the music) they are somehow to communicate this liking. In addition to filling out an evaluative scale (for the unconditioned stimulus) why not indicate approval or disapproval by consistent behavior toward the associated product itself?

10. There has been a substantial amount of interest among advertising practitioners and marketing and advertising academics regarding repetition and wear-out effects. See Sawyer (1977) and Ray (1982) for recent discussions.

References

Aaker, D. A., & Bruzzone, D. E. (1981). Viewer perceptions of prime-time television advertising. *Journal of Advertising Research, 21,* 15–23.

Aaker, D. A., Stayman, D. M., & Hagerty, M. R. (1986). Warmth in advertising: Measurement, impact, and sequence effects. *Journal of Consumer Research, 12,* 365–381.

Ajzen, I., & Fishbein, M. (1980). *Understanding attitudes and predicting social behavior.* Englewood Cliffs, NJ: Prentice-Hall.

Alba, J. W., & Hutchinson, J. W. (1987). Dimensions of consumer expertise. *Journal of Consumer Research, 13,* 411–454.

Alba, J. W., & Marmorstein, H. (1987). The effects of frequency knowledge on consumer decision making. *Journal of Consumer Research, 14,* 14–25.

Allen, C. T., & Janiszewski, C. A. (1989). Assessing the role of contingency awareness in attitudinal conditioning with implications for advertising research. *Journal of Marketing Research, 26,* 30–43.

Allen, C. T., & Madden, T. J. (1985). A closer look at classical conditioning. *Journal of Consumer Research, 12,* 301–313.

Atkin, C., & Block, M. (1983). Effectiveness of celebrity endorsers. *Journal of Advertising Research, 23,* 57–61.

Axelrod, J. N. (1963). Induced moods and attitudes toward product. *Journal of Advertising Research, 3,* 19–24.

Axelrod, J. N. (1968). Attitude measures that predict purchase. *Journal of Advertising Research, 8,* 3–18.

Baker, M. J., & Churchill, G. A. (1977). The impact of physically attractive models on advertising evaluations. *Journal of Marketing Research, 14*, 538–555.

Bargh, J. A. (1984). Automatic and conscious processing of social information. In R. S. Wyer, Jr. & T. K. Srull (Eds.), *Handbook of social cognition* (Vol. 3). Hillsdale, NJ: Erlbaum.

Bartos, R. (1977). Ernest Dichter: Motive interpreter. *Journal of Advertising Research, 17*, 8.

Batra, R. & Ray, M. L. (1983). Advertising situations: The implications of differential involvement and accompanying affect responses. In R. J. Harris (Ed.), *Information processing research in advertising.* Hillsdale, NJ: Erlbaum.

Batra, R. & Ray, M. L. (1986). Affective responses mediating acceptance of advertising. *Journal of Consumer Research, 13*, 234–249.

Belch, G. E. (1982). The effects of television commercial repetition on cognitive response and message acceptance. *Journal of Consumer Research, 9*, 56–65.

Belch, G. E. (1983). The effects of message modality on one- and two-sided advertising messages. *Advances in Consumer Research, 10*, 21–26.

Bennett, P. D., & Harrell, G. D. (1975). The role of confidence in understanding and predicting buyers' attitudes and purchase intentions. *Journal of Consumer Research, 2*, 110–117.

Bettman, J. R. (1979). *An information processing theory of consumer choice.* Reading, MA: Addison-Wesley.

Bettman, J. R. (1986). Consumer psychology. *Annual Review of Psychology, 37*, 257–289.

Bettman, J. R., Capon, N., & Lutz, R. J. (1975). Multi-attribute measurement models and multi-attribute attitude theory: A test of construct validity. *Journal of Consumer Research, 1*, 1–15.

Biehal, G., & Chakravarti, D. (1983). Information accessibility as a moderator of consumer choice. *Journal of Consumer Research, 10*, 1–14.

Bierley, C., McSweeney, F. K., & Vannieuwkerk, R. (1985). Classical conditioning of preferences for stimuli. *Journal of Consumer Research, 12*, 316–323.

Bower, G. H. (1981). Mood and memory. *American Psychologist, 36*, 129–148.

Bower, G. H., & Cohen, P. R. (1982). Emotional influences in memory and thinking. In S. Fiske & M. Clark (Eds.), *Affect and social cognition.* Hillsdale, NJ: Erlbaum.

Brooker, G. W. (1981). A comparison of the persuasive effects of mild humor and mild fear appeals. *Journal of Advertising, 10*, 29–40.

Burnkrant, R., & Page, T. J., Jr. (1982). An examination of the convergent, discriminant, and predictive validity of Fishbein's behavioral intention model. *Journal of Marketing Research, 19*, 550–561.

Burnkrant, R., & Sawyer, A. G. (1983). Effects of involvement and message content on information-processing intensity. In R. J. Harris (Eds.), *Information processing research in advertising.* Hillsdale, NJ: Erlbaum.

Calantone, R. J., & Sawyer, A. G. (1978). The stability of benefit segments. *Journal of Marketing Research, 15*, 395–404.

Calder, B. J. (1978). Cognitive response, imagery, and scripts: What is the cognitive basis of attitude? *Advances in Consumer Research, 5*, 630–634.

Calder, B. J., & Gruder, C. L. (1988). A network activation theory of attitudinal affect. Unpublished manuscript.

Carson, T., & Adams, H. (1980). Activity valence as a function of mood change. *Journal of Abnormal Psychology, 89*, 368–377.

Chaiken, S. (1980). Heuristic versus systematic information processing and the use of source versus message cues in persuasion. *Journal of Personality and Social Psychology, 39,* 752–766.

Childers, T. L., & Houston, M. J. (1984). Conditions for a picture-superiority effect on consumer memory. *Journal of Consumer Research, 11,* 643–654.

Cohen, J. B. (1982). The role of affect in categorization: Toward a reconsideration of the concept of attitude. *Advances in Consumer Research, 9,* 94–100.

Cohen, J. B. (1983). Involvement and you: 1000 great ideas. *Advances in Consumer Research, 10,* 325–328.

Cohen, J. B., & Basu, K. (1987). Alternative models of categorization: Toward a contingent processing framework. *Journal of Consumer Research, 13,* 455–472.

Cohen, J. B., & Chakravarti, D. (1990). Consumer Psychology. *Annual Review of Psychology,* in press.

Cohen, J. B., & Goldberg, M. E. (1970). The dissonance model in most decision product evaluation. *Journal of Marketing Research, 7,* 315–321.

Cohen, J. B., Moore, D. L. (1988). Postdecision consistency enhancing processes. Center for Consumer Research Working Paper No. 57, University of Florida.

Coyne, J. C. (1982). Putting humpty dumpty back together: Cognition, emotion and motivation reconsidered. *Advances in Consumer Research, 9,* 153–155.

Cummings, W. H., & Venkatesan, M. (1976). Cognitive dissonance and consumer behavior: A review of the evidence. *Journal of Marketing Research, 13,* 303–308.

Dichter, E. (1960). *The strategy of desire.* New York: Doubleday.

Dichter, E. (1964). *Handbook of consumer motivation.* New York: McGraw-Hill.

Donovan, R. J., & Rossiter, J. R. (1982). Store atmospherics: An environmental psychology approach. *Journal of Retailing, 58,* 34–57.

Edell, J. A., & Burke, M. C. (1987). The power of feelings in understanding advertising effects. *Journal of Consumer Research, 14,* 421–433.

Edell, J. A., & Staelin, R. (1983). The information processing of pictures in print advertisements. *Journal of Consumer Research, 10,* 45–61.

Fazio, R. H. (1986). How do attitudes guide behavior? In R. M. Sorrentino & E. T. Higgins (Eds.), *Handbook of motivation and cognition.* New York: Guilford Press.

Fazio, R. H., & Zanna, M. P. (1981). Direct experience and attitude-behavior consistency. *Advances in Experimental Social Psychology, 14,* 161–202.

Fishbein, M. (1967). Attitudes and the prediction of behavior. In M. Fishbein (Ed.) *Readings in attitude theory and measurement.* New York: Wiley.

Fishbein, M., & Ajzen, I. (1975). *Attitude, intention and behavior: An introduction to theory and research.* Reading, MA: Addison-Wesley.

Fiske, S. T. (1982). Schema-triggered affect: Applications to social perception. In M. S. Clark & S. T. Fiske (Eds.). *Affect and cognition: The 17th Annual Carnegie Symposium on Cognition,* Hillsdale, NJ: Erlbaum

Fiske, S. T., & Pavelchak, M. A. (1986). Category-based versus piecemeal-based affective responses: Developments in schema-triggered affect. In R. M. Sorrentino & E. T. Higgins (Eds.), *Handbook of motivation and cognition.* New York: Guilford Press.

Frank, R., Massy, W., & Wind, Y. (1972). *Market segmentation.* Englewood Cliffs, NJ: Prentice-Hall.

Friedstad, M., & Thorson, E. (1986). Emotion-eliciting advertising: Effect on long term memory and judgment. *Advances in Consumer Reseach, 13,* 111–115.

Gardner, M. P. (1985a). Mood states and consumer behavior: A critical review. *Journal of Consumer Research, 12,* 281–300.

Gardner, M. P. (1985b). Does attitude toward the ad affect brand attitude under a brand evaluation set? *Journal of Marketing Research, 22,* 192–198/

Gardner, M. P., & Siomkos, G. J. (1986). Toward a methodology for assessing effects of in-store atmospherics. *Advances in Consumer Research, 13,* 27–31.

Goldberg, M. E., & Gorn, G. J. (1987). Happy and sad TV programs: How they affect reactions to commercials. *Journal of Consumer Research, 14,* 387–403.

Golden, L. L. (1979). Consumer reactions to explicit brand comparisons in advertisements. *Journal of Marketing Research, 16,* 21–26.

Golden, L. L., & Johnson, K. A. (1983). The impact of sensory preference and thinking versus feeling appeals on advertising effectiveness. *Advances in Consumer Research, 10,* 203–208.

Gorn, G. J. (1982). The effects of music in advertising on choice behavior: A classical conditioning approach. *Journal of Marketing, 46,* 94–101.

Gorn, G. J., & Weinberg, C. B. (1984). The impact of comparative advertising on perception and attitude: Some positive findings. *Journal of Consumer Research, 11,* 719–727.

Greenwald, A. G., & Leavitt, C. (1984). Audience involvement in advertising: Four levels. *Journal of Consumer Research, 11,* 581–592.

Gresham, L. G., & Shimp, T. A. (1985). Attitude toward the advertisement and brand attitudes: A classical conditioning perspective. *Journal of Advertising, 14,* 10–17.

Haley, R. I. (1968). Benefit segmentation: A decision-oriented tool. *Journal of Marketing, 32,* 30–35.

Haley, R. I. (1983). Benefit segmentation – 20 years later. *Journal of Consumer Marketing, 1,* 5–13.

Hilgard, E. R. (1980). The trilogy of the mind: Cognition, affection and conation. *Journal of History of Behavioral Sciences, 16,* 107–117.

Hill, R. P., & Gardner, M. P. (1987). The buying process: Effects of and on consumer mood states. *Advances in Consumer Research, 14,* 111–128.

Hill, R. P., & Mazis, M. B. (1986). Measuring emotional responses to advertising. *Advances in Consumer Research, 13,* 164–69.

Hirschman, E. C., & Holbrook, M. B. (1982). Hedonic consumption: Emerging concepts, methods and propositions. *Journal of Marketing, 46,* 92–101.

Hoffman, M. L. (1986). Affect, cognition and motivation. In R. M. Sorrentino & E. T. Higgins (Eds.), *Handbook of motivation and cognition.* New York: Guilford Press.

Holbrook, M. B. (1978). Beyond attitudinal structure: Toward the informational determinants of attitude. *Journal of Marketing Research, 15,* 545–556.

Holbrook, M. B., & Hirschman, E. C. (1982). The experiential aspects of consumption: Consumer fantasies, feelings and fun. *Journal of Consumer Research, 9,* 132–140.

Holbrook, M. B., & Batra, R. (1987). Assessing the role of emotions as mediators of consumer responses to advertising. *Journal of Consumer Research, 14,* 404–420.

Howard, J. A. (1965). *Marketing theory.* Boston: Allyn & Bacon.

Isen, A. M. (1984a). The influence of positive affect on decision making and cognitive organization. *Advances in Consumer Research, 11,* 534–537.

Isen, A. M. (1984b). Toward understanding the role of affect in cognition. In R. S. Wyer, Jr. & T. K. Srull (Eds.), *Handbook of social cognition.* Hillsdale, NJ: Erlbaum.

Isen, A. M. (1987). Positive affect, cognitive processes and social behavior. In L. Berkowitz (Ed.), *Advances in experimental social psychology.* New York: Academic Press.

Isen, A. M., Shalker, T. E., Clark, M., & Karp, L. (1978). Affect, accessibility of material in memory, and behavior: A cognitive loop? *Journal of Personality and Social Psychology, 36,* 1–12.

Isen, A. M., & Hastorf, A. H. (1982). Some perspectives on cognitive social psychology. In A. H. Hastorf & A. M. Isen (Eds.), *Cognitive social psychology.* New York: Elsevier North Holland.

Isen, A. M., Means, B., Patrick, R., & Nowicki, G. (1982). Some factors influencing decision-making strategy and risk taking. In M. Clark & S. Fiske (Eds.), *Cognition and affect.* Hillsdale, NJ: Erlbaum.

Isen, A. M., & Shalker, T. (1982). The effect of feeling state on evaluation of positive, neutral and negative stimuli: When you "accentuate the positive," do you "eliminate the negative"? *Social Psychology Quarterly, 45,* 58–63.

Isen, A. M., Daubman, K. A., & Nowicki, G. P. (1987). Positive affect facilitates creative problem solving. *Journal of Personality and Social Psychology, 52,* 1122–1131.

Kahle, L. R. (1986). The nine nations of North America and the value basis of geographic segmentation. *Journal of Marketing, 50,* 37–47.

Kahneman, D., & Miller, D. T. (1986). Norm theory: Comparing reality to its alternatives. *Psychological Review, 93,* 136–153.

Kassarjian, H. H. (1978). Presidential address: Anthropomorphism and parsimony. *Advances in Consumer Research, 5,* 13–14.

Kassarjian, H. H., and Robertson, T. S. (1990). *Handbook of Consumer Theory and Research.* Englewood Cliffs, NJ: Prentice-Hall, in press.

Kisielius, J., & Sternthal, B. (1986). Examining the vividness controversy: An availability-valence interpretation. *Journal of Consumer Research, 12,* 418–431.

Kotler, P. (1974). Atmospherics as a marketing tool. *Journal of Retailing, 49,* 48–64.

Kroeber-Riel, W. (1984a). Effects of emotional pictorial elements in ads analyzed by means of eye movement monitoring. *Advances in Consumer Research, 11,* 591–596.

Kroeber-Riel, W. (1984b). Emotional product differentiation by classical conditioning. *Advances in Consumer Research, 11,* 538–543.

Krugman, H. E. (1962). The learning of consumer preference. *Journal of Marketing, 26,* 31–33.

Krugman, H. E. (1965). The impact of television advertising: Learning without involvement. *Public Opinion Quarterly, 29,* 349–356.

LaBarbera, P. A., & Mazursky, D. (1983). A longitudinal assessment of consumer satisfaction/dissatisfaction: The dynamic aspect of the cognitive process. *Journal of Marketing Research, 20,* 393–404.

Lawson, R. (1985). The effects of mood on retrieving consumer product information. *Advances in Consumer Research, 12,* 399–403.

Leavitt, C. (1970). A multidimensional set of rating scales for television commercials. *Journal of Applied Psychology, 54,* 427–429.

Loken, B. (1983). Effects of uniquely purchase information on attitudes toward objects and attitudes toward behaviors. *Advances in Consumer Research, 10,* 88–93.

Lott, A. J., & Lott, B. E. (1968). A learning theory approach to interpersonal attitudes. In A. G. Greenwald, T. C. Brock, & T. M. Ostrom (Eds.), *Psychological foundations of attitudes.* New York: Academic Press.

Lutz, R. J. (1975). Changing brand attitudes through modification of cognitive structure. *Journal of Consumer Research, 1,* 49–59.

Lutz, R. J. (1985). Affective and cognitive antecedents of attitude toward the ad: A conceptual framework. In L. F. Alwitt & A. A. Mitchell (Eds.), *Psychological Processes and Advertising Effects: Theory, Research, and Application*, Hillsdale, NJ: Erlbaum.

Lutz, R. J., & Bettman, J. R. (1977). Multi-attribute models in marketing: A bicentennial review. In A. Woodside, J. Sheth & B. Bennett (Eds.), *Consumer and industrial buying behavior*. New York: Elsevier North Holland.

Lutz, R. J., McKenzie, S. B., & Belch, G. E. (1983). Attitude toward the ad as a mediator of advertising effectiveness: Determinants and consequences. *Advances in Consumer Research, 10*, 532–539.

Mandler, G. (1982). The structure of value: Accounting for taste. In M. S. Clark & S. T. Fiske (Eds.), *Affect and cognition: The 17th annual Carnegie Symposium*. Hillsdale, NJ: Erlbaum.

Mazis, M. B., Ahtola, O. T., & Klippel, R. E. (1975). A comparison of four multi-attribute models in the prediction of consumer attitudes. *Journal of Consumer Research, 2*, 38–52.

McSweeney, F. K., Bierley, C. (1984). Recent developments in classical conditioning. *Journal of Consumer Research, 11*, 619–631.

Mehrabian, A., & Russell, J. A. (1974). *An approach to environmental pyschology*. Cambridge, MA: The MIT Press.

Milliman, R. E. (1982). Using background music to affect the behavior of supermarket shoppers. *Journal of Marketing, 46*, 86–91.

Milliman, R. E. (1986). The influence of background music on the behavior of restaurant patrons. *Journal of Consumer Research, 13*, 286–289.

Miniard, P. W. & Cohen, J. B. (1981). An examination of the Fishbein-Ajzen behavioral intention model's concepts and measures. *Journal of Experimental Social Psychology, 17*, 309–339.

Mitchell, A. A. (1981). The dimensions of advertising involvement. *Advances in Consumer Research, 8*, 25–30.

Mitchell, A. A. (1986). The effect of verbal and visual components of advertising on brand attitudes and attitude toward the advertisement. *Journal of Consumer Research, 13*, 12–24.

Mitchell, A. A., & Olson, J. C. (1981). Are product attribute beliefs the only mediator of advertising effects on brand attitude? *Journal of Marketing Research, 18*, 318–322.

Moore, D. L., Hausknecht, D., & Thamodaran, K. (1986). Time compression, response opportunity, and persuasion. *Journal of Consumer Research, 13*, 85–99.

Moore, D. L., & Hutchinson, J. W. 1983. The effects of ad affect on advertising effectiveness. *Advances in Consumer Research, 10*, 526–531.

Moore, D. L., & Hutchinson, J. W. (1985). The influence of affective reactions to advertising: Direct and indirect mechanisms of attitude change. In L. F. Alwitt & A. A. Mitchell (Eds.), *Psychological processes and advertising effects: Theory, research and application*. Hillsdale, NJ: Erlbaum.

Nord, W. J., & Peter, J. P. (1980). A behavior modification perspective on marketing. *Journal of Marketing, 44*, 36–47.

Obermiller, C. (1985). Varieties of mere exposure: The effects of processing style and repetition on affective response. *Journal of Consumer Research, 12*, 17–30.

Oliver, R. L. (1980). A cognitive model of the antecedents and consequences of satisfaction decisions. *Journal of Marketing Research, 17*, 460–469.

Oliver, R. L., & Berger, P. K. (1979). A path analysis of preventive health care decision models. *Journal of Consumer Research, 6*, 113–122.

Olson, J. C., Toy, D. R., & Dover, P. A. (1982). Do cognitive responses mediate the effects of advertising content on cognitive structure? *Journal of Consumer Research, 9,* 245–262.

Packard, V. (1957). *The hidden persuaders.* New York: Pocket Books.

Park, W. C., & Young, M. (1983). Types and levels of involvement and brand attitude formation. *Advances in Consumer Research, 10,* 320–323.

Percy, L., & Rossiter, J. R. (1983). Effects of picture size and color on brand attitude responses in print advertising. *Advances in Consumer Research, 10,* 17–20.

Petty, R. E., & Cacioppo, J. T. (1981). *Attitudes and persuasion: Classic and contemporary approaches.* Dubuque, IA: Wm. C. Brown.

Petty, R. E., Cacioppo, J. T., & Schumann, D. (1983). Central and peripheral routes to advertising effectiveness: The moderating role of involvement. *Journal of Consumer Research, 10,* 135–146.

Puto, C. P., & Wells, W. D. (1984). Informational and transformational advertising: The differential effects of time. *Advances in Consumer Research, 11,* 638–643.

Raju, P. S. (1980). Optimum stimulation level: Its relationship to personality, demographics and exploratory behavior. *Journal of Consumer Research, 7,* 272–282.

Ray, M. L. (1982). *Advertising and communication management.* Englewood Cliffs, NJ: Prentice-Hall.

Robertson, T. S., Zielinski, J., & Ward, S. (1984). *Consumer behavior.* Glenview, IL: Scott, Foresman & Co.

Rosenberg, M. J. (1956). Cognitive structure and attitudinal affect. *Journal of Abnormal and Social Psychology, 53,* 367–372.

Rossiter, J. R., & Percy, L. (1980). Attitude change through visual imagery in advertising. *Journal of Advertising, 9,* 10–16.

Russell, J. A. (1978). Evidence of convergent validity on the dimensions of affect. *Journal of Personality and Social Psychology, 36, 11,* 42–68.

Russell, J. A. (1980). A circumplex model of affect. *Journal of Personality and Social Psychology, 39,* 1161–1178.

Ryan, M. J. (1982). Behavioral intention formation: The interdependency of attitudinal and social influence variables. *Journal of Consumer Research, 9,* 263–278.

Ryan, M. J. & Bonfield, E. H. (1975). The Fishbein extended model and consumer behavior. *Journal of Consumer Research, 2,* 118–136.

Sawyer, A. G. (1977). Repetition and affect: Recent empirical and theoretical developments. In A. Woodside, J. Sheth, & P. Bennett (Eds.) *Consumer and industrial buyer behavior.* New York: Elsevier North Holland.

Schachter, S., & Singer, J. E. (1962). Cognitive, social and physiological determinants of emotional state. *Psychological Review, 69,* 379–399.

Schlegel, R. P., & DiTecco, D. (1982). Attitudinal structures and the attitude-behavior relation. In M. P. Zanna, E. T. Higgins, & C. P. Herman (Eds.), *Consistency in social behavior: The Ontario Symposium* (Vol. 2, 17–49). Hillsdale, NJ: Erlbaum.

Schlinger, M. J. (1979). A profile of responses to commercials. *Journal of Advertising Research, 19,* 37–46.

Schultz, D. E. (1979). Media research users want. *Journal of Advertising Research, 19,* 13–17.

Sherman, E., & Smith, R. B. (1987). Mood states of shoppers and store image: Promising interactions and possible behavioral effects. *Advances in Consumer Research, 15,* 251–254.

Sheth, J. M. (1968). How adults learn brand preference. *Journal of Advertising Research, 8,* 25–36.

Shimp, T. A. (1981). Attitude toward the ad as a mediator of consumer brand choice. *Journal of Advertising, 10*(2), 9–15.

Shimp, T. A., & Kavas, A. (1984). The theory of reasoned action applied to coupon usage. *Journal of Consumer Research, 11,* 795–809.

Silk, A. J., & Vavra, T. G. (1974). The influence of advertising's affective qualities on consumer response. In D. Hughes & M. L. Ray (Eds.), *Buyer/consumer information processing.* Chapel Hill, NC: North Carolina Press.

Singh, S. N., & Churchill, G. A., Jr. (1987). Arousal and advertising effectiveness. *Journal of Advertising, 16,* 4–10.

Smith, R. E., & Swinward, W. R. (1983). Attitude-behavior consistency: The impact of product trial versus advertising. *Journal of Marketing Research, 20,* 257–267.

Smith, W. R. (1956). Product differentiation and market segmentation as alternative marketing strategies. *Journal of Marketing, 21,* 3–8.

Srull, T. K. (1983). Affect and memory: The impact of affective reactions in advertising on the representation of product information in memory. *Advances in Consumer Research, 10,* 520–525.

Srull, T. K. (1984). The effects of subjective affective states on memory and judgment. *Advances in Consumer Research, 11,* 503–533.

Srull, T. K. (1987). Memory, mood, and consumer judgment. *Advances in Consumer Research, 15,* 404–407.

Staats, A. W. (1968). Social behaviorism and human motivation: Principles of the attitude-reinforcer-discriminative system. In A. G. Greenwald, T. C. Brock, & T. M. Ostrom (Eds.), *Psychological foundations of attitudes.* New York: Academic Press.

Sternthal, B., & Craig, C. S. (1974). Fear appeals: Revisited and revised. *Journal of Consumer Research, 1,* 22–34.

Stuart, E. W., Shimp, T. A., & Engle, R. W. (1987). Classical conditioning of consumer attitudes: Four experiments in an advertising context. *Journal of Consumer Research, 14,* 334–349.

Troutman, C. M., & Shanteau, J. (1976). Do consumers evaluate products by adding or averaging attribute information? *Journal of Consumer Research, 3,* 101–106.

Tsal, Y. (1985). On the relationship between cognitive and affective processes: A critique of Zajonc and Markus. *Journal of Consumer Research, 12,* 358–362.

Weinberg, P., & Gottwald, W. 91982). Impulsive consumer buying as a result of emotions. *Journal of Business Research, 10,* 43–57.

Weiner, B. (1986). Attribution, emotion, and action. In R. M. Sorrentino & E. T. Higgins (Eds.), *Handbook of motivation and cognition.* New York: Guilford Press.

Westbrook, R. A. (1980). Intrapersonal affective influences on consumer satisfaction with products. *Journal of Consumer Research, 7,* 49–54.

Wilkie, W. L. (1986). *Consumer behavior.* New York: Wiley.

Wilkie, W. L., & Cohen, J. B. (1977). An overview of market segmentation: Behavioral concepts and research approaches. In *Marketing Science Institute Report,* June, 77–105. Cambridge, MA: MSI.

Wilkie, W. L., & Pessemier, E. A. (1973). Issues in marketing's use of multi-attribute models. *Journal of Marketing Research, 10,* 428–441.

Woodruff, R. B., Cadotte, E. R., & Jenkins, R. L. (1983). Modeling consumer satisfaction processes using experience-based norms. *Journal of Marketing Research, 20,* 296–304.

206   Joel B. Cohen

Wright, P. L. (1973). The cognitive processes mediating acceptance of advertising. *Journal of Marketing Research, 10*, 53–62.

Wright, P. L. (1980). Message evoked thoughts: Persuasion research using thought verbalizations. *Journal of Consumer Research, 7*, 151–175.

Yalch, R. F., & Elmore-Yalch, R. (1984). The effect of numbers on the route to persuasion. *Journal of Consumer Research, 11*, 522–527.

Yuspeh, S. (1979). The medium versus the message. In G. Hafer (Ed.), *A look back, a look ahead,* proceedings of the 10th National Attitude Research Conference. Chicago: American Marketing Association.

Zajonc, R. B. (1980). Feeling and thinking: preferences need no inferences. *American Psychologist, 35*, 151–75.

Zajonc, R. B., & Markus, H. (1982. Affective and cognitive factors in preferences. *Journal of Consumer Research, 9*, 123–131.

Zanna, M. P., Higgins, E. T., & Herman, C. P. (Eds.) (1982). *Consistency in social behavior: The Ontario Symposium* (Vol. 2). Hillsdale, NJ: Erlbaum.

Zanna, M. P., Kiesler, C. A., & Pilkonis, P. A. (1970). Positive and negative attitudinal affect established by classical conditioning. *Journal of Personality and Social Psychology, 14*, 321–328.

Zielski, H. A. (1982). Does day after recall penalize "feeling" ads? *Journal of Advertising Research, 22*, 19–22.

Zinkhan, G. M., & Martin, C. R., Jr. (1983) Message characteristics and audience characteristics: Predictors of advertising response. *Advances in Consumer Research, 10*, 27–31.

8. Depression and sensitivity to social information

GIFFORD WEARY

Research in the area of depression has proliferated in the last 10 years, with impressive theoretical and empirical developments. One of the most exciting of these is the notion that depression, traditionally viewed as an affective disorder, may have its roots in cognitive processes. Two models, Beck's (1967) cognitive schema theory and Abramson, Seligman, and Teasdale's (1978) reformulated learned helplessness model of depression, have advocated the primacy of cognition in the development and maintenance of depression. Although much research deriving from these models has focused on the existence of cognitive predisposers of depression and the effects of such cognitions on self-attributions and self-perceptions of depressed individuals, little research has focused on the role of depressogenic cognitions in perceptions and attributions about others. In this chapter, I will present the results of several studies that have examined differences between depressed and nondepressed persons' perceptions of and attributions about the behavior of others. Before doing so, however, I will review briefly the major models of depressive cognition.

8.1. Cognitive models of depression

Reformulated learned helplessness model

Originally drawn from laboratory experiments with dogs, Seligman's (1974) learned helplessness model suggests that through exposure to uncontrollable stress or trauma, individuals learn that responses and outcomes are independent, or noncontingent. According to Seligman, "The depressed patient has learned or believes that he cannot control

207

those elements of his life that relieve suffering or bring him gratification" (p. 98). Helpless and depressed individuals presumably come to believe that active coping efforts are futile. Learned helplessness is manifested in motivational, cognitive, and emotional changes. Motivational changes are inferred from the individual's general passivity and from slow response initiation in experimental settings. Negative expectations are presumed to reflect cognitive changes. The emotional consequence of learned helplessness is depressed mood.

The helplessness model of depression has been reformulated and elaborated (Abramson et al., 1978) as a model for a subset of depression called "hopelessness depression." According to this model, individuals' expectations of a lack of control, or hopelessness, accompanied by lowered self-esteem, have been identified as sufficient causes of depressive symptoms. Although the reformulated model allows for a variety of causes of hopelessness, it focuses on individuals' causal attributions for negative events as important contributory causes of hopelessness and the subsequent depression. That is, experiencing an uncontrollable negative event may not result in depression; the depressed response may be mediated by individuals' attributions regarding the experience.

Individuals who experience negative events presumably attempt to evaluate and understand the causes of their experience. Three attributional dimensions are especially relevant to the reformulated learned helplessness model of depression – internality, stability, and globality. The internality dimension determines the impact of an event on self-esteem. For example, an attribution to a personal characteristic (internal) is more likely to have an impact on self-esteem than an attribution to an environmental cause (external). The stability dimension relates to an individual's ability to predict future experiences; a stable cause (e.g., ability) is likely to remain unchanged and is, therefore, a better predictor of future experiences than is an unstable cause (e.g., luck). The globality dimension is important in determining the generalizability of the experience. That is, a global cause is one that is likely to affect many areas of experience. According to the reformulated learned helplessness model, depression is most likely to occur with an internal, stable, global attribution for a negative uncontrollable event and least likely to occur with an external, unstable, specific attribution for the event. The depressogenic attributional style (internal-stable-global) presumably leads to a generalized expectation of uncontrollability and, consequently, to depression.

Beck's cognitive model

Beck's (1967, 1974) cognitive model of depression bears considerable resemblance to the reformulated learned helplessness model in its emphasis on the etiological significance of causal attributions for negative uncontrollable outcomes. According to Beck, depression-prone people develop a negative view of themselves, their world, and their future, and these negative conceptions, or schemas, when activated by environmental stress, lead to systematic distortions in perceptions and interpretations of information. Although Beck outlined numerous cognitive schemas involved in depression, he regarded schemas concerning causality, particularly about an inability to change a given situation, as especially important. Beck argued that depressed people attribute their negative outcomes to internal, stable factors, such as incompetence, and their good outcomes to external factors, such as luck. Such cognitive distortions presumably result in symptoms characteristic of depression.

Recent research

After reviewing both animal and human experiments, Garber, Miller, and Seaman (1979) concluded that experience with uncontrollable events leads to two primary deficits: (1) reduced motivation to respond in situations where outcomes are controllable and (2) impaired ability to learn about response–outcome contingencies in new situations. They further concluded that there are close parallels between the behavioral signs of learned helplessness following uncontrollable aversive events and the symptoms of depression.

Additional support for the association between experience with uncontrollability and depression has been reported recently by Warren and McEachren (1983). These investigators examined the relationship between depressive symptomatology and a set of demographic and psychosocial variables presumed to be depression susceptibility factors in a sample of 499 women. These investigators found that both sets of factors were related to depression but that the psychosocial factors – including less perceived life control, less perceived accomplishment, more derived identity, and less social support – accounted for most of the variance. Moreover, perceived lack of control over life events was five times more strongly related to depression than any of the other psychosocial factors.

The results of three studies concerned with the influence of depressives' experience with uncontrollability on their social perception processes are reported below. The first two experiments focused on depressed-nondepressed differences in sensitivity to social comparison information and in social information gathering activities, respectively. The third study examined the relationship between depression and a need to structure and make meaningful social situations.

8.2. Laboratory study of depressives' sensitivity to social comparison information

This study (Weary, Elbin, & Hill, 1985) was designed to examine the consequences for depressed and nondepressed individuals of receiving comparison feedback regarding their causal understanding of an event. Specifically, we examined the effects of another's similar or dissimilar causal judgments on depressed and nondepressed college students' evaluations of the other. It seems particularly important to examine the comparison of causal understandings given the role of causal attribution in the development and maintenance of depression and low self-esteem (Abramson et al., 1978). Moreover, the evaluation of others seems to be a useful place to begin a consideration of depression and the consequences of comparison feedback about attributional judgments. Negative evaluations resulting from such feedback likely produce negative interactions with comparison others, and negative social interactions have been implicated in the occurrence of depression (Coyne, 1976).

How might nondepressed perceivers respond to another's similar or dissimilar causal explanations for an event? Although it is not concerned with causal judgments, a large body of literature has focused on the evaluative reactions of individuals to another as a function of their statements of beliefs, attitudes, or values (Byrne, 1971). In general, investigators have found a strong positive relationship between perceived and actual attitude similarity and interpersonal attraction; that is, that we tend to evaluate others favorably to the degree that they express attitudes, opinions, or beliefs similar to our own.

In a recent study, Weary, Jordan, and Hill (1985) argued that the similarity–attraction relationship also should apply for statements of attributional judgments. Specifically, Weary et al. reasoned that the expression by another of similar causal explanations for an event should provide individuals with validation for their understanding of the event. Such validation should reduce individuals' uncertainty about the adequacy of the causal explanation and should lead to the feeling of positive sentiment toward the other. The expression of dissimilar causal explanations for the event, however, should provide invalidation, increase uncertainty, and lead to the feeling of negative sentiment toward the other. In this study, subjects made causal attributions for a hypothetical actor's outcome and subsequently learned that their attributions were similar or dissimilar to another participant's and were socially correct or incorrect. Weary et al. found that similarity resulted in more positive evaluations of a comparison other than did dissimilarity of causal understanding. Moreover, this effect was obtained regardless of the perceived social correctness of the causal understanding.

We might then expect nondepressed perceivers in the present study to evaluate more favorably another who makes similar rather than dissimilar causal judgments for an event. Moreover, research concerned with depression and the processing of social information suggests that this effect might be even more pronounced for depressed perceivers. Evidence suggests that depressed perceivers have a diminished sense of control over their lives (Warren & McEachren, 1983), and also are more uncertain than are nondepressed perceivers and attempt to cope with stressful events by seeking information and advice from others more than do nondepressed individuals (Coyne, Aldwin, & Lazarus, 1981). Since the reduction of uncertainty about one's judgments presumably is a major motive underlying the effects of comparison of causal judgments, it seems reasonable to expect that depressed individuals, who are assumed to have experienced heightened uncertainty associated with frequent exposure to uncontrollable life events, may be more sensitive to comparison feedback. The effects of such feedback on evaluations of the comparison other, then, should be more pronounced for depressed than for nondepressed perceivers.

In the present study, depressed and nondepressed subjects read two case summaries that supposedly were items on a test of social perceptiveness. Each of these test cases consisted of hypothetical events in which an actor received a negative outcome. Subjects made causal attributions for the hypothetical actors' outcomes and subsequently learned that their causal judgments were either similar or dissimilar to a second participant's (comparison other). On the basis of the notion that similar attributional judgments provide validation and lead to greater uncertainty reduction (Byrne, 1971), we predicted that similarity would lead to more positive evaluations of the comparison other than would dissimilarity of causal judgments. Moreover, we predicted that this effect would be more pronounced for depressed subjects.

Finally, we examined the consequences of a comparison other's similar and dissimilar causal judgments on depressed and nonde-pressed subjects' feelings about themselves. We predicted that compari-son feedback regarding subjects' causal understandings would have a greater impact on depressed than on nondepressed subjects' feelings about themselves. This latter finding would follow from the presumed sensitivity of depressed individuals to social comparison information and would provide support for the notion, based on clinical observa-tions, that depressed individuals base their feelings of self-worth on external criteria (Beck, Rush, Shaw, & Emery, 1979).

To provide baseline measures of subjects' evaluations of the compari-son other, two control conditions in which depressed and nondepressed subjects received no information regarding the second participant's causal judgments were included. It was not entirely clear whether there would be any depressed-nondepressed differences in the evaluations of control condition subjects. However, we expected that within level of depression, control subjects' evaluations would fall between those of subjects in the similar and dissimilar judgment conditions. The control conditions also permitted an assessment of depressed and nondepres-sed perceivers' attributions for the actors' outcomes. Recent evidence suggests that although depressed and nondepressed individuals may differ in their self-attributions, they make similar causal judgments for the outcome of others (Sweeney, Shaeffer, & Golin, 1982). Accordingly, we expected that similar attributions would be made by depressed and nondepressed control subjects in the present study. Such a finding would help rule out the possibility that any differences in depressed and nondepressed subjects' evaluations of the others who made similar or dissimilar causal judgments were due to a tendency to make different attributions for the hypothetical actors' outcomes.

Method

Subjects. Ostensibly as part of a study seeking normative information on several recently developed psychological scales, 345 undergraduates enrolled in introductory psychology at Ohio State University completed the Beck Depression Inventory (BDI; Beck, 1967). From this pool, groups of depressed and nondepressed subjects were selected. The criterion for inclusion in the nondepressed group was a BDI score of 3 or below, and for inclusion in the depressed group a BDI score of at least 10 was required. These subjects then were contacted to arrange for their participation in a follow-up study. From 1 to 5 weeks ensured before subjects reported for the experimental procedure. To eliminate subjects who may have been experiencing only a transient depressed state, the BDI was readministered at the time of the experiment (cf. Sacco, 1981). If the second BDI score fell below 10 for the depressed subjects or went above 3 for the nondepressed subjects, those subjects were excluded from the final sample. Thirty-three subjects fell into this transient category. The final sample included 26 depressed subjects (11 males and 15 females) and 30 nondepressed subjects (21 males and 9 females). Of the 26 depressed subjects in the experiment, 20 were mildly depressed, three were moderately depressed, and three were severely depressed.[1] For depressed subjects, the mean BDI scores for the first and second administrations were 15.42 and 14.35, respectively. For nondepressed subjects, the mean BDI scores for the first and second administrations were 1.53 and .93, respectively. Within level of depression, the subjects were randomly assigned to conditions such that all cell sizes ranged from eight to ten.

Procedure. The subjects were told that the study was concerned with the development of a test of social perceptiveness. This scale was said to be designed to measure a person's ability to form impressions about and understand another person in a variety of situations. The subjects then were informed that the entire test would contain a number of case studies describing the experiences of individuals, but that the first day they would read and answer questions about only two of the test cases. They also were led to believe that the other participant would be asked to read the same two test case studies. The experimenter next instructed the subjects to read the first case and to answer the questionnaire that followed. She then joined the confederate in the adjacent room, ostensibly to explain the experiment to her.

The two case summaries were presented in counterbalanced order; each was about 400 words in length. They described a hypothetical actor who experienced a negative outcome. In one case, the actor delivered therapy to a student suffering from an anxiety disorder, and the student became more anxious during the therapy session. In the other case, the actor's rented truck rolled down a hill during a bad rainstorm and damaged a neighbor's property. Each case was constructed so as to include multiple causal explanations for the actors' outcomes.

Following each case summary were two 9-point scales designed to measure subjects' attributions for the actors' outcomes. On these scales subjects were asked to rate (1) the extent to which the individual was personally responsible for the outcome and (2) the extent to which the negative outcome was due to situational factors beyond the individual's control. In addition, subjects were asked to indicate the amount of confidence they had in each of their attributional judgments.

When the experimenter was sure that subjects had completed reading the first case summary and answering the four questions, she rejoined them. The experimenter then explained to subjects that since the case studies ultimately might appear on the Social Perceptiveness Scale, it would be interesting for each subject to know the perceptions formed by the other subjects. The experimenter took the subjects' responses to the two attribution questions into the adjacent room, ostensibly to show to the confederate. There the experimenter made ratings on both of the attribution measures for the confederate that were either similar (within 1 point) or dissimilar (within 4 or 5 points) to the subjects' actual ratings. The confederate's supposed attributions then were shown to the subjects, and the similar or dissimilar nature of their causal judgments was noted.

The same procedure was followed for the second case study: Subjects read the passage, completed scales developed to measure their internal and external attributions for the actor's outcome as well as their confidence in these attributions, and received information indicating that both of their causal judgments were, again, similar or dissimilar to the confederate's. In summary, subjects received information on a total of four attribution scales indicating that their judgments about the two hypothetical events were (similar judgment condition) or were not (dissimilar judgment condition) consistently in accord with the other participant's judgments. The procedure for the no-attribution-information control conditions was identical except that subjects received no information regarding the other participant's attribution ratings.

In the final phase of the experiment, all subjects were asked to complete a final questionnaire. This questionnaire included several nine-point scales on which all subjects were asked to rate the other participant on each of four characteristics (reasonable, pleasant, open-minded, and friendly). In addition, experimental condition subjects were asked to complete measures designed to check on the manipulation of similarity of causal judgments and to assess the extent to which the feedback they received influenced their feelings about themselves. Control condition subjects were asked to complete a measure of their expectancies of similarity of the other participant's causal judgments. All subjects were informed that their responses to the final questionnaire would be confidential. After subjects finished the questionnaire, they were thorough-ly debriefed and dismissed.

Results

Control conditions.

  *Actor attributions.*To determine the extent to which depressed and nondepressed subjects' attributions about the actor and the situational factors for the two hypothetical outcomes differed, depressed and non-depressed no-information control condition subjects' ratings on the four attribution measures were submitted to a one-way analysis of variance. As expected, no significant effects were obtained on any of the mea-sures. Additional analyses of these measures revealed that on nine-point scales (where 9 = entirely), control subjects' mean ratings of the actors' personal responsiblity for the therapy and accident summaries were 4.35 (SD = 1.98) and 5.7 (SD = 2.94), [$t(19)$ = 1.71, $p > .05$], respectively. The mean ratings for the measure of external attributions were 6.0 (SD = 1.95) and 4.85 (SD = 2.98), [$t(19)$ = 1.15, $p > .05$], for the therapy and accident summaries, respectively. The actor and situational factors, then, were viewed as equally responsible for the actor's outcome in both case summaries.

Effectiveness of manipulation. To check on the manipulation of perceived similarity of causal understanding, subjects were asked to rate on a nine-point scale the degree to which they believed their own and the other participant's understanding of the two test cases were similar.[2] A 2 (Level of Depression) × 2 (Similar or Dissimilar Judgment) unweighted means analysis of variance of experimental condition subjects' ratings yielded a significant main effect only for similarity of judgment [$F(1,32)$ = 387.2, $p < .0001$]. Subjects in the similar judgment condition (M = 8.5) believed that their own and the other participant's understanding of the hypothetical events were significantly more similar than did subjects in the dissimilar judgment condition (M = 1.9). The manipulation of the similarity of causal understanding variable, then, was successful.

Evaluation measure. Subjects were asked to rate on four 9-point scales the extent to which the other participant seemed reasonable, pleasant, open-minded, and friendly. Subjects' ratings on these scales were high-ly intercorrelated ($ps < .001$) and, consequently, were summed and divided by 4 to yield a single evaluation index. A 2 (Level of Depression)

× 3 (Similarity of Judgment) unweighted means analysis of variance of
the evaluation index yielded a significant main effect for similarity of
causal judgment [$F(2,50)$ = 22.98, p < .0001] such that subjects in the
similar judgment condition evaluated the other participant more favorably (M = 7.23) than did subjects in the dissimilar (M = 5.18) and
no-information control (M = 5.8) conditions (ps < .05). The analysis also
yielded a significant Level of Depression × Similarity of Judgment
interaction [$F(2,50)$ = 5.14, p < .01]. Examination of the means presented in Table 8.1 revealed that similarity resulted in more positive
evaluations of the other participant than did dissimilarity of causal
judgments, with this effect being particularly pronounced for depressed
subjects. The results of a priori pairwise comparisons (Dunn's) among
experimental condition means appear in Table 8.1. Additional comparisons within level of depression between experimental and control
condition means using Dunnett's procedure (Kirk, 1968) indicated only
that depressed subjects in the no-information control condition evaluated the other participant significantly less favorably than did depressed
subjects in the similar judgment condition (p < .05) and significantly
more favorably than did depressed subjects in the dissimilar judgment
condition (p < .05).

Feelings about self. Experimental condition subjects were asked to rate on
a nine-point scale the extent to which the similarity of judgment feedback they received affected their feelings about themselves. A 2 (Level of
Depression) × 2 (Similar or Dissimilar Judgment) unweighted means
analysis of variance yielded a significant main effect for level of depres-

TABLE 8.1 *Means for the measure of positivity of evaluation*

	Similarity of judgment		
	Similar	Dissimilar	No-information control
Depressed	7.94a	4.72c	5.80d
	(8)	(8)	(10)
Nondepressed	6.67bd	5.55ce	5.80de
	(10)	(10)	(10)

Note: The higher the mean, the more positive the evaluation. The numbers in
parentheses indicate the number of subjects in each condition. Experimental
condition means sharing a common subscript are not significantly different at
the .05 level. Comparisons involving control and experimental condition means
were conducted within level of depression.

sion [$F(1,32) = 3.95$, $p = .05$] such that depressed subjects were seen to be more affected by the feedback they received ($M = 4.06$) than were nondepressed subjects ($M = 2.55$). In addition, it revealed a significant main effect for similarity of judgment [$F(1,32) = 10.9$, $p < .01$]. Subjects in the similar judgment condition ($M = 4.44$) were more affected by the feedback they received than were subjects in the dissimilar ($M = 2.0$) judgment condition. This latter finding is consistent with the notion that confirmation of individuals' causal analyses may serve their needs to see themselves as logical, consistent, and accurate interpreters of the environment (Byrne, 1971; Weary et al., 1985).

Confidence. The predictions relevant to the level of depression variable for the measures of actor evaluation and feelings about self were based on the notion that depressed subjects, because of a chronic lack of control and resultant uncertainty, would make more use of or be more sensitive to attributional comparison information. To assess uncertainty, subjects were asked to rate on four 9-point scales how confident they were in their internal and external attributions for the two cases. Because level of confidence was likely to be influenced by the manipulation of similarity of causal judgments, only the confidence ratings made for the first set of attributions (i.e., before the manipulation of similarity of judgments) were included in the analyses. A 2 (Level of Depression) × 3 (Similarity of Judgment) × 2 (Internal and External Confidence Ratings) repeated-measures analysis of variance revealed a significant main effect for level of depression [$F(1,50) = 5.92$, $p = .01$]. As expected, depressed subjects were less confident ($M = 6.77$). in their attributions than were nondepressed subjects ($M = 7.27$).

Discussion

It has been suggested that uncertainty motivates individuals to engage in social comparison in order to assess the correctness of their self-evaluations and their attitudes, opinions, and judgments (Festinger, 1954). In the present study, we argued that depressed college students, who were assumed to have experienced chronic heightened uncertainty associated with exposure to uncontrollable life events (Abramson et al., 1978; Warren & McEachren, 1983), would be particularly sensitive to social comparison information. Specifically, we predicted that subjects would evaluate the comparison other more favorably when she made similar rather than dissimilar causal judgments for the hypothetical actors' outcomes. Moreover, we predicted that this pattern of results would be more pronounced for depressed than for nondepressed subjects. Consistent with these predictions, we found that depressed and nondepressed individuals evaluated the comparison other more favorably in the similar than in the dissimilar judgment condition. Although this effect of similarity of causal understanding was more pronounced for depressed individuals, only under similar judgment conditions were the depressed-nondepressed differences in evaluation significant. It is widely recognized, however, that subjects generally are reluctant to evaluate strangers very negatively in an experimental context (Gerard, 1961). This likely floor effect may account for the failure of the depressed and nondepressed subjects' evaluations of the dissimilar comparison other to reach statistical significance.

The finding that depression results in more pronounced evaluations of similar and dissimilar comparison others may, at first, appear inconsistent with previous theorizing and research on interpersonal attraction. Byrne (1971) has argued and researchers (e.g., Govaux, 1971) have found, for example, that affective states contiguous with the evaluations of a stimulus person significantly influence the evaluation of that person. The more negative the affective state of subjects is, the more negative will be their evaluations. According to this formulation, depressed subjects in all conditions (similar and dissimilar judgment and no-information control conditions) of the present study should have responded in a more unfavorable way to the other participant. It is important to note, however, that depressed affect is only one of the symptoms of depressive syndrome. Depression also involves prominent cognitive, motor, perceptual, and behavioral symptoms (see Clarkin & Glazer, 1981, for a discussion). As such, any attempt to generalize from work on moods and interpersonal attraction to research on depression probably is unwarranted.

Further evidence suggestive of the increased sensitivity of depressives to social comparison information was provided by subjects' estimates of the degree to which the feedback influences their feelings about themselves. Results indicated that the comparison information had a greater impact on the self-evaluations of depressed than it did on those of nondepressed subjects. It is important to note that we did not assess the direction, positive or negative, of the impact of comparison feedback on feelings of self-worth. Beck (1976) has argued that depressives' tendency to compare themselves with others further lowers self-esteem since every comparison can be turned into negative self-evaluations. It is difficult to see how, in the context of the present study, the impact of similar causal understandings on depressed or nondepressed individuals' self-evaluations could be negative. However, future research will need to determine the affective nature of comparisons typically made and/or preferred by depressed individuals and the direction of self-evaluative changes that result from such comparisons. It seems possible, at least, that depressives' heightened sensitivity to social comparison information could be used to produce favorable changes in self-evaluation.

8.3. Laboratory study of depression and social information gathering

The previous study suggested that depressives experience heightened uncertainty and are more sensitive to social comparison feedback than are nondepressives. The purpose of the Hildebrand-Saints and Weary (1989) study was to assess whether depressives, who presumably feel a chronic lack of control and resultant uncertainty, are also more motivated to seek information about others than are nondepressives.

Evidence suggests that individuals seek social information in order to satisfy a need for effective control over the environment (Kelley, 1971; Kelly, 1955). It is reasonable to assume that those who have a greater need for control may be more motivated to gain social information about another. Indeed, there is evidence that individuals who have been deprived of control and then exposed to another person in a social situation are more likely to utilize information about the other (Pittman & Pittman, 1980).

Research also suggests that individuals are more likely to seek and use information about another person if they expect to interact with that person in the future. Elliott (1979) found that participants were more likely to seek information about the partner than were participants who did not believe such information could be useful during the forthcoming self-presentational task. Berscheid, Graziano, Monson, and Dermer (1976) reported that participants who were committed to a future interaction with another tended to award more attention to the other, and made more extreme and confident inferences about the other.

A recent study has looked at both control deprivation and information utility as factors affecting information seeking. Swann, Stephenson, and Pittman (1981) hypothesized that people will seek information about others when they have recently been deprived of control. This information seeking will increase if the individuals believe the information has high rather than low utility. In their study, individuals experienced uncontrollable outcomes on a problem-solving task and then were introduced to what was described as a second study, in which they expected to interview another participant. Some participants were led to believe that acquiring information about the interviewee would have high utility. This was accomplished by informing the participants that following the interview, they would be required to create additional questions to ask the interviewee during a get-acquainted period.

Swann et al. reported that participants who had been deprived of control sought more diagnostic information from their interaction partners than did nondeprived participants. In addition, those participants who believed that the information would have high utility sought more diagnostic information (that is, asked fewer nondiagnostic questions) than did participants who believed the information would have low utility. Contrary to predictions, however, information utility did not moderate the effects of control deprivation. Deprived participants sought more high than low diagnostic information in both high- and low-utility conditions. One explanation proposed by Swann et al. for this latter finding was that utility was sufficiently high in both high- and low-utility conditions that all participants believed the information would provide a useful means of exerting future control.

The method employed in the present study was quite similar to that used by Swann et al. (1981). However, instead of some participants being temporarily deprived of control, depressed subjects who presumably had experienced a chronic lack of control over outcomes were recruited. Depressed and nondepressed subjects in this study anticipated interviewing another participant. In addition, some subjects were informed that following the interview, they would be asked questions by the experimenter about their impressions of the interview, the process involved, and the other participant (high utility). Other subjects were informed that their participation would end following the interview (low utility). Subjects then were presented with the measure of information seeking.

The major prediction was that depressed subjects would be more likely to seek information about their interaction partners than would nondepressed participants. It also was expected that depressives would be motivated to engage in diagnostic information seeking whether the information had high or low utility, while nondepressives were expected to engage in diagnostic information seeking only in the high-utility conditions.

Method

Subjects. The procedures for selection of subjects in this study were identical to those employed in the preceding study. Eleven subjects were excluded from the final sample because their second BDI scores fell above 3 or below 10. The final sample included 24 depressed subjects (12 males and 12 females) and 24 nondepressed subjects (12 males and 12 females). Of the 24 depressed subjects in the experiment, 12 were mildly depressed, 11 were moderately depressed, and one was severely depressed. For depressed subjects, the mean BDI scores for the first and second administrations were 16.7 and 15.5, respectively. For nondepressed subjects, the mean BDI scores for the first and second administrations were 1.5 and 1.3, respectively. Within level of depression, subjects were randomly assigned to conditions.

Procedure. Each subject and a second participant (actually a same-sex confederate) were seated at tables in adjacent rooms. The experimenter then explained that the study was concerned with developing a videotape to be used in a study on interviewing processes. The experimenter asked the participants to help in the preparation of these videotapes by taking the roles of the interviewer and the interviewee. It was explained that in a natural interview situation, participants do not usually meet until the actual start of the interview; therefore, they had been placed in separate rooms until the start of the interview.

Subjects then were informed that they had been randomly assigned to the interviewer role. This role required that they ask the questions during the interview that the other participant would answer. The experimenter further explained to subjects that they would not be required to make up questions for the interview, but instead would be able to select questions from a list of items that the experimenter would provide.

At this point, subjects in the high-utility condition learned that immediately following the interview, the experimenter would inquire about their impressions of the interview, the processes involved, and the other participant. Subjects in the low-utility condition were informed that they were free to leave immediately following the interview.

The experimenter next introduced the measure of information seeking by first explaining that the interviews should be as natural as possible and should cover a wide range of content areas. To ensure this, the subjects were asked to select from a pool of 30 questions the 10 questions they would like to ask of the interviewee during the interview. It was emphasized that there was no right or wrong strategy in selecting the questions and that the participants should simply select the questions they were most interested in asking.

The questions used for the measure of information seeking were those selected by Swann et al. (1981) from Taylor and Altman's (1966) list of intimacy-scaled stimuli that represented 11 intimacy levels. In a pilot study, 89 psychology students at Ohio State University read each of these questions and responded to the question, "If you asked this question of a college freshman, how much do you feel you could learn about him/her from the answer?" Responses could range from 1 (nothing at all) to 6 (a great deal). Thirty questions that had the lowest standard deviations were selected from within each of three diagnosticity levels for the final experiment.[3] Eight questions were classified on the basis of pilot data as nondiagnostic, eight were classified as diagnostic, and the remaining 14 were classified as ambiguous with respect to diagnosticity (see Table 8.2). After completing the information-seeking measure, subjects completed manipulation checks so that they could be certain they understood their role in the session before the interview began. They then were fully debriefed.

Results

Manipulation check. To check on the manipulation of utility, subjects were asked to rate on a seven-point scale the degree to which they believed they would be questioned by the experimenter after the interview about their impressions of the interview, the process involved, and the other participant. A 2 (Mood) × 2 (Utility) analysis of variance of subjects' ratings yielded a highly significant main effect for utility [$F(1,40) = 505.79$, $p < .0001$]. Subjects in the high-utility condition ($M = 6.29$) believed that they would be questioned by the experimenter following that they would be questioned by the experimenter following the interview to a greater degree than did subjects in the low-utility condition ($M = 1.12$). The manipulation of utility, then, was successful.

Information seeking. Subjects were asked to select 10 questions from a list of 30 that they would like to ask the other participant during the videotaped interview. It was expected that depressed subjects would be

TABLE 8.2

Please circle the numbers of the 10 questions that you would like to ask the interviewee during the interview.

Diagnostic category	
Low	1. How do you feel about the United Nations (UN)?
Low	2. What do you think our government's policy toward Russia should be?
Low	3. What are your feelings about how good a job the President is doing?
Ambig	4. What do you think about bussing students to achieve integration?
Ambig	5. How do you feel about capital punishment for criminals?
Low	6. How do you feel about the Federal Government supporting persons who cannot find work?
Ambig	7. Do you like to do things alone or in a group?
High	8. What kind of person do you like to have as a friend?
Ambig	9. How much do you enjoy talking with other people?
Low	10. What radio and television programs interest you?
High	11. What are your favorite ways of spending spare time?
Ambig	12. How do you like to spend your summers?
Ambig	13. What annoys you most in people?
High	14. How do you feel when you have been severely criticized?
Ambig	15. How do you feel when you see a sick or hurt animal?
High	16. What does it take to hurt your feelings deeply?
High	17. When do you feel down and what brings these feelings on?
Ambig	18. How sensitive are you compared to other people?
Ambig	19. What things or situations embarrass you?
Low	20. What are your views on exercise and keeping fit?
Ambig	21. What is the greatest point of disagreement that you have (or have had) with your parents?
Ambig	22. What annoys you most about women/men?
Ambig	23. Tell me about disappointments of bad experiences that you have had in love affairs.
High	24. What kind of person do you like to date?
Low	25. How do you feel about blind dates?
Ambig	26. How much sexual freedom do you believe women/men should have?
Ambig	27. What are your feelings about the quality of schooling that you have received?
High	28. Which is more important to you – working on a job that you like or working on a job that pays a lot?
Low	29. What do you like best about school?
High	30. What kind of work would you like to do in the future?

Note: Ambig = ambiguous

more likely to select high diagnostic questions and nondepressed subjects would be more likely to select low diagnostic questions on the intrusive information-seeking measure. In addition, it was expected that depressives would select more high diagnostic questions than would nondepressives under both high- and low-utility conditions. Nondepressives, however, were expected to ask more high diagnostic questions under high-utility than under low-utility conditions.

A 2 (Mood) × 2 (Utility) multivariate analysis of variance (MANOVA) of the number of high and low diagnostic questions that subjects selected revealed a significant main effect for mood [$F(2,43) = 4.54$, $p <$ .0162]. Univariate analyses revealed that nondepressed subjects selected significantly more low diagnostic questions on the information-seeking measure ($M = 2.84$) than did depressed subjects ($M = 1.54$), [$F(1,44) =$ 9.11, $p < .004$]. Univariate analyses on the number of high diagnostic questions selected revealed a tendency, although not significant [$F(1,44)$ = 2.61, $p < .114$ for depressed subjects to select more high diagnostic questions ($M = 3.53$) than nondepressed subjects ($M = 2.99$).

It also was predicted that depressives and nondepressives would select diagnostic questions differently on the basis of the utility of the information. It was expected that depressed subjects would be more motivated than nondepressed subjects to engage in information seeking (i.e., to ask more high diagnostic questions) in both high- and low-utility conditions. On the other hand, we expected nondepressives to be motivated to engage in information seeking primarily in the high-utility conditions. These predictions were partially supported by the analyses. The overall MANOVA revealed a Mood × Utility interaction effect on the number of high and low diagnostic questions selected [$F(2,43) =$ 3.15, $p < .05$]. Univariate analyses indicated that this interaction was significant for the high diagnostic questions [$F(1,44) = 5.57$, $p < .022$]. The results of pairwise comparisons of means are presented in Table 8.3. As can be seen, in the low-utility conditions, depressed subjects selected significantly more high diagnostic questions ($M = 4.07$) than did nondepressed subjects ($M = 2.75$). In the high-utility conditions, no difference was found between the number of high diagnostic questions selected by depressed ($M = 3.00$) and nondepressed ($M = 3.24$) subjects. The expectation that nondepressed subjects would ask more high diagnostic questions in high- than in low-utility conditions was not supported. However, there was a tendency in that direction.

Univariate analyses also revealed a marginally significant Mood × Utility interaction effect on the number of low diagnostic questions

TABLE 8.3 *Means for the high diagnostic questions on the information-seeking measure*

	High utility	Low utility
Depressed	3.00a	4.07a
	(12)	(12)
Nondepressed	3.24ab	2.75b
	(12)	(12)

Note: The higher the mean, the greater the amount of diagnostic information gathering. The numbers in parentheses indicate the number of subjects in each condition. Experimental condition means sharing a common subscript are not significantly different at the .05 level (Dunn's a priori pairwise comparisons).

selected [$F(1,44) = 3.28$, $p = .077$]. The results of pairwise comparisons are presented in Table 8.4. As expected, nondepressed subjects selected more low diagnostic questions ($M = 3.34$) than did depressed subjects ($M = 1.66$) only in the low-utility conditions. Depressives, who presumably were motivated to gather information (i.e., to ask high diagnostic questions), chose fewer low diagnostic questions. These results suggest that nondepressives, when required to choose 10 questions to ask of the interviewee, were more likely than depressives to choose questions that would gain the least diagnostic information when they felt this information had little utility.

It also was expected that overall, depressives should ask more high than low diagnostic questions than would nondepressives. A 2 (Mood) × 2 (Utility) analysis of variance on the difference between the number of high and low diagnostic questions asked on the intrusive measure revealed a significant effect for mood [$F(1,44) = 6.92$, $p = .012$]. Depressed subjects asked significantly more high than low diagnostic questions ($M = 1.75$) than did nondepressed subjects ($M = .167$).

TABLE 8.4 *Means for the low diagnostic questions on the information-seeking measure*

	High utility	Low utility
Depressed	1.91a	1.66a
	(12)	(12)
Nondepressed	2.34ab	3.34b
	(12)	(12)

Note: The higher the mean, the greater the amount of diagnostic information gathering. The numbers in parentheses indicate the number of subjects in each condition. Experimental condition means sharing a common subscript are not significantly different at the .05 level (Dunn's a priori pairwise comparisons).

Discussion

It has been suggested that a lack of control motivates individuals in a social interaction to seek information presumably in order to regain some feeling of control (Swann et al., 1981). In the present study, we argued that depressed college students, who were assumed to feel a chronic lack of control (Abramson et al., 1978), would be more likely to seek out information in social situations than would nondepressed students. Specifically, we predicted that depressives would seek out more highly personal and revealing information from their interaction partners than would nondepressives. Support was found for this prediction. While depressives tended to ask highly diagnostic questions of their interaction partners, nondepressives asked significantly more low diagnostic questions.

We also predicted that depressed subjects would be motivated to engage in information seeking whether the information had high or low utility. We reasoned that the lack of control felt by depressives would be of itself sufficient to motivate information seeking even when such information had little or no apparent utility. Support for this prediction was found. Results indicated that depressed subjects were motivated to gather highly diagnostic information even when the utility of the information was low. In contrast, nondepressives asked significantly fewer high diagnostic questions and significantly more low diagnostic questions than did depressed subjects when they believed the information had low utility.

8.4. Study of depression and the need for cognition

The preceding studies suggest that depressives are more sensitive to social information and are more motivated to seek highly diagnostic information presumably because of a chronic lack of control and resultant uncertainly. Is it the case that depressed persons generally have a greater tendency to think about social situations they observe? Do they have a greater need for cognition than nondepressed persons? The need-for-cognition construct is concerned with an individual's tendency "to engage in and enjoy thinking" (Cacioppo & Petty, 1982). Cohen, Stotland, and Wolfe (1955) also have described the need for cognition as "a need to structure relevant social situations in a meaningful, integrated way. It is a need to understand and make reasonable the experiential world" (p. 291).

The purpose of this study (Kovacs, Tucker, & Weary, 1985) was to evaluate the association between depression and a need for cognition. If depressive sensitivity to and need for social information is related to a general need for cognition, we would expect a positive correlation between scores on the Need for Cognition Scale (Cacioppo & Petty, 1982) and the BDI (Beck, 1976).

Method

Subjects completed several measures as part of a large study ostensibly concerned with gathering information relevant to the psychometric properties of the scales. Among these were the BDI and the short form of the Need for Cognition scale (Cacioppo, Petty, & Kao, 1984). Subjects were 241 male and female undergraduate students at Ohio State University.

Results and discussion

BDI scores ranged from 0 to 32, and the range of the Need for Cognition scores was –72 to +72. A Pearson product–moment correlation was calculated between subjects' scores on the depression and need for cognition measures. Contrary to expectations, the correlation was found to be significant and negative ($r = -0.29$, $df = 239$, $p < .001$). As depression increased, the tendency to engage in and enjoy cognition decreased.

Although depressives seem to experience a chronic lack of control had heightened uncertainty over their social environments, it does not seem to motivate them to engage in more thought about social events. We must, however, caution that it is possible that the Need for Cognition scale is tapping primarily one goal underlying the need for cognition, the enjoyment of cognition. If this is the case, then a scale that measures an uncertainty reduction goal might find evidence for a positive association between depression and the need for cognition. Further investigation is needed on order to clarify these findings.

8.5. Concluding remarks

In this paper, I have examined the role of depression in processes of perception and attribution about others. The results of the studies presented converge to suggest that depressives, because of chronic experience with uncontrollability and resultant uncertainty, are more sensitive to and motivated to seek out social information. However, one limitation of the present research needs to be mentioned. The depressed subjects employed in the reported research were college students and were, for the most part, mildly depressed. It is reasonable and important to investigate social perception processes of mild depressives. However, it is possible that the relationship between amount of uncertainty and sensitivity to social information may be an inverted U–shaped function. That is, low levels of uncertainty may enhance sensitivity, whereas more extreme levels may lead to a decrease in sensitivity. Whether and to what degree the results obtained in the present research generalize to severely depressed persons, who presumably experience extreme uncertainty, will need to be determined.

Hopefully, the research reported in this paper will raise many questions for the reader and stimulate more research on the role of depression in social perception. However, before concluding, I would like to raise what is for me perhaps the most interesting of these – the likely behavioral consequences for depressives of their sensitivity to and gathering of social information.

It may be, as I have argued, that depressives are more sensitive to and gather more social information in an attempt to assuage their feelings of uncertainty. It is important to note that while postmeasures of uncertainty were obtained in the first study reported in this chapter, premeasures were not included in any of the studies because of highly probable reactivity effects. However, such measures would help to determine if depressives' sensitivity and increased information gathering in fact serves to decrease or, paradoxically, to *increase* uncertainty. It could be that more information is not always better. Hypersensitivity to social information may lead depressed persons to be painfully aware of positive and negative evaluations of them and their behaviors, and of the various action alternatives in social situations. The resulting abundance of options or choices for behavior may leave depressed persons immobilized by ever-increasing uncertainty about their perceptions, judgments, and behaviors.

Notes

1. Beck's (1967, 1976) depth of depression cut-off points for the BDI are: 0–9 = no depression, 10–15 = mild depression, 16–23 = moderate depression, 24+ = severe depression.
2. Initial analyses on all measures revealed no significant main or interaction

effects for case summary or for order of presentation of the summaries. Consequently, all subsequent analyses excluded these variables. In addition, the only significant effect associated with subject sex was a main effect of sex on the evaluation index; male subjects (M = 6.46) evaluated the female confederate more favorably than did female subjects (M = 5.33), [$F(1,44)$ = 12.42, p .001].

3. The three diagnosticity levels derived from pilot data were as follows: The nondiagnostic category included questions with mean scores of 3.11 to 3.88 on a scale from 1 (nothing at all) to 6 (a great deal). The ambiguous diagnostic category included questions with mean scores of 4.06 to 4.29, and the highly diagnostic category included questions with mean scores of 4.44 to 4.80. All standard deviations are 1.05.

References

Abramson, L. Y., Seligman, M., & Teasdale, J. P. (1978). Learned helplessness: Critique and reformulation. *Journal of Abnormal Psychology, 87,* 49–74.

Beck, A. T. (1967). *Depression: Causes and treatment.* Philadelphia: University of Pennsylvania Press.

Beck, A. T. (1974). The development of depression: A cognitive model. In R. J. Friedman & M. M. Katz (Eds.), *The psychology of depression.* Washington, DC: V. H. Winston.

Beck, A. T. (1976). *Cognitive therapy and the emotional disorders.* New York: International Universities Press.

Beck, A. T., Rush, J. A., Shaw, B. A., & Emery, G. (1979). *Cognitive therapy of depression.* New York: Guilford Press.

Berscheid, E., Graziano, W., Monson, T., & Dermer, M. (1976). Outcome dependency: Attention, attribution, and attraction. *Journal of Personality and Social Psychology, 34,* 978–989.

Byrne, D. (1971). *The attraction paradigm.* New York: Academic Press.

Cacioppo, J. T., & Petty, R. E. (1982). The need for cognition. *Journal of Personality and Social Psychology, 42,* 116–131.

Cacioppo, J. T., Petty, R. E., & Kao, C. F. (1984). The efficient assessment of need for cognition. *Journal of Personality Assessment, 48,* 306–307.

Cohen, A. R., Stotland, E., & Wolfe, D. M. (1955). An experimental investigation of need for cognition. *Journal of Abnormal and Social Psychology, 51,* 291–294.

Clarkin, J. F., & Glazer, H. I. (1981). *Depression; Behavioral and directive intervention strategies.* New York: Garland STPM Press.

Coyne, J. C. (1976). Toward an interactional description of depression. *Psychiatry, 39,* 28–40.

Coyne, J. C., Aldwin, C. & Lazarus, R. S. (1981). Depression and coping in stressful episodes. *Journal of Abnormal Psychology, 90,* 439–447.

Elliott, G. C. (1979). Some effects of deception and self-monitoring on planning and reacting to a self-presentation. *Journal of Personality and Social Psychology, 37,* 1282–1292.

Festinger, L. (1954). A theory of social comparison processes. *Human Relations, 7,* 117–140.

Garber, J., Miller, W. R., & Seaman, S. F. (1979). Learned helplessness, stress, and the depressive disorders. In R. A. Depue (Ed.), *The psychobiology of the depressive disorders: Implication for the effects of stress.* New York: Academic Press.

Govaux, C. (1971). Induced affective states and interpersonal attraction. *Journal of Personality and Social Psychology, 20*, 37–43.

Hildebrand-Saints, L., & Weary, G. (1989). Depression and social information gathering. *Personality and Social Psychology Bulletin, 15*, 150–160.

Kelley, H. H. (1971). Attribution in social interaction. In E. E. Jones et al. (Eds.), *Attribution: Perceiving the causes of behavior.* New York: General Learning Press.

Kelly, G. A. (1955). *The psychology of personal constructs.* New York: Norton.

Kirk, R. E. (1968). *Experimental design: Procedures for the behavioral sciences.* Belmont, CA: Brooks/Cole.

Pittman, T. S. & Pittman, N. L. (1980). Deprivation of control and the attribution process. *Journal of Personality and Social Psychology, 39*, 377–389.

Sacco, W. P. (1981). Invalid use of the Beck Depression Inventory to identify depressed college-student subjects: A methodological comment. *Cognitive Therapy and Research, 5*, 143–147.

Seligman, M. E. P. (1974). *Helplessness: On depression, development, and death.* San Francisco: Freeman.

Swann, W. B., Stephenson, B., & Pittman, T. S. (1981). Curiosity and control: On the determinants of the search for social knowledge. *Journal of Personality and Social Psychology, 40*, 635–642.

Sweeney, P. D., Shaeffer, D., & Golin, S. (1982). Attributions about self and other in depression. *Personality and Social Psychology Bulletin, 8*, 37–42.

Taylor, D. S., & Altman, I. (1966). *Intimacy-scaled stimuli for use in research on interpersonal exchange* (Technical Report No. 9, MF022.01.03-1002). Bethesda, MD: Naval Medical Research Institute.

Warren, L. W., & McEachren, L. (1983). Psychological correlates of depressive symptomatology in adult women. *Journal of Abnormal Psychology, 92*, 151–160.

Weary, G., Elbin, S. D., & Hill, M. G. (1987). Attributional and social comparison processes in depression. *Journal of Personality and Social Psychology, 52*, 605–610.

Weary, G., Jordan, J. S., Hill, M. G. (1985). The attributional norm of internality and depressive sensitivity to social information. *Journal of Personality and Social Psychology, 49*, 1283–1293.

9. Children's strategies for the control of emotion in themselves and others

CHARLES L. McCOY AND JOHN C. MASTERS

Over the past two decades there has been increased attention in psychological research and theory to the role of cognition and other internal processes in mediating the relation between situations and behavior (see Mischel, 1973). There has been a corresponding retreat from views that behavior is controlled primarily by factors external to the person (Skinner, 1953) or by relatively insular intrapsychic forces (S. Freud, 1923). In the current view, the person is seen as being involved in a reciprocal interaction with the environment (Bandura, 1977), and person variables such as expectancies, competencies, and values are considered as necessary factors in an adequate explanation of behavior (Mischel, 1973).

The greater acceptance of the active role of the person in determining behavior has fostered interest in issues previously not considered in depth. One such issue is children's ability to exert strategic control over internal and external events – that is, their formulation and implementation of strategies for achieving desired ends. This ability has been discussed generally in terms of self-regulation and more specifically in terms of a child's self-control, broadly conceived to include the inhibitive control of behavior such as resistance to temptation (Mischel & Patterson, 1976); facilitative control, as in persistence at an effortful task (Masters & Santrock, 1976), and even the control of cognitive processes such as memory (Keeny, Cannizzo, & Flavell, 1967) or academic learning (Brown & Smiley, 1978).

Various mechanisms of self-control have been posited, such as the self-manipulation of environmental contingencies (see Thoresen & Mahoney, 1974) or the use of overt and covert self-statements that guide behavior (Luria, 1961; Masters & Binger, 1978; Meichenbaum, 1976; Vygotsky, 1962). Another domain of strategy formulation and implementation is that of "social control" – the influence individuals exert on the behavior and cognitions of other people. Examples are children's strategies for reaching social goals, such as entrance into the peer group (Mize & Ladd, 1984; Taylor, & Asher, 1984), and the manipulation of emotion in others (Felleman, Barden, Carlson, Rosenberg, & Masters, 1983).

The role of emotion in psychological processes is a second topic that has received attention as psychologists have increasingly recognized the importance of internal processes. Two methodological developments have aided the empirical investigation of emotion. The first has been the development of valid and reliable procedures for inducing emotion in children either experientially (Barden, Garber, Leiman, Ford, & Masters, 1985; Isen, Horn, & Rosenhan, 1973) or cognitively (Masters, Barden, & Ford, 1979). These procedures have made possible controlled studies of the influence of emotional states on children's behavior and cognition (Masters, Felleman, & Barden, 1981). The second methodological advance concerns the reinterpretation of introspective procedures. Self-reports are no longer taken to reveal mental structure as they were in early introspectionist psychology (Marx & Hillix, 1979) but are interpreted as reflecting persons' implicit theories of their own or another person's psychological processes (Mischel, 1968, 1973). This advance has furthered the study of children's understanding of emotion (see Masters & Carlson, 1984; Schwartz & Trabasso, 1984).

There is an emerging literature on the area of overlap between the study of control strategies and the study of emotion. This area is children's strategies and the study of emotion. The ability to control one's own emotions is thought to be a hallmark of competent personal and social development (A. Freud, 1946). The social control of emotion – that is, influencing the emotional state of another person – is also considered an important aspect of one's adjustment. Such skills are likely, for example, to be related to a child's general popularity and specific friendships (Dodge, in press; Masters & Furman, 1981).

The purpose of this chapter is to provide an integrative review of research into children's strategies for controlling their own and others' negative emotional states. The first section will set some conceptual points of departure for the literature review. It begins with a discussion of general issues concerning control strategies and illustrates these issues by reviewing one research program into children's behavioral self-control. The section then provides a working definition of "emotion control strategies" and ends with a proposed model for the emotion control process. The second and third sections address, respectively, children's strategies for the self-control of emotion and their strategies for the social control of emotion. Both sections review research on children's understanding of strategies and their implementation of them. The fourth and final section will present issues for future research and will emphasize the need for greater attention to the specificity of emotion control strategies, their effectiveness, and their acquisition.

9.1. Fundamental considerations

What constitutes a strategy?

A strategy, as discussed in this chapter, is a plan of action for obtaining a desired outcome. This meaning can be illustrated in a review of the work of Mischel and his colleagues on children's abilities to delay gratification and to resist temptation. Three periods can be identified in this research. During the first period, Mischel examined personal and situational factors that influence children's self-control. Mischel and Metzner (1962), for example, found that a child's age and the length of projected delay are related to willingness to delay. Older children choose more often than do younger children to wait for a highly desirable reward rather than accept one that is less desirable but immediately available. Children of all ages are more likely to choose delay if the delay period will be short.

After investigating the influence of these and other determinants of delay, Mischel examined effective means of increasing self-control. This work initially focused on cognitive and attentional processes in children's delay of gratification. Mischel, Ebbesen, and Zeiss (1972) found that preschool children instructed to think about distracting "fun things" when the reward was present delayed gratification longer than did children instructed to think about the reward itself or those given no instructions. In a subsequent study, Mischel and Baker (1975) attempted to identify the properties of reward-focused ideation that undermines ability to delay. Children were instructed to concentrate either on the reward's consummatory qualities (e.g., if the reward was a marshmallow, to think about how marshmallows are sweet, chewy, and fun to eat) or on its nonconsummatory qualities by cognitively transforming the reward into a nonedible item (e.g., to think of marshmallows as white, fluffy clouds). Children concentrating on the nonconsummatory qualities delayed gratification longer than did the other children.

Another means of increasing delay studied by Mischel and his colleagues is the talking to themselves that children do in situations requiring self-control. Mischel and Patterson (1976, 1978) studied pre-school children's ability to utilize self-instruction in persisting at a task in the face of a highly attractive alternative activity. Children were given one of three types of self-instruction: "temptation-inhibiting" plans exhorting oneself not to give in to the distracting activity, "task-facilitating" plans to continue concentrating on the assigned task, and "reward-oriented" plans emphasizing the positive consequences of persistence. The structure of the plans was also varied such that half of the children in each condition were given specific verbal scripts for the assigned plans ("elaborated plans") and half were given only the general purpose of the plan ("unelaborated plans"). Children given elaborated temptation-inhibiting plans or elaborated reward-oriented plans resisted temptation more successfully than did the other children.

The effectiveness of the strategies suggested to children raised the possibility that children can spontaneously alter their cognitions in order to increase their ability to delay gratification. Mischel's research thus moved increasingly toward studying factors under the child's control. The third period of Mischel's research has focused on children's understanding of strategies for self-control. Mischel and Mischel (1983) questioned preschool children, third graders, and sixth graders about what types of reward-focused thinking would enhance ability to delay gratification. Only the older children understood that concentrating on abstract, nonconsummatory qualities of the reward would lead to longer delay than would thinking about its consummatory qualities. This is particularly interesting in light of the finding that preschoolers' increased delay when instructed to engage in nonconsummatory ideation (Mischel & Baker, 1975): They are able to implement the strategy successfully even if they cannot think of it on their own.

Mischel's work is instructive not only in illustrating an empirical approach to goal-oriented strategies but also in suggesting possible avenues of effective emotion control. Consider the greater delay shown by children who occupied themselves in the delay period by thinking about distracting events rather than the reward itself. This suggests that an effective strategy for controlling a negative emotion such as anger may be to engage in distracting ideation such as counting to 10 or thinking about the eventual benefits of exercising control. Moreover, it is possible that the more detailed or elaborated one's strategy for controlling emotion, the more effective it will be. Before possibilities such as these are considered some specification is needed concerning what constitutes an emotion control strategy.

What constitutes an emotion control strategy?

There is neither room nor need in the present context for a review of theories and definitions of emotion. These topics have been covered fully by others (e.g., Strongman, 1978). Let it suffice to say that a multiplicity of definitions and theories exist, each emphasizing one or more antecedent, component, or consequence of emotion. What is required for the present purpose is a working definition of emotion control strategy that will provide some boundaries for this review.

As discussed in this chapter, an emotion control strategy will be any act or cognition having the goal of (1) altering one's own or another person's experience of an ongoing negative emotional state, (2) preventing the experience of a negative state, or (3) maintaining the experience of a positive emotional state. This definition specifies both a strategy's purpose and its target. In terms of its purpose, only acts specifically intended to change emotion are considered to be strategies and acts that incidentally alter emotion are excluded from discussion. Thus, giving a present to a friend who, unknown to the giver, is feeling sad would not constitute a strategic attempt to control emotion. The act of giving the present may have the incidental effect of cheering the recipient but would not qualify as a strategic attempt at emotion control strategy since there was no intent for emotional intervention on the giver's part.

The definition specifies that the target of an emotion control strategy is the person's actual experience of an emotional state rather than the behavior resulting from that emotion. The behavioral expression of an emotional state can have varied relations to the underlying state. At times it may be manipulated to hide the emotion actually felt, in which case display rules are said to be operating concerning which emotions can be appropriately expressed in which situations (e.g., facial display rules; Saarni, 1979). We will not consider the implementation of such display rules to be emotion control strategies. In instances of emotion control, thought or behavior is manipulated in the service of influencing emotional state (whether to prevent, alter, or maintain – for example, buying something when one is feeling sad or diverting attention to positive outcomes or events).

Finally, a strategic intervention can be characterized in terms of its timing relative to an emotionally provocative event. The intervention is preventative if it precedes an emotionally potent experience and thus inhibits induction. It is remedial or maintaining if it follows induction of an emotion and thus alters or sustains, respectively, an ongoing emotion. As we shall see, researchers have paid more attention to the issues of remediation and maintenance of emotional states than they have to prevention.

A model of the emotion control process

One of the earliest and most complete statements concerning the role of control sequences in human behavior is Miller, Galanter, and Pribram's (1960) book, *Plans and the Structure of Behavior*. The authors advocated a view of psychology in which strategic control processes construed as "TOTE units" replace stimulus – response associations as the basic level of analysis. The TOTE unit, a concept derived from cybernetics, is a description of a general control process by which an organism achieves goals through: (1) testing (T) its present state against some desired state, (2) operating (O) by the implementation of a strategy for altering its state if a match between actual and desired does not exist, (3) testing (T) the newly obtained state against the desired state, and (4) exiting (E) the control process if a match has been reached. If a discrepancy still exists, however, other strategies will be implemented until the goal has been achieved.

The model proposed here for emotional control is based on Millet et al.'s TOTE unit and extends it to include instances of preventative, sustaining, and remedial control. Figure 9.1 illustrates the TOTE model as adapted to the case of emotion control. For example, remedial emotion control may be conceived as a four-step process that is initiated after an event has elicited an undesired emotional reaction either in oneself or in another person and proceeds as follows:

1. *Monitoring* of emotion. This requires attention to emotional cues and correct recognition of emotional states.
2. *Activation of motivation* to intervene. This is derived from a discrepancy between the current emotional state and a desired state.
3. *Formulation* of a strategy for intervention. Drawing on one's beliefs or knowledge about emotion, one generates or selects a plan for remediation.
4. *Implementation* of the strategy for altering emotion. Intervener monitors the change in emotional state to determine the success of the intervention.

At this point, the intervener may exit the process if the desired end has been achieved or may, if the second test fails and adequate motivation remains, resume the process by reinstating the strategic attempt or formulating and implementing another strategy.

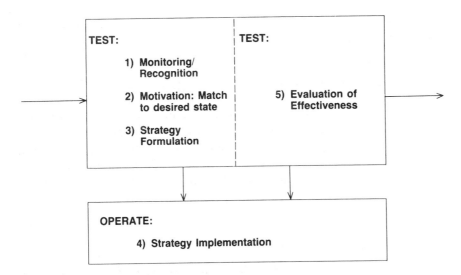

Figure 9.1. Model of emotion control process for the remediation of negative emotional states. (Adapted from Miller, Galanter and Pribram, 1960)

This model is offered primarily as a heuristic device in that it helps organize discussion. Despite its intuitive appeal, the model's validity as an actual psychological process remains largely untested and is, in itself, an issue for future empirical investigation. Aspects of the process have, however, been studied in isolation. For example, it has been found that children as young as 4 and 5 years of age are able to recognize spontaneous facial displays of others' emotions (Felleman et al., 1983), are not influenced by their own emotional state in inferring others' emotions (Carlson, Felleman, & Masters, 1983), and depend increasingly with age on contextual cues rather than expressive cues for these inferences (Reichenbach & Masters, 1983). Moreover, children indicate they are motivated to intervene into others' negative emotions, particularly if they will be the agent of intervention (Carlson et al., 1983). (Suprisingly, little research has addressed children's recognition of their own emotional states or their motivation to alter these states.) Finally, children have consensual beliefs about the determinants of emotion (Barden, Zelko, Duncan, & Masters, 1980) that may serve as a knowledge base for emotion control in themselves and others by suggesting intervention strategies likely to be effective. In short, children possess a relatively sophisticated understanding of emotion and, as a group, appear to have the requisite skills for emotion control. The emerging literature on how they formulate and implement strategies for controlling their own and other persons' emotions will be reviewed in the next two sections.

9.2. Strategies for the self-control of emotional states

This discussion of strategies for the self-control of emotion is divided into two parts. The first addresses children's formulation of control strategies as reflected in their nomination of methods for controlling their own emotions. The second addresses children's spontaneous implementation of control strategies. The implementations of behavioral, experiential, and cognitive means of self-intervention are discussed in turn.

Strategy formulation

Strategies for the remediation of negative emotional states. Two studies have examined children's articulation of strategies for remediating their own negative emotions. In the first, Harris, Olthof, and Terwogt (1981) interviewed 6-, 11-, and 15-year-old children about their strategies for remediating their own sadness, anger, and fear. The strategies nominated were assigned to one of seven categories, depending upon the mechanism invoked. These were situational change (altering one's immediate situation, such as by playing with friends), inner redirection (redirecting one's thoughts), display (changing the apparent emotion by displaying another emotion), crying (stopping crying), failure of inner redirection (asserting that mental processes cannot be manipulated), or autonomous (asserting that the emotion cannot be altered). Strategies that could not be classified into one of the above categories were assigned to a residual category. Note that only the first two of these categories fit the currently adopted definition of emotion control strategies. Children of all three ages nominated strategies involving situation change (e.g., "I would go play with friends"), but cognitive strategies such as inner redirection (e.g., "I would try to think about something happy") were nominated predominantly by the older children. This age difference in nominating cognitive strategies was particularly true for altering sadness.

The Harris et al. study documents that children have consensual strategies for altering their emotions. Moreover, these strategies change with age in a manner consistent with children's growing cognitive sophistication (Harris & Olthof, 1982). Future research may need to consider the categories into which children's strategy nominations are classified. As noted above, not all of the categories in the Harris et al. study seem truly to address the remediation of the emotional state per se. Furthermore, over 24 percent of the subjects nominated strategies classified only as residual. This was particularly true for the youngest subjects, nearly half of whom nominated residual strategies. Consequently, much information on children's emotion control strategies was lost. Additionally, Harris et al. did not address children's ability to generate strategies for emotional self-intervention while actually experiencing an emotional state or the influence of the emotion's cause upon the intervention strategy. Since emotion self-control strategies are by definition utilized in the experience of an emotion and since one is likely to know the cause of the emotion, the ecological validity of the Harris et al. study is compromised.

Strategies for the maintenance of positive emotional states. There is an even greater paucity of research on this topic, the only study being one by Harris et al. (1981) exploring children's understanding of ways a positive emotional state might be maintained. These investigators also asked children how they would intensify an already existing emotional state. As was found for controlling sadness, a developmental increase was found for the nomination of cognitive strategies. We may conclude, then, that children can formulate strategies for the maintenance of positive emotional states, but further research is needed to reveal the general character of such strategies and the different categories into which they fall.

Strategies for the prevention of negative emotional states. We have included this section largely as an implicit call for research. Despite attention to vulnerability and invulnerability in children in terms of their resiliency in the face of stress (e.g., Garmezy & Rutter, 1983), at the time of this writing there had been no direct investigation of children's ability to nominate strategies to prevent the occurrence of negative emotional reactions. Although the research on remediation and maintenance strategies is sparse, it nevertheless suggests that the self-control of emotion is something about which even very young children have some common strategic knowledge. The degree to which self-control strategies may be conceived of in anticipatory (preventative) ways remains an important topic for investigation.

Conclusion. Although children are clearly able to nominate strategies for emotional self-control and are influenced by developmental and situational factors in their strategies, little is known about the character of the strategies (especially about maintenance and prevention strategies) and even less about the processes underlying children's ability to nominate them. There is some indication that children typically assess the causal context of the emotional state in devising intervention strategies (McCoy & Masters, 1985), suggesting that they may rely on observed causes as models for intervention strategies (to the extent that they might manipulate such causes). In general, however, children's formulation of emotion control strategies remains a relatively unexplored domain.

Given that children can formulate emotion self-control strategies, the next question is whether they are able to implement such strategies. Below, the spontaneous implementation of behavioral, experiential, and cognitive self-control strategies is discussed.

Strategy implementation: behavioral strategies

The bulk of research on children's behavioral strategies for the self-control of emotion has focused on remediation and maintenance of emotional states through self-gratification (acquiring rewards for oneself) or generosity (giving rewards to peers). These studies will be reviewed.

Strategies for the remediation of negative emotional states. Increased self-reward when one is in a negative mood has long been interpreted as being a strategy for the remediation of that mood (Masters, 1972; Underwood, Moore, & Rosenhan, 1973). The influence of negative emotions on self-gratification has also been found to be mediated by the cause of the mood and the contingencies for self-gratification. Children in negative moods resulting from thinking about unhappy events subsequently engage in greater self-gratification than do children who have thought about neutral events (Barden, Garber, Duncan, & Masters, 1981; Rork & Masters, 1989; Rosenhan, Underwood, & Moore, 1974; Underwood et al., 1973). However, when the negative mood is induced experientially through failure on a task, children's self-gratification is not enhanced for self-reward contingent upon task performance ("take as many as you deserve") but is enhanced for noncontingent self-reward ("take as many as you want") (Masters, 1972; Masters & Peskay, 1972). Moreover, experiences of negative social comparisons have been found to increase self-gratification when the inequity was material (i.e., receiving fewer tokens than a peer) (Masters, 1968) but not when the inequity was social (i.e., receiving less social nurturance from an adult; Masters & Santrock, 1982).

The studies reviewed indicate that the presence of a negative emotional state is not in itself sufficient to elicit implementation of a specific type of remediation strategy. For example, material self-reward will follow experiences of negative social comparison only when the social inequality was itself materially based. Such selective implementation of self-gratification suggests that children tailor their emotion control strategies to the specific cause of the emotion, which is consistent with the findings presented earlier that children are attentive to the causal context of a state when formulating control strategies (McCoy & Masters, 1985).

Developmental differences in the influence of a negative mood on subsequent generosity have been interpreted as reflecting the impact of socialization upon children's emotion remediation strategies for themselves as well as others (Cialdini & Kenrick, 1976). Older children in negative states are more generous than are younger children in negative states (Cialdini & Kenrick, 1976), but this enhanced generosity may occur only when the generous act will be known to others ("public generosity") and not when it is known only to oneself ("private generosity") (Isen et al., 1973; Kenrick, Baumann, & Cialdini, 1979). Moreover, the social nature of the event causing the negative mood mediates generosity (e.g., thinking about someone else's misfortune enhances generosity while thinking about one's own misfortunes does not; Barnett, King, & Howard, 1979). These findings suggest that generosity to others is indeed used by children in an attempt to remediate their own state when the condition of generosity or the character of their own emotional state is such that generous behavior will have a positive effect on their own state (e.g., eliciting public recognition or addressing another's negative state). This is well illustrated in a study by Rork & Masters (1989) that was designed to demonstrate that young children's generosity to others may indeed be a functional strategy to influence their own state. In this study, children were given the opportunity to donate rewards to others, but this opportunity involved either sharing (in which each reward donated to a peer was one less for the donor) or assignment (in which any rewards left after donation were returned to a common pool). Sad children tended to reduce their generosity when rewards were to be shared, but not when they had the opportunity only to assign rewards to others, indicating that their generosity was influenced by an implicit opportunity for self-gratification that might be used to remediate their own negative emotional state.

In general, then, children's keeping of tokens rather than giving them to peers is likely to reflect an acquisitive motive similar to that underlying self-gratification. This may be particularly true for young children. (Subsequently, as socialization proceeds, reinforcement for prosocial acts such as sharing with other children and an appreciation of other's positive emotional states may imbue generosity with reinforcing quality.) Because it is reinforcing, generosity thus becomes a direct means of enhancing or improving one's mood.

Strategies for the maintenance of positive emotional states. Increased self-reward or generosity while one is in a positive mood has been interpreted as an attempt to maintain that mood. Positive emotional states have consistently been found to increase children's self-gratification (e.g., Mischel, Coates, & Raskoff, 1968; Rosenhan, Underwood, & Moore, 1974). Positive emotional states have generally been found to enhance children's generosity to peers (e.g., Isen et al., 1973; Rosenhan et al., 1974).

However, the evidence of children's actual motivated use of generosity for the maintenance of a positive emotional state is not clear. Rork & Masters (1985) failed to find increased generosity by happy children in general. They did find that an other-focused happy state inclined children to show increased generosity, which might be interpreted to mean that the other focus increased the ability for generosity to others to have a maintaining "feedback" effect for their own state. In general, however, the evidence for any broad behavioral tendencies for children to maintain their own positive affective states is not yet compelling. Because of the small number of studies, the hypothesis that children do indeed implement behavioral strategies to maintain positive states remains viable, but certainly merits more research. This may be especially necessary since it seems reasonable that motives to maintain positive states will be less strong or urgent than motives to remediate negative ones, so the implementation of behavioral strategies to do so will be less frequent, intense, and broadly invoked.

Strategies for the prevention of negative emotional states. Again, we include this section largely to illustrate how issues of prevention have not yet received attention in the research literature, though we would earmark the notion of children's invulnerability (cf. Garmezy, 1981; Garmezy & Neuchterlein, 1972) to psychopathology as the first inroad to this area. Certainly, these issues merit further consideration, in terms of the prevention of negative emotional reactions in normal children, the response to "typical" life stressors, and the prevention of psychopathological conditions.

Conclusion. Self-gratification and generosity have been by far the most studied strategies for the behavioral self-control of emotion. It is likely, however, that other behavioral strategies play a role in emotion remediation (becoming involved in some enjoyable activity may, for example, be a means for altering one's negative emotions). Although it might be argued that the investigation of behavioral self-control strategies should lag behind research on children's strategy formulation, this argument is not totally compelling. Children may have behavioral strategies that they invoke without awareness or voluntary intent that have been effective in the past. Such behavior may violate our rather strict definition of a strategy (where we rely heavily upon notions of intent), but the more general point is that our knowledge about children's ability to initiate behavior that exercises, inadvertently or otherwise, systematic self-control over their own emotional states is woefully inadequate. The increased interest in this topic, as illustrated by this volume, provides hope that this important topic will receive greater attention in the near future.

Strategy implementation: experiential strategies

Studies of the experiential antecedents of emotion indicate that children are responsive to a variety of experiences, including success or failure (Fry, 1976), social acceptance or rejection (Barden, Garber, Leiman, Ford, & Masters, 1985), reinforcing or punishing social interactions (Furman & Masters, 1980), and positive or negative social comparisons (Masters, Carlson, & Rahe, 1985). The obvious effectiveness of experiences as inducers of emotion raises the question of whether they could be used strategically for remediating ongoing emotions. To a great extent, individuals may control their own experiences by setting them up (e.g., planning a party) or simply exposing themselves to a context in which certain experiences are likely to occur (e.g., calling a friend who is likely to say nice things). Many experiences, particularly those that can be purchased (e.g., movies, carnivals at shopping centers) or that are available via the media (e.g., television, music), are readily accessed and (especially in the case of the media) freely available to young children as well as older ones and adults.

Strategies for the remediation of negative emotional states. A recent study by Masters, Ford, and Arend (1983) examined the hypothesis that children might use experiences provided by the media (television) in an apparent attempt to reinstate a negative emotional state. In this study, 4- and 5-year-old children participated in social interactions during which they received from an adult less nurturance than did a peer, more nurturance than the peer, or the same amount of nurturance as the peer. After these interactions, children were given the opportunity to watch either a highly nurturant television program *(Mister Rogers' Neighborhood)* or a children's news program. Boys who had been in the aversive social interaction watched the nurturant program for a longer period than did boys who had experienced positive or neutral interactions. However, girls in the three conditions did not differ in the duration of their viewing.

In consistency with findings discussed earlier indicating that attempts to remediate negative emotion (self-justification or generosity, in particular) are linked in highly specific ways to the conditions under which an emotional state is aroused (self vs. other focus, material vs. social deprivation), these findings suggest a contextual specificity to children's spontaneous implementation of experiential strategies for the self-control of emotion, and a sex difference in strategies. The boys matched cause and intervention by seeking additional social nurturance as a means of remediating the emotional effects of having received relatively little social nurturance. Of course, the finding that only boys increased their television viewing of a nurturant content may also reflect the fact that the nurturant figure, Mr. Rogers, was also male.

In order to assess the effectiveness of any remediation strategies children might adopt, Masters et al. (1983) monitored children's emotional states at various points throughout the study by videotaping their facial expressions. It was found that even though boys who had experienced a nonnurturant interaction increased their viewing of nurturant television content, this viewing experience did not effectively remediate their negative state. This suggests that the actual implementation of remediation strategies for intervention may be undertaken even though, in the end, they prove ineffective. The issue of the effectiveness of children's self-control strategies for their own emotional states, experiential or otherwise, has not been explored in any depth and clearly merits further attention.

So far as we can determine, there have been no other studies directly examining children's attempts to manipulate their own experiences in ways that appear strategically designed to influence their emotional states. Given the emerging interest in the affective consequences of social experience or media content (primarily television), this seems a particularly important topic for future research.

Strategies for the maintenance of positive emotional states. There appears to have been no research directly examining children's manipulation of their own experiences in ways designed to maintain positive emotional states. Some findings in the social interaction literature are consistent with the hypothesis that such strategies exist, but they are open to alternative interpretations. For example, the early report by Charlesworth and Hartup (1967) and Hartup, Glazer, and Charlesworth (1967) that a consequence of positive social reinforcement in the nursery school classroom was the continuation of the behavior or activity that was reinforced might be interpreted to indicate that children continued that activity to elicit reinforcement by others, thus maintaining the positive affective state presumably induced by such reinforcement (Furman & Masters, 1980). On the other hand, it is probably more parsimonious to interpret this as a simple effect of reinforcement on the maintenance of behavior. This topic also merits more attention, though as noted earlier, the likelihood that maintenance motives for positive states would be weaker than ones for the remediation of negative states suggests that children may only infrequently manipulate experiences in pursuit of the maintenance of positive effect.

Strategies for the prevention of negative emotional states. Although the study by Masters et al. (1983) was intended to investigate children's manipulation of experience in a remedial fashion, an inadvertent finding suggests the possibility that some of the children attempted to prevent negative affect from being induced during the period of nonnurturant treatment by an adult. As noted earlier, only the boys watched a nurturant television program longer after a negative affective state had been induced through the nonnurturant treatment than they did after a positive affective state had been induced. During the nurturance manipulation, children were given a cover task of puzzles on which they might work while the adult interacted with them in a nurturant or nonnurturant fashion. It was found that girls completed significantly more puzzles during non-nurturant treatment than they did when treated nurturantly or in a neutral fashion, and they also completed significantly more puzzles than did boys in this condition.

Therefore, it is possible that girls did not attempt subsequent remediation of negative affect because they had already implemented a preventative strategy. The work on the puzzles may have provided a means of self-distraction from the nonnurturant social treatment. It might also have been an effort designed to elicit praise (nurturance) from the nonnurturant adult for meritorious performance. Whereas further research is necessary to clarify these interpretations, the findings suggest self-distraction and impression management as two strategies, one personal and the other social but both designed to manipulate experience, that may be used to prevent the induction of a negative emotional state. It should be noted, however, that there was no indication that the girls' preventative strategy, if that is what it was, was any more effective than the remedial one the boys used in modifying negative affect, and at the end of the experiment girls who had been treated nonnurturantly continued to display facial expressions indicative of sadness.

Strategy implementation: cognitive and attentional strategies

Admonitions to "count one's blessings" when feeling sad or to "look on the bright side" when faced with an undesired outcome attest to the common belief that thoughts can change our undesirable feelings. Interest in cognitive means of reducing or avoiding noxious emotions has a long history within psychology as well. Early in the development of psychoanalysis, Sigmund Freud (1896) suggested that cognitive processes could be used as defenses against unacceptable wishes or memories and the disturbing affect associated with them. Later analysts extended this notion of "defense mechanisms" to the study of children (A. Freud, 1946). Despite the accumulation of extensive case study reports on the functioning of defense mechanisms, it has been difficult to define these constructs adequately for experimental investigation. Although the recent development of methods to induce emotion has permitted new approaches to the study of cognition–affect relations, the issue continues to be the focus of great debate (Lazarus, 1984; Zajonc, 1984).

Strategies for the remediation of negative emotional states. Consider some ways in which cognitions could be manipulated to alter one's emotional state. In the case of negative affect induced by failure on a task, one could, for example, (1) manipulate one's expectations for future performance (e.g., "I didn't do well that time, but now I know how to do it and I'll do better next time"), (2) alter one's attributions concerning the cause of failure (e.g., "I was just nervous that time"), (3) compensate by thinking of one's personal assets (e.g., "I may not be good at spelling but I'm really good at math"), or (4) discount the importance of the task or experience ("I really don't care how I did – it's just a game").

Of these possible cognitive manipulations, relatively consistent empirical support has been found for only one, attributions following failure. Adults who have failed on a task are less likely to attribute their outcome to internal factors than are adults who have succeeded (e.g., Fitch, 1970; Miller, 1976; Weary, 1980; Wollert, Heinrich, Wood, & Werner, 1983). On the other hand, chronically depressed adults have been found to attribute failures or other negative events to internal or stable factors more often than do nondepressed adults (Harvey, 1981; Kuiper, 1978; Litman-Adizes, 1978; Menapuce & Doby, 1976; Rizley, 1978). These results suggest that adults who are not clinically depressed may defend against failure-related affect by altering their beliefs about the cause of that failure.

The literature concerning children's attributions following failure is less extensive but indicates that at least some children utilize defensive attributional processes as a means of controlling negative emotion. Nicholls (1975), for example, found that elementary school girls blame themselves for their failures but that boys blame external causes. In a study of helpless children (i.e., those who feel unable to overcome failure), Diener and Dweck (1978) found that such children blame themselves for failures but that mastery-oriented children focus not on the cause of their failure but on means of correcting it. The developmental course of such strategies has yet to be studied extensively.

The literature on attributions following failure contains the most direct implications for the potential use of one type of cognition in a remedial fashion. But attributions are not the only class of cognition associated with affect that might serve a remedial function. If one assumes a reciprocity between affect and cognition, studies of the effect of negative emotion on cognition may suggest ways that cognitions, in turn, might affect emotion. Generally, however, this literature contains inconsistent results. Some studies have found that negative states elicit mood-congruent cognitions (memory for negatively valenced material, Nasby & Yando, 1982; expectancies for performance outcomes, Wright & Mischel, 1982; evaluation of neutral stimuli, Isen & Shalker, 1982), while others have found no effect (expectancies for serendipitous outcomes, Masters & Furman, 1976; memory for negatively valenced materials, Isen, Shalker, Clark, & Karp, 1978; Mischel, Ebbeson, & Zeiss, 1976; Teasdale & Fogarty, 1979; attention to personal liabilities, Mischel, Ebbeson, & Zeiss, 1973). The general absence of findings that mood states elicit cognitive consequences that are contrary to the valence of the mood state suggests that this is a strategy that children may nominate (e.g., Harris et al., 1981) but that is seldom implemented by either children or adults.

Strategies for the maintenance of positive emotional states. Children's cognitive strategies for prolonging a positive emotion such as happiness have not been studied directly. Nevertheless, possible strategies are suggested by established links between induced positive states and cognition or cognitive processes. Generally, positive emotions have been found to elicit mood-congruent cognitions. Positive moods increase children's expectancies for serendipitous events (Masters & Furman, 1976), facilitate their learning (Masters, Barden, & Ford, 1979), increase children's and adults' memory for positively valenced material (Isen, et al., 1978; Mischel et al., 1976; Nasby & Yando, 1982; Natale & Hantas, 1982; Teasdale & Fogarty, 1979), increase adults' expectancies for good performance outcomes (Wright & Mischel, 1982), increase adults' attention to personal assets (Mischel et al., 1973), and dispose adults toward more favorable evaluation of their belongings (Isen et al., 1978) and of neutral stimuli (Isen & Shalker, 1982).

In studies of children's attributions following success on a task, an experience presumably leading to a positive emotional state, it has been found that children tend to endorse internal factors such as effort (Nicholls, 1975) or ability (Ruble, Parsons, & Ross, 1976) as the causes for their outcome more than do children who have failed. These findings have been interpreted as reflecting children's logical or commonsense use of performance feedback – i.e., one's doing well logically means that one tried harder or is better at a task than if one had done poorly. Success could, however, just as logically be attributed to the ease of the task or to luck. Interpreting the greater endorsement of ability or effort as reflecting common sense begs the question of why these attributions are invoked and not others. One possibility is that these internal attributions are biased such that they enhance a child's self-esteem and ensure the continuation of the positive state brought about by the success. Children's use of such self-enhancing attributions deserves construed examination.

Strategies for the prevention of negative emotional states. Carlson (1985) has demonstrated the preventative utility of a positive, self-focused emotional state in preventing the affective effects of negative social comparison in preschool children. In this study, a happy or neutral emotional state related to personal experience (self-focus) or the experience of another person (other focus) was induced in 4- and 5-year-old children. Follwing this, children were given the opportunity to compare their reward outcomes with those of another child, and these comparisons revealed either a negative inequity (the other child received more), a positive inequity, or equality. Earlier work had shown that a negative inequity revealed by social comparison induced a negative emotional state (Masters, Carlson, & Rahe, 1985), but Carlson hypothesized that a self-focused, positive emotional state would "inoculate" children against the negative emotion-inducing properties of the negative social comparison. The hypothesis was supported. The findings of this study indicate that an emotional state itself may serve a preventative function, but its effects are influenced by more than its valence alone. Specifically, it was found that while a self-focused positive state prevented negative emotion in response to negative social comparison, an other-focused positive state of equal intensity did not have that effect. This underscores, once again, the emerging theme of specificity between the character of an emotional state and its behavioral, cognitive, or in this case, emotional consequences.

Self-control strategies: an overview

Despite long-standing interest in behavioral self-regulation, there has been relatively little research on the self-control of emotional states by children or adults. The literature that does exist is relatively recent, suggesting that attention is now being turned to this important topic.

Although it is certain that research has not fleshed out the full gamut of strategies children can nominate for the self-control of emotion or how these strategies develop, there seems little question that children do share common knowledge or beliefs about such strategies, and that the strategies they nominate change with age in a manner consistent with general cognitive development and socialization experience. There is also evidence that children implement at least some of these strategies, in particular behavioral ones (self-gratification and generosity). It also appears that children make some attempts to alter their experience in ways designed to influence their emotional states. Finally, although cognitive strategies for the self-control of emotion are nominated, the literature has yet to demonstrate that they are readily implemented. This lack of evidence may simply reflect the difficulty of studying covert self-control processes. However, given the indications that cognitions are more likely to be consistent with an emotional state than remedial, plus other findings that cognitive processes may not be particularly effective in changing an ongoing state (Barden et al., 1985), it may be that children do not implement cognitive strategies for the remediation of negative states because they are difficult to generate while in that state and also are likely to prove ineffective. It seems more likely that cognitive strategies would play a role in the maintenance of positive states.

The evidence thus far suggests that children are motivated to attempt the remediation of negative states, and to a lesser extent the maintenance of positive ones. While there is some indication that the prevention of negative states is also attempted, this topic merits further exploration. There is some evidence that children may spontaneously attempt to prevent a negative state while they encounter an experience that induces it. It has also been found that an ongoing emotional state itself may preventatively inoculate a child against the induction of a different state, though there is no evidence that children strategically use their own emotional states in this fashion.

Finally, there is little indication that self-control strategies for the remediation or prevention of negative emotional states are effective. It would be premature to conclude that this is invariably the case, but the effectiveness of emotion control strategies is a topic meriting careful theoretical and empirical attention at this time, given the accumulating evidence regarding children's ability to formulate and implement such strategies.

9.3. Strategies for the social control of emotional states

In addition to being a "person variable" (Mischel, 1973) and a private, covert (in part), and reactive experience, emotion is also a social phenomenon, influencing social behavior and being influenced by it. It is well documented that children regulate the display of emotion (Gnepp, in press; Saarni, 1979, 1981), that they can readily and accurately recognize common emotional states in peers (Felleman et al., 1983; Reichenbach & Masters, 1983), and that they express motives to remediate negative emotional states or enhance positive ones in other children (Carlson et al., 1983). The issues at hand include to what degree they are able to nominate strategies to do so, whether they implement such strategies, and whether there is any evidence of their effectiveness. As for children's self-control strategies, we will deal in turn with the strategic remediation, maintenance, and prevention of emotional states in others (although there is as yet no evidence of motives for the latter dimension of emotion control).

Strategy formulation

Strategies for the remediation of negative emotional states. Two studies of children's strategies for altering other people's negative emotions have been reported. In the first, Burleson (1982) interviewed first- to twelfth-grade children about their strategies for verbally comforting hypothetical distressed friends. He found a developmental increase in the number of such strategies a child offered, the variety of these strategies, and the degree to which they accounted for the other person's point of view.

This study revealed that even the youngest children typically had strategies for verbally comforting others, but because it focused solely on verbal strategies, it did not permit subjects to nominate other strategies for intervention that they may have been able to formulate or even have preferred. In a more recent study (McCoy & Masters, 1985), we interviewed 5-, 8-, and 12-year-old children about their social intervention strategies. Children were shown slides of target children spontaneously displaying sadness, anger, happiness, or a neutral state. In half of the instances, children were also read a vignette describing an experience that could have led to the emotion pictured. Children were then asked to tell what they could do to change the target child's emotional state. For the negative emotional states there was a developmental increase in the nomination of verbal nurturance to alter either sadness or anger, of social nurturance to change sadness, and of helping to remediate anger. There was a concomitant decrease with age in the nomination of material strategies to alter sadness or anger. Moreover, while children of all ages tended to nominate strategies relevant to the experiential context of the target child's emotion (i.e., suggesting a strategy that addressed the cause of the emotion when that was known), this was particularly true of older children. Finally, children of all ages tended to avoid social interventions with angry target children (e.g., ask target child to one's house).

Strategies for the maintenance of positive emotional states. Despite the finding by Carlson et al. (1983) that children are motivated to intervene in positive as well as negative emotional states experienced by peers, primarily to enhance rather than to maintain them, there appears to be no research dealing with children's ability to nominate strategies to do so. Although there has been greater interest in issues of remediation than in those of maintenance, the psychological literature concerned with yea-saying, social desirability, and aspects of social influence has addressed, if only indirectly, the maintenance or enhancement of positive affect in others. However, adult subjects have been the primary interest, and the role of emotion has not been central.

Thus, we have another area in which research is still to be done, in this case about children's knowledge of strategies to maintain or enhance positive emotion in others. While the remediation of negative states in others – social repair (cf. Walton & Sedlak, 1982) – may be a topic of more compelling interest than the maintenance of positive ones, it seems plausible that the general fabric of social interaction among children as well as adults must contain some reciprocal processes targeting the maintenance of positive affect as part of positive social relations. On the other hand, it should be noted that there have been recent observations regarding the preponderance of neutral behaviors in children's social exchanges (Furman & Masters, 1980), and so it may be that the maintenance of positive affect in others is indeed not as significant a social activity as might be otherwise thought.

Strategies for the prevention of negative emotional states. This is another empty section, there having been no research we can identify regarding children's formulation of preventative strategies. As noted earlier, there is also no indication that children are motivated to prevent the occurrence of negative states in others; however, there seems no reason to expect them not to be, especially to the extent that negative emotion in others is itself distressing to the observer (cf. Radke-Yarrow & Zahn-Waxler, 1976, discussed below).

Children's understanding of the experiential causes of emotion appears to be relatively sophisticated (e.g., Barden et al., 1980), suggesting that by observing what happens to others they can anticipate emotional reactions. With respect to preventative strategies, it might be expected that many would be linked to the anticipation of experiences likely to induce a negative state, especially when the individual is instrumental in the experience that induces a negative state in the target. For example, the bearer of ill tidings may wait for an opportune moment or engage in preliminary social interaction designed to be mood elevating before conveying the bad news. A child who wants another's toy may attempt to share rather than to commandeer the toy, at least in part to avoid a negative emotional reaction by the peer.

In short, we would not expect children's strategies to prevent negative states in others to be independent of the anticipation of an emotional reaction to an experience that has not yet occurred. However, it remains for future research to reveal any link between children's ability to anticipate emotional reactions, their motives to intervene to prevent such reactions, and their ability to nominate strategies for such intervention.

In summary, though there has been relatively little research, it seems clear that even very young children can formulate strategies to remediate negative emotional states in others, and these strategies change in a manner consistent with general cognitive and social development. Little is currently known, however, about children's ability to nominate maintenance or preventative strategies. These studies indicate that children have an understanding of experiential and cognitive means of altering other people's emotional states.

Strategy implementation

Children's implementation of strategies for the social control of emotion has generally been studied in terms of children's responses to other persons' actual or staged expressions of globally defined distress. Studies differ in the amount of detail reported about children's prosocial interventions, and, unfortunately, most have reported only the frequency of occurrence of prosocial interventions and not the use of specific intervention strategies. Although the focus of this review is children's use of specific emotion control strategies, the less detailed studies will also be reviewed because they reveal children's willingness to act upon their motivations to intervene.

Strategies for the remediation of negative emotional states: the willingness to act.
Radke-Yarrow and Zahn-Waxler (1976) observed 3- to 7½-year-old children's attempts to comfort an adult who was apparently distressed over pinching her finger in a drawer or reading a sad story. Overall, 37 percent of the children attempted some form of prosocial intervention. Interestingly, younger children were more likely than older children to intervene. The authors also report that the adult's manner of expression of her distress influenced children's prosocial interventions. Children were more reluctant to approach the adult when she appeared to be crying.

Sawin (cited in Radke-Yarrow, Zahn-Waxler, & Chapman, 1983) observed 3- to 7-year-olds' spontaneous responses to peers' crying in naturally occurring situations. Thirty-two percent of the children made some attempt to intervene prosocially by attempting to console the peer directly (17 percent), seeking aid from an adult (10 percent), or threatening the child who had caused the peer's distress (5 percent). Most of the remaining children responded with a concerned facial expression. Only 21 percent of the children evidenced no empathetic response.

Finally, Staub (1970) observed kindergarteners' to sixth graders' attempts to help a crying peer. A tape recording of a 7-year-old crying was played in the room adjacent to that in which the subject was seated alone. Responses were categorized as "active helping" (going to the other room or trying to find the experimenter), "volunteering" (informing the experimenter of the crying child when the experimenter returned to the room), and "no helping" (no active or passive attempt at helping). A curvilinear relationship was found between age and combined active helping and volunteering: The mid-age children helped most often, and the oldest or youngest helped the least.

These studies document that children will make attempts to intervene into both adults' and other children's distress. Moreover, consistent with Carlson et al.'s (1983) finding that children are more motivated to intervene into emotional states if they are to be the agent of intervention, it has been found that children tend to intervene personally more readily than they do by seeking the assistance of a third party (Sawin, cited in Radke-Yarrow et al., 1983; Staub, 1970). The initiation of such interventions is, however, mediated by situational factors such as the others' expression of emotion and by personal factors such as the potential intervener's age and possible assessment of the situation. Radke-Yarrow and Zahn-Waxler (1976) suggest, for example, that the age effects they observed may have resulted from older subjects' belief that the adult could handle the situation or would be embarassed by intervention.

Two other studies have taken a more detailed look at the precise strategies children utilize for social intervention. These will be reviewed next.

Strategies for the remediation of negative emotional states: the implementation of specific instructions. Zahn-Waxler, Friedman, and Cummings (1983) observed children's responses to a distressed infant. Preschool through sixty-grade children heard an infant crying in an adjacent room. Shortly afterward, the infant's mother entered the subject's room in search of the infant's bottle. Children's attempts to help were observed and categorized as being gestural (e.g., pointing to bottle), verbal (e.g., expressing sympathy toward the infant), or physical (e.g., fetching the bottle or feeding the baby). While a majority of children at each age level attempted some form of help, older children were more likely to do so than younger children. In addition, verbal strategies were more frequent among the older children, gestural strategies were used more often by the oldest and youngest children than by the mid-age children (first and second graders), and physical strategies were implemented more by the mid-age children.

Zahn-Waxler and Radke-Yarrow (1982) trained mothers to categorize their infants' responses to others' actual distress. Infants between the ages of 9 months and 2½ years were observed. Infants were found to make some form of response to distress in 80 to 90 percent of the instances. The most frequent responses of the youngest children to naturally occurring distress were sustained orientation, crying, seeking the care giver, laughing, and smiling.

The older children were more likely to react with some form of prosocial intervention. Indeed, from 18 months on, such interventions were made in about one-third of the instances of distress. The youngest children's prosocial interventions consisted primarily of physical contacts such as patting or of presenting objects to distress victims. Although physical interventions remained frequent with increasing age, the exact nature of these strategies changed from relatively gross touching to more refined physical contact such as hugs and kisses. Other forms of prosocial strategies that appeared with age included verbal expressions of concern, sympathy, or reassurance (evidenced by 87 percent of the children between the ages of 1½ and 2½), instrumental helping such as getting a sweater for a chilly grandmother (81 percent), and enlisting the aid of a third person (62 percent). The sophistication exhibited by these young children is described by the authors as follows: "They express verbal sympathy, they give suggestions about how to handle problems, they are sometimes judgmental in their helping, they appear to try to cheer others up, and they sometimes try alternative helping responses when a given technique was not effective" (Zahn-Waxler & Radke-Yarrow, 1982, p. 126).

Zahn-Waxler and Radke-Yarrow's study indicates that even 1- and 2-year-old infants have a surprising variety of strategies for altering others' negative moods, and reliability checks indicated that these observations were not biased reports on the mothers' part. It is difficult, however, to know exactly what children are responding to in such studies. Neither naturalistic studies nor semistructured laboratory investigations such as Zahn-Waxler et al.'s (1983) necessarily lend themselves to identification of specific elicitors of behavior. Thus some of the developmental differences found by Radke-Yarrow and Zahn-Waxler could reflect variations in the situations or people encountered with age rather than solely the child's greater social sophistication. Structured studies in which children have the opportunity to intervene would be helpful in specifying the exact conditions needed for implementation.

In a recent study, Rork and Masters (1989) studied children's use of material nurturance (generosity) as a means of intervening into their own emotion as well as that of a peer. Children's generosity was greater toward sad peers than toward happy or neutral peers. When both the subject and the target child were sad, however, personal intervention motives were predominant, and children's generosity was reduced when the mood resulted from thinking about their own sad experiences. This finding illustrates how motives for the self-control and social control of emotion may compete and suggests that, all other things being equal, there may be a tendency for personal interest to prevail.

Strategies for the maintenance of positive emotional states. Just as there is a dearth of information about children's ability to nominate strategies to maintain positive emotional states in peers, there is also a general absence of knowledge about any tendencies to engage in behavior that appears intended to do so. Again, early work on social interaction may be cited to suggest that such strategies exist. For example, the finding by Hartup et al. (1967) that the positive social reinforcement dispensed by a child is correlated with the amount received is consistent with the notion of a reciprocal "fugue" (cf. Lewis, Sullivan, & Michaelson, 1984) of social behavior in which there is a dyadic maintenance of positive affect in the participants. Evidence that social reinforcement elicits positive affect supports the possibility that such interaction would have the effect of maintaining positive affect, but whether affect maintenance is operating as a motive to promote such changes has not been demonstrated. Initially, it seems unlikely that all, or perhaps even a majority, of such interactions would be founded on such a motive alone, although it might be one among several factors promoting children's positive social interaction.

Strategies for the prevention of negative emotional states. Despite clear evidence that children implement systematic, strategic efforts to repair social interactions gone awry (Walton & Sedlak, 1982), there has been no research on children's strategic action to prevent, anticipatorily, the occurrence of negative emotion in others.

Conclusion

In summary, children do spontaneously implement specific strategies for social intervention into emotional states. Our present understanding is limited, however, in terms of the range of strategies children utilize and the specific factors that elicit intervention. For example, studies have tended to examine children's responses to "distress" rather than to more specific emotional states. In general, children's articulation of strategies for the social control of emotion takes into consideration such factors as the other's particular emotion and the cause of that state. There is a clear need for greater attention to children's implementing maintenance and, especially, preventative strategies for the control of emotion in others.

Social-control strategies: an overview

From a surprisingly young age, children have and use strategies for remediating other persons' emotional states. Our understanding of these strategies, however, is severely limited by the methodologies used in much of the research. There is a marked need for greater refinement in specification of the interventions children utilize and of the situational or experiential factors that mediate implementation. Finally, there is a need to expand the scope of concern beyond the remediation or repair of negative emotions in others. While maintenance strategies merit some attention, children's strategic efforts for the anticipatory control of emotional reaction in others (prevention strategies) seem to be a particularly important issue for investigation given their implicit relation to children's social knowledge about the causes of emotion.

9.4. Issues for future research

Research suggestions and methodological refinements have been made throughout this review. In this concluding section, we have selected three issues to examine in greater detail: children's psychological knowledge and beliefs underlying emotion control strategies, their effectiveness for such strategies, and their acquisition.

Children's implicit theories of emotion and strategies for the control of emotions in themselves and others

Children's proposed interventions tend to be specific to a particular emotion and to its structural or experiential cause; this is true even among very young children. "Specificity" is used in this context to refer to the match between the cause of an emotional state and the intervention used to remediate it, a match both in terms of the *content* of the cause or intervention and the cognitive or experiential *process* involved in each.

Further research on the range of the emotion control strategies that children are able to formulate and implement will contribute to our understanding of how children comprehend and grapple with emotionality as a part of their own and others' personalities. However, the more basic issue seems to us to be the processes governing (1) children's personal and social knowledge about emotion and its control, and (2) their behavioral and cognitive attempts to implement such control. That children tailor their proposed and enacted interventions to the emotional state and its causal context suggests that their personal and social knowledge plays a role and that emotion control is at least in part a cognitive problem-solving endeavor. Relevant issues meriting attention include the acquisition of such knowledge (see below) as well as its effective implementation in either the derivation or performance of control strategies.

We can immediately identify some issues worthy of attention, though there are surely a number of others. Processes such as self-monitoring are clearly germane to the development and appropriate implementation of self-control strategies. The concept of social monitoring might be proposed as a process beyond mere observational learning that would contribute to children's knowledge and use of social control strategies. State variables, such as a child's own emotional state, will surely influence both the generation and implementation of strategies, especially those targeting self-control, through both cognitive and motivational factors. Developmental changes in emotion control strategies beyond those reflecting increased cognitive and verbal competencies also seem of interest. Here we look to the interface between emotion control and developmental progression in social cognition and general social interaction skills.

The general proposal therefore is for a more concerted integration of the social/personal cognition and social/personal behavior parameters of emotion control. The fruitfulness of this is perhaps best illustrated through the almost totally unstudied topic of prevention strategies. Social or personal knowledge about the causes of emotion in the self and others is surely a prerequisite to motives, strategy formulation, and strategy implementation of this type.

Effectiveness of emotion control strategies

In few studies of emotion control has the postintervention affect been measured, and therefore evaluation of the strategy's effectiveness has generally been precluded. The only study examining the effectiveness of children's spontaneous emotion control strategies (Masters et al., 1983) found that selective self-exposure to nurturant social stimuli was not effective in remediating negative affect. Nor was self-distraction effectively preventative. This discouraging finding is tempered by the results of two studies focusing on the remediation of negative emotion.

In the first study, Barden et al. (1981) examined 4- and 5-year-old children's self-gratification and generosity after two consecutive cognitive inductions of emotion. Children who had undergone an initial induction of sadness continued to show the enhanced self-gratification and diminished generosity characteristic of sad children even after a succeeding induction of a happy or neutral state. Children's facial expressions of emotion, however, mirrored the more recent induction. These results suggest that at least the behavioral aspects of a cognitively induced emotional state, those usually interpreted as attempts at remediation, persist despite cognitive remediation attempts.

In a follow-up study, Barden et al. (1985) examined a "process specificity" hypothesis of emotion repair suggesting that the most effective strategy for remediating a negative emotion is one that matches the experience or cognition that induced the state. In line with earlier findings, the authors also hypothesized that cognitively induced emotional states would be more resistent to remediation than would experientially induced states. To examine these hypotheses, a sad emotional state was induced in 7- and 8-year-old children in one of four ways: (1) children thought about a personal experience of social rejection (cognitive self-focus), (2) children thought about a social rejection experience that happened to a peer (cognitive other focus), (3) children actually experienced social rejection by a peer (experience of self), or (4) children observed a peer experiencing social rejection (experience of other). Children in all four conditions then either experienced social acceptance personally, observed a peer being socially accepted, thought about a personal experience of social acceptance, or thought about a peer's experience of social acceptance.

It was found that experientially induced negative affect with either a self-focus or other focus could be effectively remediated by experiences of social acceptance and that cognitively induced moods with an other focus could be remediated effectively by thinking about a peer's acceptance. Cognitively induced moods having a self-focus, however, were resistent to remediation. These findings suggest that effective remediation is often possible but that the most effective remedial strategy is one that matches the process (cognitive vs. experiential), the content (e.g., social acceptance or rejection), and the focus (self vs. other) of the emotion's cause.

Therefore, one possible explanation of the lack of effectiveness found by Masters et al. (1983) is that the remediation strategy available involved symbolic (televised) nurturance rather than actual nurturance and the preventative strategy either involved self-distraction, not a nurturant experience at all, or was an attempt to elect nurturance that failed. Since the induction experience was an actual aversive interaction, neither the remediation nor the preventative strategies were an effective match.

In general, then, it seems reasonable to call for further research to demonstrate the *effective* use of strategies for the self-control or social control of emotion and to identify the factors influencing such effectiveness. Several examples immediately come to mind regarding fruitful directions for such research. To the extent that they are based on past experiences of successful and unsuccessful emotional control attempts (through self-monitoring or social monitoring), it might be expected that children's strategies would gradually come to reflect a realistic understanding of the specificity of effective strategies. Similar strategies (e.g., cognitive ones) may also differ in effectiveness with age, and there are certain to be variations in the skill with which a general strategy (e.g., social nurturance) will be implemented and, consequently, effective. Finally, broader issues such as those of emotional vulnerability or invulnerability (Garmezy, 1981; Garmezy & Neuchterlein, 1972) might well be examined, not merely from the perspective of whether strategies can be formulated or implemented but also in terms of factors influencing their effectiveness for the child in question.

To the extent that they are based on past experiences of successful and unsuccessful emotional control attempts (through self-monitoring or social monitoring), children's strategies might be expected to gradually come to reflect a realistic understanding of the specificity of effective strategies.

Acquisition of emotion control strategies

At present, there are no data concerning children's acquisition of specific strategies for the control of emotion. It is not known, for example, how the rudimentary self-regulatory and self-calming abilities of the infant (Doxsey West, 1984; Kopp, 1982; Vaughn, Kopp, & Krakow, 1984) may develop into the experiential and cognitive remediation strategies of childhood and beyond. Numerous possible mechanisms of acquisition include direct tuition (e.g., "Count to 10 when you're angry"), observation of other persons' attempts at self-control and social control, self-monitoring of early, potentially "automatic" or imitative interventions (cf. Radke-Yarrow & Zahn-Waxler, 1976), or monitoring the affective consequences of others' interventions into one's own moods from the perspective of both the actor (a social intervener) and the observer (the self whose emotions are influenced). This last possibility may be particularly important. A child's experience of what does and does not work for himself or herself could form the basis of a set of expectations concerning potentially effective strategies for personal or social implementation. These expectations would guide the formulation of specific strategies on occasions when there is motivation to exert control on one's own emotional responding or that of another.

Another issue related to the acquisition of strategies is the potential efficacy of the explicit, perhaps therapeutic training of children in their use. Such training could address either self-control or social control strategies. For example, consider both the cognitive approach and be-havior skills required for the successful emotion control. Deficits in any of these factors may be relevant to emotional disorders of varying degrees. Thus, depressed children (or adults) might be able to recognize their emotional state, be motivated to alter it, but be unable to formulate or implement a successful remedial strategy. Depressed children, for example, could be instructed in the formulation of self-control strat-egies, and their subsequent implementation of strategies could be ex-amined in natural or laboratory settings. Or consider the training of nondepressed children in social intervention strategies for use with depressed peers. Finally, a better understanding of preventative strat-egies and their acquisition might be of particular relevance for develop-ing intervention programs for children (or adults) at risk for depression reactions.

Conclusion

Studies of children's understanding and control of emotion in them-selves and others generally reveal surprising competencies in such skills. Although the amount of research on various issues varies widely, it seems reasonable to conclude that children are able to recognize emotional states, are motivated to intervene into negative moods, have systematic beliefs about the experiential/causal determinants of emo-tion, and are able to articulate and implement strategies for altering their own and other persons' emotional states. Given the important role of affect in early behavior and interactions (Sroufe, 1979; Sroufe & Waters, 1977), the rapid development of these competencies is perhaps quite adaptive and, consequently, not so surprising after all. Predominant theories of child development have, however, tended to emphasize children's lack of competency or realism in handling emotions (e.g., Freudian or Piagetian theories). Zahn-Waxler and Radke-Yarrow (1982) point out that existing theories are equally unable to account for the early appearance of prosocial behavior they found in infants. These and other newly recognized competencies in children (Masters, 1981) are challenging old conceptions of development and are demanding the formulation of new theories that acknowledge such skills yet simulta-neously account for their transformation across time. In the present case, many issues relating to the self-control and social control of emo-tion have not yet received either the theoretical or the empirical atten-tion they merit or that is needed to complete our understanding of this important aspect of children's personal and social competence.

References

American Psychiatric Association. (1980). *Diagnostic and statistical manual of mental disorders* (3rd ed.). Washington, DC: Author.

Bandura, A. (1977). *Social learning theory*. Englewood Cliffs, NJ: Prentice-Hall.

Barden, R. C., Garber, J., Duncan, S. W., & Masters, J. C. (1981). Cumulative effects of induced affective states: Remediation, inoculation, and accentuation. *Journal of Personality and Social Psychology, 40*, 750–760.

Barden, R. C., Garber, J., Leiman, B., Ford, M. E., & Masters, J. C. (1985). Factors governing the effective remediation of negative affect and its cognitive and behavioral consequences. *Journal of Personality and Social Psychology, 49*, 1040–1053.

Barden, R. C., Zelko, F. A., Duncan, S. W., & Masters, J. C. (1980). Children's consensual knowledge about the experiential determinants of emotion. *Journal of Personality and Social Psychology, 39*, 968–976.

Barnett, M. A., King, L. M., & Howard, J. A. (1979). Inducing affect about self or other: Effects on generosity in children. *Developmental Psychology, 15*, 164–167.

Brown, A. L., & Smiley, S. S. (1978). The development of strategies for studying tests. *Child Development, 49*, 1076–1088.

Burleson, B. R. (1982). The development of comforting communication skills in childhood and adolescence. *Child Development, 53*, 1578–1588.

Carlson, C. R. (1985). *Children's emotions and their responses to social comparisons.* Presentation at the biennial meeting of the Society for Research in Child Development. Toronto, Canada, April.

Carlson, C. R., Felleman, E. S., & Masters, J. C. (1983). Influence of children's emotional states on the recognition of emotion in peers and social motives to change another's emotional state. *Motivation and Emotion, 7*, 61–79.

Charlesworth, R., & Hartup, W. W. (1967). Positive reinforcement in the nursery school peer group. *Child Development, 38*, 994–1002.

Cialdini, R. B., & Kenrick, D. T. (1976). Altruism as hedonism: A social developmental perspective on the relation of mood states and helping. *Journal of Personality and Social Psychology, 34*, 907–914.

Diener, C. I., & Dweck, C. S. (1978). An analysis of learned helplessness: Continuous changes in performance, strategy, and achievement cognitions following failure. *Journal of Personality and Social Psychology, 36*, 451–462.

Doxsey West, P. (1984). Individual differences in self-calming abilities of infants. Unpublished doctoral dissertation. Department of Psychology and Human Development, Peabody College of Vanderbilt University, Nashville, TN.

Dodge, K. A. (in press). Group behavior and social status. In S. R. Asher and J. D. Coie (Eds.), *Peer rejection in childhood: Origens, consequence, and intervention*. New York: Cambridge University Press.

Dodge, K. A. (1985). Facets of social interaction and the assessment of social competence in children. In B. H. Schneider, K. H. Rubin, & J. E. Ledingham (Eds.), *Peer relationships and social skills in childhood: Issues in assessment and training*. New York: Springer-Verlag.

Felleman, E. S., Barden, R. C., Carlson, C. R., Rosenberg, L., & Masters, J. C. (1983). Children's and adult's recognition of spontaneous and posed emotional expressions in young children. *Developmental Psychology, 19*, 405–413.

Fitch, G. (1970). Effects of self-esteem, perceived performance, and choice on causal attributions. *Journal of Personality and Social Psychology, 16*, 311–315.

Freud, A. (1946). *The ego and the mechanisms of defense* (Revised ed.). New York: International Universities Press, 1946.

Freud, S. (1923). *The ego and the id.* In J. Strachey (Ed. and Trans.), *The standard edition of the complete psychological works of Sigmund Freud* (Vol. 19, pp. 3–36). London: Hogarth, 1961.

Freud, S. (1896). *Further remarks on the neuro-psychosis of defence* [sic]. In J. Strachey (Ed. and Trans.), *The standard edition of the complete psychological works of Sigmund Freud* (Vol. 3, pp. 162–185). London: Hogarth, 1962.

Fry, P. S. (1976). Success, failure, and self-assessment ratings. *Journal of Consulting and Clinical Psychology, 44,* 413–419.

Furman, W., & Masters, J. C. (1980). Affective consequences of social reinforcement, punishment, and neutral behavior. *Developmental Psychology, 16,* 100–104.

Garmezy, N. (1981). Children under stress: Perspectives on antecedents and correlates of vulnerability and resistance to psychopathology. In A. I. Rabin, J. Aronoff, A. M. Barclay, & R. A. Zucker (Eds.), *Further explorations in personality.* New York: Wiley Interscience.

Garmezy, N., & Neuchterlein, K. (1972). Invulnerable children: The fact and fiction of competence and disadvantage (Abstract). *American Journal of Orthopsychiatry, 42,* 328–329.

Garmezy, N., & Rutter, M. (Eds.). (1983). *Stress, coping, and development in children.* New York: McGraw-Hill Book Company.

Gnepp, J. (1986). Children's understanding of verbal and facial display rules. *Developmental Psychology, 22,* 103–108.

Harris, P. L., & Olthof, T. (1982). The child's concept of emotions. In G. Butterworth & P. LIght (Eds.), *Social cognition: Studies of the development of understanding.* Chicago: University of Chicago Press.

Harris, P. L., Olthof, T., & Terwogt, M. M. (1981). Children's knowledge of emotion. *Journal of Child Psychology and Psychiatry, 22,* 247–261.

Hartup, W. W., Glazer, J. A., & Charlesworth, R. (1967). Peer reinforcement and sociometric status. *Child Development, 38,* 1017–1024.

Harvey, D. M. (1981). Depression and attributional style: Interpretations of important events. *Journal of Abnormal Psychology, 90,* 134–142.

Isen, A. M., Horn, N., & Rosenhan, D. L. (1973). Effects of success and failure on children's generosity. *Journal of Personality and Social Psychology, 27,* 239–247.

Isen, A. M., & Shalker, T. E. (1982). The effect of feeling state on evaluation of positive, neutral, and negative stimuli: When you "accentuate the positive," do you "eliminate the negative?" *Social Psychology Quarterly, 45,* 58–63.

Isen, A. M., Shalker, T. E., Clark, M., & Karp, L. (1978). Affect accessibility of material in memory and behavior: A cognitive loop? *Journal of Personality and Social Psychology, 36,* 1–12.

Keeny, T. J., Cannizzo, S. R., & Flavell, J. H. (1967). Spontaneous and induced verbal rehearsal in a recall task. *Child Development, 38,* 953–966.

Kenrick, D. T., Baumann, D. J., & Cialdini, R. B. (1979). A step in the socialization of altruism as hedonism: Effects of negative mood on children's generosity under public and private conditions. *Journal of Personality and Social Psychology, 37,* 747–755.

Kopp, C. B (1982). Antecedents of self-regulation: A developmental perspective. *Developmental Psychology, 18,* 199–214.

Kuiper, N. A. (1978). Depression and causal attributions for success and failure. *Journal of Personality and Social Psychology, 36,* 236–246.

Lazarus, R. S. (1984). On the primacy of cognition. *American Psychologist, 39,* 124–129.

Lewis, M., Sullivan, M. W., & Michaelson, L., (1984). The cognitive-emotional fugue. In C. E. Izard, J. Kagan, & R. Zajonc (Eds.), *Emotions, cognition and behavior*. New York: Cambridge University Press.

Litman-Adizes, T. (1978). An attributional model of depression: Laboratory and clinical investigations. *Dissertation Abstracts International, 39*, 5007B.

Luria, A. R. (1961). *The role of speech in the regulation of normal and abnormal behavior*. New York: Pergamon Press.

Marx, M. H., & Hillix, W. A. (1979). *Systems and theories in psychology* (3rd ed.). New York: McGraw-Hill.

Masters, J. C. (1968). Effects of social comparison upon subsequent self-reinforcement behavior in children. *Journal of Personality and Social Psychology, 10*, 391–401.

Masters, J. C. (1971). Effects of social comparison upon children's self-reinforcement and altruism toward competitors and friends. *Developmental Psychology, 5*, 64–72.

Masters, J. C. (1972). Effects of success, failure, and reward outcome upon contingent and noncontingent self-reinforcement. *Developmental Psychology, 7*, 110–118.

Masters, J. C. (1981). Developmental psychology. In M. R. Rosenzweig & L. W. Porter (Eds.), *Annual review of psychology* (pp. 117–151). Palo Alto, CA: Annual Reviews.

Masters, J. C., Barden, R. C., & Ford, M. E. (1979). Affective states, expressive behavior, and learning in children. *Journal of Personality and Social Psychology, 37*, 380–390.

Masters, J. C., & Binger, C. G. (1978). Interrupting the flow of behavior: The stability and development of children's initiation and maintenance of compliant response inhibition. *Merrill-Palmer Quarterly, 24*, 229–242.

Masters, J. C., & Carlson, R. C. (1984). Children's and adults' understanding of emotion. In C. E. Izard, J. Kagan, & R. Zajonc (Eds.), *Emotion, cognition, and behavior*. New York: Academic Press.

Masters, J. C., Carlson, C. R., & Rahe, D. F. (1985). Children's affective, behavioral, and cognitive responses to social comparison. *Journal of Experimental Social Psychology, 21*, 407–420.

Masters, J. C., Felleman, E. S., & Barden, R. C. (1981). Experimental studies of affective states in children. In B. B. Lahey & A. E. Kazdin (Eds.), *Advances in clinical child psychology* (Vol. 4, pp. 91–118). New York: Plenum.

Masters, J. C., Ford, M. E., & Arend, R. A. (1983). Children's strategies for controlling affective responses to aversive social experience. *Motivation and Emotion, 7*, 103–116.

Masters, J. C., & Furman, W. C. (1976). Effects of affective states on noncontingent outcome expectancies and beliefs in internal or external control. *Developmental Psychology, 12*, 481–482.

Masters, J. C., & Furman, W. (1981). Popularity, individual friendship selection, and specific peer interaction among children. *Developmental Psychology, 17*, 344–350.

Masters, J. C., & Peskay, J. (1972). Effects of race, socioeconomic status, and success or failure upon contingent and noncontingent self-reinforcement in children. *Developmental Psychology, 7*, 139–145.

Masters, J. C., & Santrock, J. W. (1976). Studies in the self-regulation of behavior: Effects of contingent cognitive and affective events. *Developmental Psychology, 12*, 334–348.

Masters, J. C., & Santrock, J. W. (1982). Social reinforcement and self-gratification: Effects of absolute and socially compared levels of nurturance. *The Journal of Genetic Psychology, 140,* 59–69.

McCoy, C. L., & Masters, J. C. (1985). The development of children's strategies for the social control of emotion. *Child Development, 56,* 1214–1222.

McCoy, C. L., Sarmiento, P., & Masters, J. C. (in preparation). The development of children's strategies for the self-control of emotion. Vanderbilt University, Nashville, TN.

Meichenbaum, D. (1976). Toward a cognitive theory of self-control. In G. E. Schwartz & D. Shapiro (Eds.), *Consciousness and self-regulation: Advances in research* (Vol. 1, pp. 223–260). New York: Plenum.

Menapuce, R. H., & Doby, C. (1976). Causal attributions for success and failure for psychiatric rehabilitees and college students. *Journal of Personality and Social Psychology, 34,* 447–454.

Miller, D. T. (1976). Ego involvement and attributions for success and failure. *Journal of Personality and Social Psychology, 34,* 901–906.

Miller, G. E., Galanter, E., & Pribram, K. (1960). *Plans and the structure of behavior.* Palo Alto, CA: Stanford University.

Mischel, H. N., & Mischel, W. (1983). The development of children's knowledge of self-control strategies. *Child Development, 54,* 603–619.

Mischel, W. (1968). *Personality and assessment.* New York: Wiley.

Mischel, W. (1973). Toward a cognitive social learning reconceptualization of personality. *Psychological Review, 80,* 252–283.

Mischel, W., & Baker, N. (1975). Cognitive appraisals and transformations in delay behavior. *Journal of Personality and Social Psychology, 31,* 254–261.

Mischel, W., Coates, B., & Raskoff, A. (1968). Effects of success and failure on self-gratification. *Journal of Personality and Social Psychology, 10,* 381–390.

Mischel, W., Ebbeson, E. B., & Zeiss, A. R. (1972). Cognitive and attentional mechanisms in delay of gratification. *Journal of Personality and Social Psychology, 21,* 204–218.

Mischel, W., Ebbeson, E. B., & Zeiss, A. R. (1973). Selective attention to the self: Situational and dispositional determinants. *Journal of Personality and Social Psychology, 27,* 129–142.

Mischel, W., Ebbeson, E. B., Zeiss, A. R. (1976). Determinants of selective memory about the self. *Journal of Consulting and Clinical Psychology, 44,* 92–103.

Mischel, W., & Metzner, R. (1962). Preference for delayed reward as a function of age, intelligence, and length of delay interval. *Journal of Abnormal and Social Psychology, 64,* 425–431.

Mischel, W., & Patterson, C. J. (1976). Substantive and structural elements of effective plans for self-control. *Journal of Personality and Social Psychology, 34,* 942–950.

Mischel, W., & Patterson, C. J. (1978). Effective plans for self control in children. In W. A. Collins (Ed.), *Minnesota Symposia on Child Psychology,* Vol. 11.

Mize, J., & Ladd, G. W. (1984). Preschool children's goal and strategy knowledge: A comparison of picture-story and enactive assessment. In G. Ladd (Chair), *From preschool to high school: Are children's interpersonal goals and strategies predictive of their social competence?* Symposium conducted at the annual meeting of the American Education Research Association, New Orleans, April.

Nasby, W., & Yando, R. (1982). Selective encoding and retrieval or affectively valent information: Two cognitive consequences of children's mood states. *Journal of Personality and Social Psychology, 43,* 1244–1253.

Natale, M., & Hantas, M. (1982). Effect of temporary mood states on selective memory about the self. *Journal of Personality and Social Psychology, 42*, 927–934.

Nicholls, J. (1975). Causal attributions and other achievement-related cognitions: Effects of task outcome, attainment value, and sex. *Journal of Personality and Social Psychology, 31*, 379–389.

Radke-Yarrow, M., & Zahn-Waxler, C. (1976). Dimensions and correlates of prosocial behavior in young children. *Child Development, 47*, 118–125.

Radke-Yarrow, M., Zahn-Waxler, C., & Chapman, M. (1983). Children's prosocial dispositions and behavior. In P. H. Musson (Ed.), *Carmichael's Manual of Child Psychology*, vol. 4 (4th Ed.). New York: Wiley.

Reichenbach, L., & Masters, J. C. (1983). Children's use of expressive and contextual cues in judgments of emotion. *Child Development, 54*, 993–1004.

Rizley, R. (1978). Depression and distortion in the attribution of causality. *Journal of Abnormal Psychology, 87*, 32–48.

Rork, R., & Masters, J. C. (1989). Personal versus social motives to maintain and repair emotional states. Unpublished manuscript Department of Psychology, Vanderbilt University, Nashville, TN.

Rosenhan, D. L., Underwood, B., & Moore, B. (1974). Affect moderates self-gratification and altruism. *Journal of Personality and Social Psychology, 30*, 546–552.

Ruble, D. N., Parsons, J. E., & Ross, J. (1976). Self-evaluative responses of children in an achievement setting. *Child Development, 47*, 990–997.

Saarni, C. (1979). Children's understanding of display rules for expressive behavior. *Developmental Psychology, 15*, 424–429.

Saarni, C. (1981). Emotional experience and regulation of expressive behavior. Paper presented at the biennial meeting of the Society for Research in Child Development, Boston.

Schwartz, R. M. & Trabasso, T. (1984). Children's understanding of emotions. In c. Izard, J. Kagan, & R. Zajonc (Eds.), *Emotions, cognition, and behavior*. New York: Cambridge University Press.

Skinner, B. F. (1953). *Science and human behavior*. New York: MacMillan.

Sroufe, L. A. (1979). Socioemotional development. In J. D. Osofsky (Ed.), *The handbook of infant development*. New York: Wiley.

Sroufe, L. A., & Waters, E. (1977). Attachment as an organizational construct. *Child Development, 34*, 1184–1199.

Staub, E. (1970). A child in distress: The influence of age and number of witnesses on children's attempts to help. *Journal of Personality and Social Psychology, 14*, 130–140.

Strongman, K. T. (1978). *The psychology of emotion* (2nd ed.). New York: Wiley.

Taylor, A. R., & Asher, S. R. (1984). Children's interpersonal goals in game situations. In G. Ladd (Chair), *From preschool to high school: Are children's interpersonal goals and strategies predictive of their social competence?* Symposium conducted at the annual meeting of the American Education Research Association, New Orleans, April.

Teasdale, J. D., & Fogarty, S. J. (1979). Differential effects of induced mood on retrieval of pleasant and unpleasant events from episodic memory. *Journal of Abnormal Psychology, 88*, 248–257.

Thoresen, C. E., & Mahoney, M. J. (1974). *Behavioral self-control*. New York: Holt, Rinehart, & Winston.

Underwood, B., Moore, B. S., & Rosenhan, D. L. (1973). Affect and self-gratification. *Developmental Psychology, 8*, 209–214.

Vaughn, B. E., Kopp, C. B., & Krakow, J. B. (1984). The emergence and consolidation of self-control from eighteen to thirty months of age: Normative trends and individual differences. *Child Development, 55,* 990–1004.

Vygotsky, L. S. (1962). *Thought and language.* Cambridge, MA: MIT Press.

Walton, M. D., & Sedlak, A. J. (1982). Making amends: A grammar-based analysis of children's social interaction. *Merrill Palmer Quarterly, 28,* 389–412.

Weary, G. (1980). Examination of affect and egotism as mediators of bias in causal attributions. *Journal of Personality and Social Psychology, 38,* 348–357.

Wollert, R., Heinrich, L., Wood, D., & Werner, W. (1983). Causal attributions, sanctions, and normal mood variations. *Journal of Personality and Social Psychology, 45,* 1029–1044.

Wright, J., & Mischel, W. (1982). Influence of affect on cognitive social learning person variables. *Journal of Personality and Social Psychology, 43,* 901–914.

Zahn-Waxler, C., Friedman, S. L., & Cummings, E. M. (1983). Children's emotions and behaviors in response to infant's cries. *Child Development, 54,* 1522–1528.

Zahn-Waxler, C., & Radke-Yarrow, M. (1982). The development of altruism: Alternative research strategies. In N. Eisenberg (Ed.), *The development of prosocial behavior.* New York: Academic Press.

Zajonc, R. B. (1984). On the primacy of affect. *American Psychologist. 39,* 117–123.

Author Index

269

Subject Index